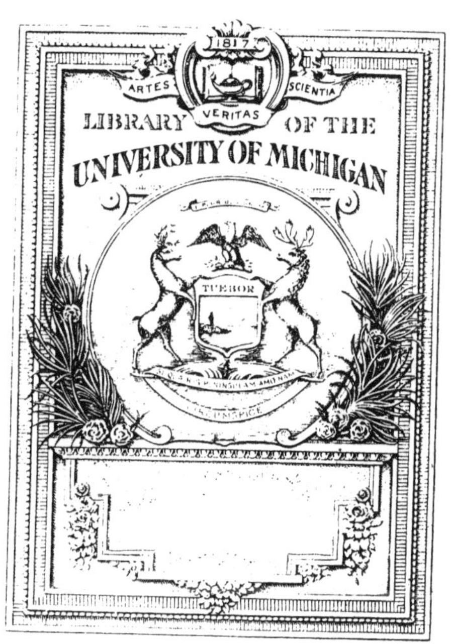
1817
ARTES
SCIENTIA
VERITAS
LIBRARY OF THE
UNIVERSITY OF MICHIGAN
TUEBOR

I0833966

ANGLO-AMERICAN

LITERATURE AND MANNERS:

FROM THE FRENCH OF

PHILARÈTE CHASLES,
PROFESSOR IN THE COLLEGE OF FRANCE

NEW YORK:
CHARLES SCRIBNER, 145 NASSAU STREET.
1852.

C. W. BENEDICT,
Stereotyper and Printer,
201 William Street.

TRANSLATOR'S NOTE.

One or two words are judged necessary for the better understanding of this book, and the quitting of the translator's conscience.

The author is fully rendered into English, with the exception of certain long extracts from well known or unknown English writers, analyses of such familiar works as Melville's Typee, and a chapter from American history, the chapter of Arnold and Andre.

The use of the words "Puritan" and "Calvinist" will strike the reader; who is to remember that M. Chasles is a Frenchman, and that to a Frenchman Calvinism means simply "Protestantism," of which the only form known in France is a modified Calvinism.

It is trusted that readers will remember that the *whole* United States is spoken of, and that what may not be true of their own immediate society, may be very true of some other portion of this vast community—indeed, what is there not in this huge country?

It is hoped that few errors will be found in this translation; and that the transcendant merit of the original will be appreciated, even in this present English version. Such appreciation of the merit and of the profound thoughtfulness and discriminating delicacy of M. Chasles, will reward the translator for his trouble, which has not been small.

THE TRANSLATOR.

No. 4 Amity Place, New York,
May 12, 1852.

AUTHOR'S PRELIMINARY NOTICE.

This volume contains several "studies" on North America, and the development of literature and manners there. You will find here no pretension to direct the age, nor to preach new doctrines—a merit, by the way, sufficiently rare in these times.

The Americans of the United States, last-born of the great Anglo-Saxon race, and founders of the federal republic of the United States, have conquered, in the civilized world, a place which does not permit the observer to pass them by in silence.

For a scientific analysis of their institutions, I refer the reader to the excellent works of M. de Tocqueville and of M. Michael Chevalier. My object is different. I propose to exhibit, in a series of faithful pictures, the details of manners, traits of character, phenomena and singularity, observed upon the spot by foreign travellers, or shown forth by Americans themselves.

CONTENTS.

CHAPTER I.

CHAPTER II.

CHAPTER III.

CHAPTER IV.

CHAPTER V.

CHAPTER VI.

CHAPTER VII.

CHAPTER VIII.

CHAPTER IX.

ORIGIN AND PROGRESS

OF

LITERATURE AND ELOQUENCE IN THE UNITED STATES.

SECTION I.

THE MAY-FLOWER—PURITAN COLONISTS—FIRST EFFORT OF ANGLO-AMERICAN LITERATURE.

IN 1630 there was seen in the harbor of Delft, in Holland, a little vessel of poor appearance and meanly equipped. It was called the May Flower. It was anchored in the harbor, waiting for its cargo and its passengers, the former very trifling, the latter a knot of poor enough fellows.

The May-Flower sailed, carrying with her a dozen English Puritans, for the most part old, weary, mournful, in threadbare black coats, and fortified with their Calvinist Bibles, a provision of biscuit, and more or less ham. When they had crossed the Atlantic, these worthy people, who were seeking a peaceable spot where they might worship God in their own fashion, set to work to found colonies, which became Philadelphia, New York, and Boston. They had, as you know, to fight against much hardship. When their dust was mingled with the soil of America, there issued from it a magnificent Empire.

They had brought with them something more powerful than credit, riches, or armies, they possessed Moral Force; they were depositories of that sacred spark from which empires are created; they had sincerity, belief, perseverance, courage. There is nothing to show that they were very clever or even well instructed; they certainly expected no great fortune, but their souls were strong. Suppose in their place, brave gentlemen of France or Spain, the most courtly lords of the Court of Charles I. or of Charles II.; they would not have held up three years against the savages, the bears and the ennui of the solitude. American society would not have been founded. Our Puritans believed; they knew how to wait, fight, suffer, and these are great qualities.

Half a century later, Bayle sought an asylum in another city of that same Holland, refuge and workshop of revolutionary intellects during two hundred years. Bayle was certainly one of the rarest minds that can be cited, and if we were in search of a man to oppose to our Puritans, we could not find a better one.

He lodged near the statue of Erasmus, and when, at night, he illumed his lamp, its sceptic light fell upon the bronze robe of his sceptic precursor. He was, throughout the whole of his laborious life, more brilliant, more active, more influential, than Erasmus himself.

Yet after all, in what did he succeed? in furnishing Voltaire and Diderot with excellent epigrams. The Puritans had done better; they had deposed in the soil of America, the germ of a colossal empire. The power of faith and courage, even with genius, is in fecundity and grandeur, singularly greater than cleverness. Bayle, the charming thinker, " the

Story-teller of the Universe," as M. Villemain paints him with one profound and ingenious touch, gave to the 18th century an immense arsenal of arguments, facts, doubts, and railleries—he has, in playing with it, sapped certainty and destroyed credulity and glory. That is all. I would not sacrifice to courageous souls all independence and spiritual grace; but I say that the one builds, where the other destroys. I say that Moral Force is essential to the creation, maintenance and greatness of society.

Now this Moral Force existed in its highest degree in the little Puritan colony carried by the May Flower. Its true originality was neither chivalric grace nor intellectual brilliancy. The colonists had only that Calvinist energy, that vigorous courage, about to struggle with nature, that force which the author of Robinson Crusoe, the old Puritan, Daniel Defoe, has dressed in epic robes. Profound reverie, highly colored fiction, tragic starts, refined metaphysics, clever style, harmonious choice of language, none of all these could suit these colonists; savage in their austerity, cruel by force of virtue, Art could not live in the hardness of their souls.

It was not until late, after the first efforts at colonization, when the red men had been forced to retire into their woods, when a considerable strip of land had been cleared upon the borders of the Atlantic, that a sort of literature was born in America.

Feeble, timid, imitative, with no pretension to sublimity or passion, a stranger to greatness, half rustic, half citizen, was it—in a word, it was inspired by the Spectator and Robinson Crusoe.

The beginner of this literature, amiable and subtle scholar of Defoe and Addison, was Benjamin Franklin. He announced the advent of a milder and more indulgent civilization. Addison's apologue and delicacy; the popular, plain-speaking of Defoe and Bunyan, were softened and melted into a pleasant composition, which characterised the first essays of colonial literature, essays remarkable for the sobriety of their tone, and the absence of high color.

Imagination, magnificent and dangerous gift, is not found in the works of Franklin, nor do any of his cotemporaries or friends possess it. Nor Washington, nor Jefferson, nor Gouverneur Morris, nor John Quincy Adams. Only to-day some sparks from its prism are thrown upon the pages of Prescott and Longfellow, of Washington Irving and Cooper.

What is the cause of this intellectual phenomenon? In view of those green savannahs, those virgin forests, those lakes which are seas, those rivers whose banks are too far apart to be seen, the manly virtues of the Puritans have grown; but their imagination has rested mute. Problem of curious resolution.

SECTION II.

WHAT IS IMAGINATION?—THE UNITED STATES WANT HISTORICAL PERSPECTIVE, NOT GREATNESS.

What is imagination? It is remembrance idealized.

Of all the striking images evoked by the mind of man there is but one which does not emanate from the memory. Unite the forms of the man and the horse, of the fish and the woman, of the goat and the youth, and you create the Centaur, the Syren, the Faun. Submit yourself to the laws of Nature, and if there be any harmony or proportion in your new combination, your chimera will be the fruit of a happy imagination. If your remembrances, badly united, clumsily adjusted, do not succeed in composing a whole, you give birth to monsters. In either hypothesis, the common source from whence you draw is the Memory. Endowed with a more or less vivid or ardent power of remembrance, you will have what is vulgarly called fecundity or sterility of imagination; but in your books, pictures, songs, poems, statues, what you fancy that you invent—though you were Dante, Phidias, or Raphael—will always be an impression of your childhood or youth, something which you have seen or felt; treasure of remembrance whose poverty constitutes what is called stupidity, whose confusion results in extravagance, whose riches and plenitude constitute Genius.

One abuses the elasticity of language, when one speaks of *creative intelligences;* for there is no creation: to reproduce, to imitate, is enough for us. If Homer, Cervantes, Ariosto, Byron had lived, shut up in a dungeon, what would they ever have imagined? What creation would they have given to the world? Their empty brain, their inert thought would have produced but mean or gross ideas, such as belong to hunger, thirst, the material wants of man. But they led lives of agitation; a thousand varied impressions were profoundly engraved upon their minds which were endowed by Nature with a great aptitude to receive such impressions. Dante had seen Florence; he created a Hell: Theologian, he created the Paradise: Lover, he produced Beatrice. Was it wanting in him, that quality falsely designated, but which must be called by its vulgar name, *Imagination;* to him who has not introduced into his "Comedy" celestial, infernal or expiatory, one single word which was not a remembrance, one single idea which was not taken from Nature or History?

The critics, born in such days as ours, only talk of creation, invention, imagination. It is precisely when all images have been reproduced, when all ideas have been a thousand times repeated, that they demand of art an impossible fecundity and originality. Hence the monsters produced by the old Literature when it fell into barbarity ; hence the unheard-of personages who people our romances.

One goes beyond Nature, yet fancies that he imagines ; one is prodigal of falsehood, and thinks that he invents ; one builds upon vulgar realities all manner of grotesque novelties. The expression becomes as forced, as the idea is exaggerated and absurd. Yet after all, these disproportions, these monsters, these daubs, are but remembrance ill-employed, the dreams of a sick man, the incoherent phantoms of delirium ; a confused evocation of facts and ideas without harmony. The imagination of men of genius, produces the passions and scenes of the world, as a faithful and polished mirror reproduces a beautiful country or a regular visage ; false imagination is like those twisted mirrors, which the optician has made so as to produce no exact reflection ; where all appears immeasurably shortened or elongated. One is to the other what caricature is to portrait.

And as it is impossible for a man without remembrance to have imagination, so that intellectual quality cannot belong to a people born yesterday, whose whole Past dates from yesterday. The United States of America, for so many reasons remarkable and grand, are essentially modern ; their genius is material and mechanic ; their force lies in their good sense, their patient observation and industry. It is—as we have just said—a country without imagination because without memories. Countries grown old in sorrow, Ireland, Scotland, for instance, lend much to the imagination. They have bought that brilliant faculty dear ; not a castle whose walls are not blood-stained, whose legend does not tell of a murder ; not a fortress whose echoes do not bring to you from afar the sound of violence; the atmosphere of the Gaelic hills is peopled with phantoms, every lake has its fay, every cavern its enchanter: the shadow of Bruce wanders through those sombre chapels; the name of Wallace sounds with the sough of the wind through these ruined arches.

The United States, by a phenomenon which we have just explained, wants that dawn and penumbra which give perspective. The very tongue is not native to the soil; it has crossed the sea, and naturalized itself on that side the ocean. To preserve the purity of their style, American writers are forced to keep their regards constantly fixed upon the mother country where are found their types and their models. If they innovate, they fear vulgarity or emphasis. In this respect they are like those modern writers, who use a dead language, and fancy that they can thus restore to us Cicero, Demosthenes, Livy; forgetting that it is the social life of a people which gives energy and life to a language, and that an idiom detached from national society and manners, is a branch detached from the tree, and deprived of its sap. Scotland, even, is proud of her dialect: she has her poet Burns, whose inspiration was at once extinguished when he became unfaithful to the patois of his province.

The republicans of the United States, a virgin people, full of grandeur, whose struggle with nature is not yet ended; all of whose energy must necessarily be directed to the foundation of cities and the development of industry; a nation whose Future is their country; who have no Past—hardly born and already a giant—which had no infancy, no childhood, and whose maturity precedes its youth—not recognizing in their history any of those transitions from feebleness to virility; any of those epochs, the chain of which, ornamented by tradition, receives later, the consecration of poetry.

Here are soldiers, legislators, artisans, a strong, noble race sufficient for to-day. Poets will be born, hereafter.

The first of her writers is an artisan-legislator, it is Franklin.

SECTION III.

BENJAMIN FRANKLIN—SIR JOHN CREVECŒUR—LETTERS OF AN AMERICAN PLANTER—JONATHAN EDWARDS.

I have already spoken of Franklin, type of the national genius; consummate politician, subtle dialectician, a lover of the useful. His style has the qualities of his thought: good sense, lucidity, benevolence, delicate and sportive unction. He addresses himself neither to souvenirs, nor to hopes; not one shadow of passion mingles with his language. It is rustic and pleasing, a prudence which smiles. Call him prosaic and vulgar, it will not offend his shadow. His charming "Parable against Persecution," his "Poor Robin," a manual written for an infant people, whose leading-strings still guide its uncertain march; his "Examination before the Privy Council" are chefs-d'œuvre of political sagacity. One finds there, under ingenuous and ingenious forms, the suppleness of a most rare mind.

A little while before the American Revolution broke out, a book—now little known—appeared, the tone and style of which are characteristic—"The Letters of an American Cultivator." Sir John Crevecœur, author of this work, published under the pseudonym of Hector St. John, merits an honorable place in the list of modern writers. Landscape, manners, language, sentiment, all are essentially American The existence of the colonist is reproduced with energy and simplicity; neither epithet nor coloring is exaggerated. You find not only the objects, but also the sensations and ideas of a new country; you see the author attaching his child's wagon to the plough which he guides, and so conducting along the furrows traced by the share, his little one and his plough, while his wife, seated under a tree at the other end of the field, knits the woollen vestments for the winter. In another place you have a duel between two serpents, the recital of which is grave and solemn as a battle of Homer; the author's strong impressions are all revealed by the style; he could not have chosen nobler words, had his heroes been Hector and Patroclus. He has vivid and graceful shading for whatever strikes him; he does not paint Nature in his closet, nor make himself a descriptive poet, but as he sees her, so he repeats her. He does not busy himself about what the saloons of London or Paris may think of his work; or whether the journals will criticise it. With what good will he mingles in the amusements of the Nantucket people! What alacrity, what a power of industry and labor are in his pages; how his heart beats in unison with every heart; how he compels us to associate ourselves with the perils of the whale-fishery; to take interest in the joyous feasts which reward those perils! How admirable in all latitudes are those two things, Strength and Joy! And is it not a rare and remarkable talent to paint them so as to make the reader share in them? This writer, so little read, attains in some parts of his work to a degree of dramatic interest very uncommon. The American war is about to break out; the low murmurs of the tempest rumble from afar; the Indians are menacing to raise the war-whoop and to pour down upon the inland plantation. The colony hardly formed, may fall. These presagings sadden you; and when you close the book, you have need to be reassured by History and to convince yourself that the terrors of the Colonist have not been realized, that the Colonial Hercules has strangled the serpents which attacked his cradle.

The third remarkable writer whom we encounter in the literary annals of America, is a logician whose celebrity does not seem to have been widely propagated in Europe, but whose merits cannot be denied. Jonathan Edwards, an ecclesiastic, born in Massachusetts, has written a "Treatise on the Will," which ranks him with the subtlest writers. It is a man who does not wish to persuade you but to convince himself. He has not a subterfuge, not an evasion, not a sophism. If an objection presents itself he does not strive, either to disguise or enfeeble it. Read him, and you will think Hobbes dogmatic and Priestly insolent. It is with perfect good faith that he tries to clear up the inextricable difficulties into which his thought is plunged as soon as he approaches the theories of Free will.

In these three writers you admire a fertile naïveté, a happy facility, a ripened, sagacious reason—but no imagination. The American Cultivator only, by the freshness of his pictures, exhibits a sort of originality.

Franklin is like Fenelon, Bunyan, Addison. In Jonathan Edwards there is something of the firm, neat, pressing argument of Descartes; impassioned eloquence and poetic imagination are wanting to the whole three.

SECTION IV.

GOUVERNEUR MORRIS—THE AMERICAN ARISTOCRAT—PARIS OBSERVED FROM 1789 TO 1792 BY A FOUNDER OF THE AMERICAN CONFEDERATION.

Imagination is not found either in Gouverneur Morris, a diplomatist, a distinguished observer, an intelligent and an honest man, endowed with a quick enough sagacity, a right judgment, and a coolness which serves him in a crisis, and which permits him to pass peaceably through the French Revolution.

Morris never exposed himself rashly; never went to meet danger; but when there was necessity, urgency, duty, he halted, showed a calm face and braved the peril; it is one of the finest qualities of the American character. His speeches in Congress and his notes contributed powerfully to the good organization of the confederate democracy, and above all of American finance. Friend of Washington, he became intimate with every one of those strangers who offered their services to the new Republic during its struggle—the Marquis de Lafayette—"The others," (says Washington, in a letter to Morris,) "are adventurers whom the waste of their own resources sends to us, or spies paid by foreign governments to watch our movements, or men whose souls are given up to a vain desire of glory, which would make them sacrifice the holiest interests to their personal ambition."

When that great and fine Revolution of America, so little stained with innocent blood, so noble and so grave, was terminated, and Washington, instead of seeking the first rank in the new federal empire, sought by every honest means to escape from his own glory, and the ordinary recompenses of ambition, Gouverneur Morris, whose fortune was considerable, whose social position excellent, desired to visit Europe. Washington gave him several letters to his friends, and charged him—a characteristic detail—"to buy him at Paris, a flat gold watch, without any ornament; not," says the letter, "the watch of a fool or of a man who desires to make a show, but of which the interior construction shall be extremely well cared for, and the exterior air very simple."

Morris started for France, from whence he wrote to his friends, between 1789 and 1792 a great many letters, which Jared Sparks, one of the most indefatigable biographers of the United States, published in 1802 with the life of his compatriot Morris. Biography, treated as Jared Sparks treats it, is by no means amusing; it is a Chinese screen, without perspective, where all is on the same flat, all the incidents have the same importance. Yet I like this style without style, this good faith of an honest business man better than the charms of the rhetoric biographer.

The political acts of Morris, citizen of the United States, were honorable without being brilliant. The qualities of his mind were essentially American; a penetrating good sense, and a great taste for order and economy; a gentle and benevolent severity in his way of judging men; and in matters of fortune a consummate prudence and exemplary patience. The spirit of *a-propos* and clever sally was not wanting to his character any more than to Franklin: not the only likeness between them, for they had the same cool temperament, the same Socratic look into things. Morris having never been obliged to fight against fortune, nourished more epicurean tastes, and resigned himself more easily to the brilliant and conversational idleness of great cities. He had also some good old habitual sins, gastronomy, for instance, and the love of doing nothing, which put him upon a level with the France of Louis XV., and associated him with its movement.

Morris is an admirable observer; never has the French Revolution been judged by so impartial a witness, by a man come from the other world to assist at this great drama, by an American, a member of the Congress where Washington and Franklin sate. Democrat by fact and not by theory he knows how liberty is established. He does not recall the memory of Athens and Rome, his own remembrances suffice him. He handled the interests of a nation which created itself a republic in spite of its metropolis, and which has also had its noble contests, its terrible crises, its moments of exaltation, its violent revolutions, its martyrs, its heroes, its obstacles to overcome.

How will Gouverneur Morris appreciate the new liberty of France? The movers of this grand change will pass before his eyes and will exhibit to him all their resources. It is curious to examine their portraits, made by a man who had no interest in deceiving. How will he regard those ardent theories, those philosophic vapors, by whose constant eruptions society is melted to be recast. Does he consider this vehemence as a pledge of duration; this powerful ebulition as a proof of strength? He has seen our Mirabeaus, our Camille Desmoulins; he has watched them as they worked; he has consigned his reflections to a journal, which is now published. How has he prophesied? You will not accuse him of judging after the blow was struck; nor of yielding to the predilections of an aristocratic birth. If he shows severity, it will be the severity of a friend. What leaning can this son of American colonists have towards the nobles of France? And this enemy of England, who has just revolted against the tyranny of the metropolis, can he be a partisan of Pitt, of Coburg?

Let us follow him. Let us listen to him.

It was in 1789; minds were in motion in France, heads were fermenting. Morris disembarking at Havre, formed the acquaintance of a little gentleman who appeared to him a phenomenon; it was the first specimen of this sort which had offered itself to his notice; a universal reformer; a man of plans and systems; a little gentleman, whose brain was boiling with politics, philanthrophy and philosophy; a genius who could regulate the destinies of twenty empires better than Lycurgus or Alfred the Great. Something worth observing is this: the immense surprise of the good Morris in presence of this legislative gentleman, Morris, who had himself just been a legislator and the founder of a state. He makes a note of this curious and uneasy individual, and goes on his way.

He arrives in Paris Feb. 3, 1789. Paris flashing with luxury, sparkling with cleverness, saturated with pleasure, where the awful scene of the "States General" is about to open.

The first persons whom he visits are Jefferson, Minister Plenipotentiary of the United States, in France, and M. de Lafayette, for whose character he professes a high esteem, without sharing in his feelings, or his manner of judging. The physiognomy of reforming France astonishes him. The impression produced upon him by the universal enthusiasm, by the manner of the court, by the blundering fervor of the advocates, the lawyers, the men of letters, is far from favorable. He finds no where that religious profundity of sensation and decision which is a pledge of a people's future. Instead of admitting the zeal for a purely theoretic liberty; instead of getting inflamed by the noisy logomachy of orators and writers; instead of associating himself with that popular superstition, which, in six years, was to become an ardent fanaticism, our American, who goes to the bottom of things, and earnestly seeks in the wild chaos, the germs of veritable independence, of real liberty, recognizes with sorrow, that no such germs are to be found there. From the first day he predicts the inevitable and bloody fall of the French Republic about to be established.

His political opinions never agree with those of his friend M. de Lafayette. The first time that this celebrated name appears in his journal, he says—"Lafayette is too full of politics; he appears to be too republican for the genius of his country."

It is in vain that you say to Morris, "We want the liberty which you have acquired." He replies obstinately, "This is not our American liberty." M. de Lafayette shows him a copy of the celebrated "Declaration of the Rights of Man," which he intends to read in the National Assembly. Morris, always a man of sense, says that words are not things, and that dogmatic assertions are of very little importance to the happiness of the masses. "I gave him my opinions, and suggested several amendments tending to soften the high-colored expression of freedom. It is not by sounding words that revolutions are produced."

Alas! Morris touched the wound with his finger. There were certainly too many sounding words in all that—the man of letters and the rhetorician had too much to do with our first revolution. Men had too much faith in words, and sacrificed things to them with too much inconsiderateness. The people thought they could make liberty as Rousseau had made virtue—by declamation. This frightened a foreigner who had seen a true liberty develop itself by mere moral force. He could not forget that he had taken a very active part, played a very essential role in a revolution crowned with success, with fortune, with power.

How could Morris help fearing that abortion would result from all this Spartan, Roman bombast? Founder of a democracy, he had seen no Greek memories in the cradle of the institutions which he had helped to form. What seems to him incompatible with the establishment of liberty is the violent fury for renovation, the blind and childish confidence of those who hope to found durable institutions on enthusiasm and phrases.

You must turn to the memoirs of Morris, to see how a friend of Washington appreciates those paper politicians, who issue from the Registry and the Sorbonne to regulate kingdoms. The disdain of this republican for republican talkers reaches sometimes even injustice. He has not indulgence enough for an old civilized country, overladen with colleges and academies, impregnated with Greek and Latin ideas; for a capital which has known the Regency and Louis XV.; for men who have read Rousseau after leaving the *petit souper*, and who though kneaded in monarchy are yet drunk with patriotic desires, and who run with the passions of a child towards the ideal goal from which their habits and their wishes separate them. Morris keeps too constantly under his eyes America, the new country, where manners are simple, interests not complicated; ideas, serious and strong—a nation which does not care to imitate Epaminondas, or to have a Demosthenes, so long as they can make the port of Boston free; so long as the Stamp Act does not diminish their profits. How could Morris do otherwise than pity the metaphysical discussions, and endless speculations of the French. Politics are no matters of sentiment and passion, and Morris was both frightened and alarmed at what he saw. "They reform here," he says, "with unparalleled giddiness. Every body has something to do with it. Each man has a plan, each man a theory. The physicians of the social body are multiplied. There is not an attorney, no matter how little, how ignorant of rhetoric, who does not become a reformer. Where is the moral and intellectual force which alone can rescue France? A little energy, and better morals would do her far more good than all these words."

During the various crises of the French Revolution from 1789 to 1794, Morris, who had been taught bloody lessons, grew firmer in his opinions, and did not cease to cry out to every party that they were losing themselves and ruining the liberty of their country. At last, his disapprobation became so thorough and so distinct, that the French republicans, annoyed by the presence of such a censor, solicited his recall in 1794, for Morris had replaced Jefferson as Chargé d'Affaires for the United States. Nothing appeared easier than for a minister of the American Republic to go hand in hand with the chiefs of the French Republic. But these latter had gone so far in so short a time that Washington, Franklin, Morris, had been left behind. After being two or three times put upon the list of the "suspected," our republican went home, where he lived peaceably at his estate of Morrisiana, and died not a very great while ago.

SECTION V.

MORRIS AT PARIS FROM 1789 TO 1792—PRELUDES TO THE REVOLUTION—JEFFERSON'S OPINION ON THE FRENCH REVOLUTION.

I think that no other observer was so happily placed as Morris, to get a view of our Revolution. Minister Plenipotentiary of a friendly republic, rich and independent, his relations with those in power were habitual, easy and confidential. As American and Member of Congress, he had a right to the favor of the more exalted revolutionists. Well brought up and educated, and a friend of de Lafayette, he was admitted to the drawing rooms of the nobility, and the cabinets of the dying monarchy. While he sympathized in the movement of the people towards liberty, he never hid his pity for an aristocracy which had flourished so long and which was so suddenly uprooted. Therefore all doors were opened to him, those of the boiling revolutionary clubs, those of the hotels where the trembling relics of the monarchical party united. There are a thousand curious little traits, a thousand light-giving anecdotes, jotted down upon the tablets of the traveller.

You see there how marquises and counts amused themselves on the eve of a fearful catastrophe ; how lords, old and young, whose heads would soon be in danger, attached, in the chapel and during the mass, a lighted candle' to the cassock of a fashionable abbé ; what politico-romantic discussions were heard at the restaurateurs' of Versailles ; how the expiring monarchy looked everywhere for advice, counsel, direction, accepting all and following the worst. Side by side with these details, the observant American places his prophetic reflections ; the date is there and the date is remarkable ; Morris predicts the events of more than one year.

The Republic is about to be established, and he announces it ; the Republic will be changed into a Dictature and a Tyranny ; he says so in 1791. If he appreciate a person, if he predict a result, time proves, that the man was well-judged, the result inevitable.

Let us look how he describes the materials of the coming revolution.

" The materials for a revolution in this country are very indifferent. Everybody agrees that there is an utter prostration of morals ; but this general position can never convey to an American mind the degree of depravity. It is not by any figure of rhetoric, or force of language, that the idea can be communicated. A hundred anecdotes, and a hundred thousand examples, are required to show the extreme rottenness of every member. There are men and women who are greatly and eminently virtuous. I have the pleasure to number many in my own acquaintance; but they stand forward from a background deeply and darkly shaded. It is, however, from such crumbling matter, that the great edifice of freedom is to be erected here. Perhaps, like the stratum of rock, which is spread under the whole surface of their country, it may harden when exposed to the air; but it seems quite as likely that it will fall and crush the builders."

We are tempted, by our love for France, to accuse the American of injustice; nevertheless when we examine, without prejudice, the epoch of which he speaks, when we look at the *Memoires de Bachaumont*, the *Correspondence de Grimm*, the Works of *Laclos*, the letters of *Madame d'Epinay*, that sentimental *rouée*, the letters of *Mademoiselle de Lespinasse*, who loved with so naïvely-philosophic a passion, three men at once, and the *facetiæ* of M. de Caylus, and the prettinesses of our friend Crebillon the younger;—we must agree with Morris that there is not much republic in all that;—that the affair of the Queen's collar, the lawsuit of Beaumarchais, the scandal about Madame d'Eon, the antecedents of Mirabeau, the favor of the abbé-cardinal de Bernis, form a strange portal through which to enter into an austere democracy. We must excuse Morris, nurtured, as he was, in respect for the law, for marriage, for an oath, for the sanctity of the family; who has seen flourish, in the midst of this respect and this morality, not the shadow, the bloody phantasmagoria of a republic, but a true Republic, industrious and calm.

Sometime after having written the above letter to Washington, he writes to Mr. Jay:

"When I reflect how very little this nation is prepared by habits or education, to enjoy complete liberty, I fairly tremble for it; it will overshoot the mark, or rather, I fear, has already done so. They have felt too long the heavy weight of royal authority. Now they look with pleasure upon whatever can restrain or break it; they seek a republic, but how will they sustain it? France does not yet know all the evils to which the exaggerated feebleness of the executive power necessarily exposes itself. She only fears the tyranny of power, which can no longer touch her; she does not arm herself against anarchy, the most fearful danger which now threatens her."

This was written in 1789.

We have already remarked in Morris, a mixture of severe morality, and of skilful social finesse. He has just enough of American puritanism not to excuse the slightest vice; and enough experience of the world not to be the dupe of a single false appearance. Add to this that he does not draw brilliant portraits to win your admiration, or his own; that his opinions are neither exaggerated nor wanting, but singularly redoubtable. He shows no favor to pretension. Does a vanity hide itself under a virtue; does a feebleness put on the robe of glory, the American is inexorable. Penetrating without malignity, sagacious without ambition, thrown into a stormy society which marches blindly towards its ruin, had he identified himself with it, like Anacharsis Clootz and Thomas Paine, he could not have judged it; had he only hated and despised it, like Burke, he would have been unjust. But he marched with it, yet kept apart from its follies, its furies, its intoxication. He kept his eyes open, his glance clear, his soul accessible to what was noble in the efforts of France.

French society, so well represented in its greatness and littleness by Voltaire; and which like him is a lover of humanity, like him *prime-sautiere*;* drawn on by instinct, and seduced by a *bon mot*; destructive, *roué*, light-headed, capricious, violent; desiring the good, doing the evil; talking virtue, pedantic without knowing it; a drunken marquis, who with trembling steps, in cloth of gold with ragged sleeves runs, singing, headlong towards the abyss;—all this astonishes and revolts Morris, who has never imagined anything like it. Morris has just left Washington. The most honest people of Paris seem to him somewhat crazy. As for the craziest, they are wild beasts for him.

In the midst of these morals and these men, he is yet quite at ease, tells the truth to all the world, and plays his part of "peasant from the Danube." Instead of getting angry at his frankness, they are charmed by its novelty; duchesses smile on him, countesses applaud him, ministers listen to him.

"I have dared," he says, "to utter hard words, which they are little accustomed to. I told some grave truths, and they heard them joyfully; satiated as they were with prettiness and flattery. Truth is a new and singular dish, which pleases them. It is an unexpected contrast and they like it. I will not, however, give them too much of it."

For his part he does not exchange flatteries with his hosts. Far from esteeming French politeness too highly, he sees, with clear glance, how much of false and of hollow there is in that brilliant and pleasant lie.

"It is agreeable," he says, "but you must be a fool to believe it." Still, he let himself be charmed by a conversation which is easy, always ready, which characterized the time, and which now begins to be merely a tradition. As soon as the first symptoms of agitation manifest themselves, he sees clearly the future of France. "The court," he says, "is

* Said of a person who expresses himself with great readiness.

extremely feeble ; morals are very much relaxed, and the first effort of the nation will overthrow the throne." He attends the opening of the States General; and notwithstanding the solemnity of the scene, he discovers a much greater interest than the frivolous one excited by a mere outside ceremony. He expects a total change in French life. When he sees the Queen, already humiliated, abase her Austrian pride, devour her tears in silence, and all trembling, salute the people who disdain her ; when he hears nobles declaiming against feudal tyranny, and observes the enormous power usurped by the faculty of eloquence and the strength of language he foresees Robespierre, Thermidor, Bonaparte.

"I have seen," he says, "the curtain fall upon the first act of a terrible drama. The first step of grandeur descending towards the tomb, has been taken before my eyes ; it is very sad and more deserving of pity and reflection that the last catastrophe will be." Whosoever will recal the time in which these words were written, will find them prophetic and beautiful.

His conversation with Jefferson, whose republican opinions were much more ardent and decided than those of Morris, prove that Jefferson, then Minister for the United States, judged France precisely as his compatriot did.

"June 3d—Go to Mr. Jefferson's. Some political conversation. He seems to be out of hope of any thing being done to purpose by the States General. This comes from having sanguine expectation of a downright republican form of government. The literary people here, observing the abuses of their monarchical form, imagine that everything must go the better in proportion as it recedes from the present establishments, and in their closets they make men exactly suited to their systems ; but unluckily they are such men as exist nowhere else ; and least of all in France. I am more than ever persuaded that the form, which at first appeared to be most fit for them, is that which will be adopted; and exactly to my idea, but probably in a much better manner."

Morris not content with writing all this in his note-book uttered it in the drawing-rooms. Judge if French society were surprised; the liberty with which the American spake such opinions, seemed strange in those days when all was hope, fire, ardor, attraction towards the social felicity which men dreamed of. Honorable and dishonorable, feeble and intelligent, Mirabeau and Marat, were all travelling in idea towards a political Eldorado. Morris desired to put off or to check this flight; he was in consequence reproached as faithless to his own cause, and as a traitor to that independence which as an American he was bound to propagate.

"At dinner I sit next to Monsieur de Lafayette, who tells me that I injure the cause, for that my sentiments are continually quoted against the good party. I seize this opportunity to tell him, that I am opposed to the democracy from regard to liberty. That I see they are going headlong to destruction, and would fain stop them if I could. That their views respecting this nation are totally inconsistent with the materials of which it is composed; and that the worst thing, which could happen, would be to grant their wishes. He tells me, that he is sensible that his party are mad, and tells them so, but is not the less determined to die with them. I tell him, that I think it would be quite as well to bring them to their senses and live with them."

Of the same sort is his judgment of men and character; austere as Truth, calm and simple as she is, armed with an unepigramatic irony, less bitter than satire, yet of a farther-reaching blow.

Let our readers judge whether his opinion of M. Necker,

for instance, is like that which history has at last adopted. We will extract from the diary of Morris, a simple recital of unpretentious memoranda, sometimes ungrammatical, the relation of his first interview with the Minister of Finance, a man so variously appreciated.

"I dined with M. and Madame Necker. Our society was composed of academicians and great lords. If M. Necker be really a great man, I deceive myself; so do I if he be not a great worker * * * * The courtiers in their anguish curse Necker and his acts; but he is less the cause than the instrument of their sufferings. The nation loves in him the man detested by the court. If the nobles did not try to destroy him, the republicans would not sustain him; his position is factitious; he is not listened to. Dictator a fortnight ago, he has now lost his influence. Then, he decided all; now, nothing. They keep him because they fear to do otherwise; lest his removal should prove a pretext for a popular commotion. The giant will soon fall.

"Necker's reputation seems to be false and inflated, a very common thing in this country. His enemies pretend that his character as a banker is not stainless, but Parisian judgments are too much exaggerated to be readily subscribed to. Necker is a man of probity; in his administration of the public money, he has always shown himself honest and disinterested. Apparently, he is more vain than vicious; he ruins himself to retain a high post, sought by others as a means of self-enrichment. The source of his great renown in France would be thought singular in America; it is the emphasis of his writings, the philosophic and false sensibility which makes the fortune of modern romances, and which he puts into his books upon finance; that pleases the French. Here one likes to read, if you do not make him reflect. He has talent as a writer, and his wife has finesse; but neither one nor the other know what a minister is. His financial education has taught him economy; and all he knows of mankind is their monied interests. All our other passions escape him."

Whether this portrait be exact or not, the predictions of Morris have been accomplished to the letter; the giant fell a few days after his elevation; his popularity *collapsed*, as Morris announced, and his reputation for probity remained stainless. The brilliant conversation of his daughter, Madame de Staël, frightened Morris, who by no means spares her in his journal, though he renders justice to her fine qualities, mental and spiritual; you see that she made him nervous, that he could hardly accustom himself to a nature which had nothing feminine but its sprightliness and mobility, but borrowed from the other sex audacity, strength, impetuosity, eloquence: Morris was too severe towards this extraordinary woman.

"After dinner (Madame de Tessé having told her that I am *un homme d'esprit*) she singles me out, and makes *a talk*. Asks if I have not written a book on the American constitution. "Non Madame, j'ai fait mon devoir en assistant a la formation de cette constitution." "Mais Monsieur, votre conversation doit étre très intéressante, car je vous entends cité de toute part." "Ah, Madame, je ne suis pas digne de cet éloge." How I lost my leg? It was unfortunately not in the military service of my country. "Monsieur, vous avez l'air très imposant," and this is accompanied with that look, which without being what Sir John Falstaff calls the "leer of invitation," amounts to the same thing. I answered affirmatively, and would have left the matter there; but she tells me that Monsieur de Chastellux often spoke of me. This leads us on, but in the midst of the chat arrive letters. one of which is from her lover (Narbonne) now with his regiment. It brings her to a little recollection, which I think, a little time will again banish. She enters into a conversation with Madame de Tessé, who reproves most pointedly the approbation she gave to Mirabeau, and the ladies became at length animated to the utmost bound of politeness."

The light ridicule, the frivolity applied to the gravest interests, the mingling of silliness with striking and easy grace, did not escape Morris.

"March 1st.—Sup with Madame de la Suse. A small party absorbed in Quinze. Monsieur de B. for want of something else to do, asks me many questions about America, in a manner which shows he cares little for the information. By way of giving him some adequate idea of our people, when he mentioned the necessity of fleets and armies to secure us against invasions, I tell him, that nothing would be more difficult than to subdue a nation, every individual of which, in the pride of freedom, thinks himself equal to a king; and if, sir, you should look down on him, would say, "I am a man; are you anything more?" "All this is very well; but there must be a difference of ranks, and I should say to one of these people—'You, sir, who are equal to a king, make me a pair of shoes.'" "Our citizens, sir, have a manner of thinking peculiar to themselves. This shoemaker would reply: 'Sir, I am very glad of the opportunity to make you a pair of shoes. It is my duty to make shoes, and I love to do my duty,—Does your king do his?' This manner of thinking and speaking, however, is too masculine for the climate I am now in."

I must quote one more scene, which says enough of the religious spirit of the great, and of their occupations on the eve of a catastrophy.

"June 11th.—This morning I go to Reinsi. Arrive at eleven. Nobody yet visible. After some time the Duchess (of Orleans) appears, and tells me that she has given Madame de Chastellux notice of my arrival. This consists with my primitive idea. Near twelve before the breakfast is paraded; but, as I had eaten mine before my departure, this has no present inconvenience. After breakfast we go to mass in the chapel. In the tribune above, we have a Bishop, an Abbé, the Duchess, her maids, and some of their friends. Madame de Chastellux is below on her knees. We are amused above by a number of little tricks played off by Monsieur de Ségur and Monsieur de Cabières with a candle, which is put into the pockets of different gentlemen, the Bishop's among the rest, and lighted, while they are otherwise engaged (for there is a fire in the tribune), to the great merriment of the spectators. Immoderate laughter is the consequence. The Dutchess preserves as much gravity as she can. This scene must be very edifying to the domestics, who are opposite to us, and the villagers who worship below. After this ceremony is concluded, we commence our walk, which is long and excessively hot. Then we get into batteaux, and the gentlemen row the ladies, which is by no means a cool operation. After that, more walking; so that I am excessively inflamed, even to fever heat. Get to the Château, and doze a little, *en attendant le diner*, which does not come till after five. A number of persons surround the windows, and doubtless form a high idea of the company, to whom they are obliged to look up at an awful distance. Ah, did they but know how trivial the conversation, how very trivial the characters, their respect would soon be changed to an emotion extremely different."

Three years after, the people had discovered the hollowness of the walls; and Morris, who had pitied their imbecile veneration, saw it changed into a frightful hatred.

The Bastille is taken: Versailles rests calm and mute. "It

is considered in good taste at court," says Morris, "to seem to believe that all is tranquil. To-morrow, perhaps, when they see the walls of the smoking citadel, they may go so far as to allow that there has been some disturbance in Paris." Full of contempt for this apathy of the courtiers, who continue their mystifications and their *petits soupers*, Morris does not neglect to interest himself in the families blazoned with antique glory. He mocks the fallen art, and the artists of the day, who take so little interest in the commotion, and who, in face of the French Revolution, busy themselves about academies, smiling nymphs, and chubby cupids. A painter, a pensioner of the king, showed to Morris a handsome Æneas and Anchises, which covered a large canvas. "You would do better," said the American, "to paint the taking of the Bastille. It is less heroic, but rather more interesting for us.

The feebleness of Louis XVI., his entire want of decision and of intellectual courage in great circumstances, inspired in Morris a sort of disdain; he is not for a moment deceived as to the fate of the king, whose probity he esteems and whose situation he pities, surrounded as he is by perfidious friends and inexorable enemies. He receives a deposit of money from the hands of the Monarch, and in several very remarkable notes, gives him excellent advice which is never followed. A plan of a Constitution for France, drawn up by Morris is peculiar by the fact, that with the exception of some modifications, especially an hereditary peerage which seemed necessary to Morris, the plan indicated by the American in 1790, as the only salvation for France, is precisely that under which she tried to exist from 1830 to 1848, a mixed government, slightly aristocratic, very favorable to industry, giving but little latitude to the personal wishes of the Sovereign, ensuring extended supervision to the deliberative chambers, and leaving to talent ready access to power. An ultra-federalist in his own country, Morris would appear to most of us, to-day, to sustain ultra-monarchical principles; how then could he be otherwise than complained of when the Revolution boiled over; when one dreamed of no other social condition but Spartan equality!

He cannot get along with Lafayette; their friendship soon cools; and on Morris' side does not rekindle, until Lafayette, placed in a false position between the sovereign people and the overthrown king, unable to arrest one or to save the other, and crushed by the collision, falls, is cursed alike by the power he had weakened, and the democracy which he had served but not followed

SECTION VI.

M. DE LAFAYETTE—THE FRENCH ÉMIGRÉS.

This American Morris, accused of coldness for Utopias and indifference for enthusiastic systems, performs noiselessly several noble and very generous actions; devoted yet prudent hero, he saves the life of Madame de Lafayette, and becomes suspicious to the republicans, who send him away in 1793. His journal had ceased to be detailed; Morris, always circumspect, felt that it would be absurd to risk his head for the pleasure of making certain notes, and under date of January, 1790, you may read these words, the last written in his French journal:

"The situation of affairs is such, that I cannot continue my journal without compromising myself and many others

If I do not write useless and insignificant memoranda, I can write nothing. I prefer therefore to stop altogether."

Driven from France by the republicans, he travelled in England, Prussia, and Austria. There was then in Europe an interesting and scattered nation, a nation unfortunate, noble, brilliant, eccentric—the émigrés. We have no where a complete picture of their fortune, their absurdities, their strength of soul. Morris, who recommences his journal as soon as he is out of France, throws some light upon that curious subject. Without insulting any misfortune, without adding any derogatory or painful reflection to the observations of Morris, we will content ourselves with copying certain lines relative to the life of the émigrés abroad.

"July 11th.—I call on the Count Woranzow, and show him the draft of a manifesto by the new King of France, which I gave to Lord Grenville last Wednesday, and which he has returned with his wish, that it may arrive in season. The Count Woranzow is well pleased with it, and thinks the Duc d' Harcourt should give money to the person who will carry it to the king. I tell him that is a matter to be settled among them. He gives me an account of the strange levity and wild negociations of the Count d' Artois, and the pitiful folly of M. Serrene to whom he gives his confidence. He fears that when arrived at Vendée, he will surround himself by such *petit maîtres*, and disgust the chiefs, who have acquired the confidence of the people in that quarter, viz. Puisaye, Labourdonnaye, Charette, Stoflet, and wishes me to caution some of his entours. I tell him that would have no other effect than to lead the person to whom I might give such caution, into a communication of it to all those who are about the Prince, and by that means to produce the mischief we mean to avoid."

"*Dresden*, August 19th.—In the streets are many French

emigrants, who are travelling eastward to avoid their countrymen. They are allowed to stay only three days. Unhappy people! Yet they employ themselves in seeing everything curious which they can get at, are serene, and even gay. So great a calamity could never light on shoulders which could bear it so well. But alas! the weight is not diminished by the graceful manner of supporting it. The sense, however, is less, by all that spleen and ill-humor could add to torment the afflicted. Doubtless, there are many among them, who have a consciousness of rectitude to support them."

Three months afterwards, he returns to the chapter of the émigrés, again praises the elegance of their manners, and their courage under affliction, but he does not forget the reverse of the medal.

"Return home and write for the post. After dinner I visit Madame Audenarde who asks me if it be true that I am charged here with a mission from Congress to ask the liberty of Lafayette. I laugh at this a little, and then assuring her that there is no truth in that suggestion, say that it is a piece of folly to keep him prisoner. This brings her out violently against him, and to the same effect the Count Dietrichstein, who indeed is as much prompted to defend the Austrian administration, as to side with his friend. We examine the matter as coolly as their prejudices will admit; and, on the point of right, he takes the only tenable ground, viz., that the public safety being the supreme law of princes, the Emperor, conceiving it dangerous to leave Lafayette and his associates at large, had arrested them, and keeps them still prisoners for the same reason. Lavaupallière, who comes in during the conversation, shows still more ill-will to this unfortunate man than any one else. He seems to flatter himself that there is yet some chance of getting him hanged. He treats him not only as having been deficient in abilities, but as having been most ungrateful to the king and queen, from which last charge I defend him, in order to see what may be the amount of the inculpation; and it resolves itself into two favors received from the court. First, pardon for having gone to America, notwithstanding an order given him to the contrary; and next, promotion to the rank of marèchal de camp over the heads of several who were, many of them, men of family. To crown all, he accuses him of the want of courage, and declares that he has seen him contumeliously treated without resenting it. To this I give as peremptory a negative as good-breeding will permit, and he feels it.

"Indeed, the conversation of these gentlemen, who have the virtue and good fortune of their grandfathers to recommend them, leads me almost to forget the crimes of the French Revolution; and often, the unforgiving temper and sanguinary wishes which they exhibit, make me almost believe that the assertion of their enemies is true, viz., that it is the success alone which has determined on whose side should be the crimes, and on whose the misery."

While the émigrés, driven by democracy from their native soil, vowed hatred and vengeance against the prisoner of Olmutz, the French democrats had for him only the same malediction. His destiny, a truly frightful one, was to find pity from neither side.

In 1796, Madame de Staël, whose generous heart and noble enthusiasm are well known, wrote to Morris the following letter, never published even in America until the appearance of the Life of Morris, and which you will like to see here, as a new proof of respect due to this illustrious woman.

"I have no right to take this step in addressing you. I esteem you most highly; but who would not esteem you? I admire your talents, for I have listened to you, and in this

I am not singular. But what I have to ask of you is so much in accordance with your own feelings, that my letter will only repeat to you their dictates in poorer expressions. You are travelling through Germany, and whether on a public mission or not, you have influence ; for they are not so stupid as not to consult a man like you. Open the prison door of M. de Lafayette, you have already saved his wife from death ; deliver the whole family. Pay the debt of your country. What greater service can any one render to his native land, than to discharge her obligations of gratitude ! Is there any severer calamity than that which has befallen Lafayette ? Does any more glaring injustice attract the attention of Europe ; I speak to you of glory, yet I know a more elevated sentiment is the motive of your conduct.

"The unhappy wife of M. de Lafayette has sent a message, in which she begs her friends to *apply to him who has already been her preserver.* I had no difficulty in recognising you, under this veil. In this period of terror, there are a thousand virtues by which they, who fear to pronounce your name, may distinguish you. For myself, who am more afflicted, I believe, than any one, by the fate of M. de Lafayette, I shall not have the presumption to imagine that my solicitations can influence you in his favor. But you cannot prevent me from admiring you, nor from feeling as grateful to you, as if you had granted to myself alone that which humanity, your own glory, and both worlds expect of you.

"NECKER DE STAEL."

Morris replied very coldly to this earnest letter, and contented himself with acting prudently, without going too fast, without hazarding anything. He forwarded, to the Emperor of Austria, the letter by which Washington requested the enfranchisement of M. de Lafayette. Again Madame de Staël wrote to Morris.

"The place where your letter was written, is enough to give me some hope. It is impossible you should be there without succeeding. Such glory is reserved for you, and there is none more delightful, or more brilliant, for you, or for any man. It is possible the opposition may have been indiscreet; but could the unfortunate man, of whom they spoke, have solicited it of them? It appears certain that his wife was kindly received by the emperor; that he permitted her to write to him; and that he has never received her letters. Humane and just as we are assured he is, would he have suffered the wife and children to be treated in the same manner? The wife and children! What a reward for such a noble self-devotion! It is as cruel as the condition from which you once before saved her. What do they expect? Do they wish that the earliest enemies of the unhappy man should be roused to claim that a period should be put to his misfortunes?—that they should imitate the demand of the Romans from the Carthagenians? It seems to me, if you were to speak for a single hour to those on whom his fate depends, all would be well. I have such experience of your influence over opinions which were even opposed to your own, that I am tempted to ask,—What effect would you not produce were you to lend your intelligence and talent to second the persuasions of interest? Should you ask this, as the reward of your counsels, could it be refused? In short, the idea that this calamity may be terminated by your exertion, this idea excites in me so much emotion, that without disguising to myself the indiscretion of a second letter, I could not deny myself the expression of this belief, which arises as much from admiration of you, as from pity for him.

"NECKER DE STAEL."

Happily the arms of Bonaparte aided the eloquence of Coppet, the diplomacy of Morris, and the letters of Washington.

M. de Lafayette was freed, and one of the most absurd and atrocious injustices of modern times was put an end to. The majority of historians, Walter Scott among them, give all the credit of the liberation to Bonaparte; the documents furnished by Morris, prove that the proposition came from Austria, solicited by Morris and the President of the United States.

Another European wreck, another fragment of revolutionary lava, a name famous, proscribed, a victim, General Moreau, suddenly presents himself to Morris in his agricultural establishment where he now only occupies himself in making his orchards prosper and in planting his park.

"November 10th, 1807.—General Moreau comes to breakfast. Walk with him and endeavor to dissuade him from his projected journey to New Orleans. He is at length shaken, and would renounce it if his preparations were not too far advanced.

"I persist, and at length render it doubtful in his mind. I am certain this journey will be imputed by many evil meaning men to improper motives. He treats the chattering of idlers with contempt. But I tell him that such idlers form a power in Republics. That he must not suppose himself as free here as he would be in an absolute monarchy; that his reputation makes him a slave to public opinion; that he cannot with impunity do many things here which would be of no consequence in a country where he was surrounded by spies in the service of government; because there, the Ministers having convinced themselves that his views are innocent, and his conduct irreproachable, he might safely laugh at the suspicions both of the great vulgar and of the small; but here where the same modes of knowing what men do are not adopted, every one is at liberty to suspect, and will decide rashly on appearances, after which it may be impossible to deracinate the ideas hastily, lightly, and unjustly assumed.

In the course of our conversation, touching very gently the idea of his serving (in case of necessity), against France, he declares frankly, that when the occasion arrives he shall feel no reluctance; that, France having cast him out he is a citizen of the country in which he lives, and has the same right to follow his trade here, as any other man. And as it would be unjust to prevent a French hatter, whom Bonaparte might banish, from making hats, so it would be unjust to prevent a French General from making war. I assent to the truth of this observation, not because I believe it true, but because I will not impeach the reasons he may find it convenient to give to himself for his own conduct, should he hereafter be employed in our service."

What was false and trivial in Moreau's words has been sufficiently punished.

How different the result of different revolutions!

Moreau, wandering through the world, denies his country and dies by a French cannon; Governeur Morris ends his honored old age in the bosom of the liberty he has founded, of the land he has served.

SECTION VII.

BROCKDEN BROWN—WASHINGTON IRVING.

Morris is very like a clever English naval officer, mingling in the good society of the XVIIIth century; Jonathan Edwards like a Scottish theologian of the XVIIth; Benjamin Franklin is not far from the qualities which distinguish Goldsmith and his charming Vicar. All three lack originality.

Brockden Brown, an American, resolved to break the charm ; he looked for originality, unfortunately it was not his own. Lewis, author of the Monk, head of the funereal and demoniac school was in full fashion; Brown took him for model.

He understood and could express passion. Instead of yielding to the timid scruples of his compatriots, he braved criticism and only looked for effect; effect, factitious and exaggerated. Brown's demons are false demons ; his monsters result from predetermination; his efforts of imagination are the struggles of an intelligence which wishes to create but which produces chimeras. There is a ridiculous super-excitement in these productions ; all is forced, violent, incoherent. Nothing spontaneous, natural, simple; but always convulsions, perpetual emphasis, and horrors crowded upon horrors.

Whence comes this vehement exaggeration? Why this unheard-of tendency to the pathetic, the immense, the romantic, fantastic, marvellous? Because American society has nothing fantastic in it; the drama and the dithyrambic are exotics in the United States. Brown is already forgotten. It is the inevitable fate of all outré literature. False colors soon fade ; their own exaggeration destroys them.

Washington Irving, more modest and happier, has not pretended to so much grandeur ; he owes the renown which encircles him, not to sallies of the imagination, creative thought or a lofty mental flight, but to a graceful imitation of old English literature. It is a somewhat timid copy, upon silk paper, of Addison, Steel and Swift. All that he writes glows with the gentle, agreeable lustre of watered silk. Correct and agreeable, he pleases but does not move you: the sensations which he excites lack power. It is like a young lady of good family, well brought up, a slave to propriety, never elevating the voice, never exaggerating the tone, never guilty of the sin of eloquence, and careful not to have any energy, energy being often vulgar. Our intention is not to lower a really great merit, to depreciate a talent which we love. None know better than we, the excellence of a style without pretension and without emphasis, though not without grace, the coloring of which is harmonious and its form pure; but we cannot dissemble, that there is a certain feebleness under these qualities.

We may add that the characteristic merit of Mr. Irving has nothing American in it. All his thoughts direct themselves towards England alone; for her his wishes, his memories; he has for her a singularly superstitious and poetic worship, and takes her as the writers of Queen Anne's day exhibit her. Do not tell him that Addison's England is an embellished ideality, he will not hear you; do not try to prove to him that Sir Roger de Coverley is a creature like Don Quixotte, a half-symbolic personage, to whom the man of talent has lent action, speech and costume. For Washington Irving, all that the cotemporaries of Pope have written is gospel. He reproduces their phrases, he borrows their language. He loves even the noisy drunken hospitality of that day. This writer, who traces his lines not far from the savannahs of the Ohio, or in some square house in Boston, lives in thought in St. James' Park; he wanders, in his reveries, through the shadowy alleys of Kensington; he talks with Sterne; he shakes hands with Goldsmith. He will soon don the rose-colored buckram and jerkin of the seventeenth century. Do not wake him; he dreams of losing himself in the sinuous alleys of the old city; he is listening to the winds which whistle by the great arched windows of the feudal mansions, or agitates the immense sign boards, so spoken against by Addison. All Irving's poetic Past is there; it is the charm of his works. The velvety and golden dream which enchants him, gives a delicious illusion to olden time, and makes of him the Wouvermans of Anglo-American literature.

This delightful story-teller, is the son of a Scotchman established in New York and of an English lady. His feeble infancy and delicate youth, were passed in the neighborhood and in the city itself; "which at that time," says an American, "was little like a metropolis or even a city of Europe." You still found an ingenuous morality in this growing city, where all the pleasures of a progressing prosperity, all the enjoyments of an internal well-being, were combined with the pleasant liberty and easy pleasures of an almost country life.

"The advantageous situation of the port caused an affluence of dollars to the coffers of the merchant, for the inhabitants of other parts of the province had not yet come to colonize this fortunate spot and to demand their share of its profits. The elders of the city saw the falling of the commercial manna, and busied themselves rather in enjoying the present, than in thinking of the future. They had not yet recognized the necessity of habituating their children to the discipline of labor and prudence. The cupidity engendered by gain, the close egotism of local concurrence, had not yet dried their hearts. You saw in these rapidly enriched families, patriarchal manners; they believed in domestic happiness; they did not resign their children for ten hours a day to the mercenary care of the pedagogue; they feared the suffocating atmosphere of the school-room; they found time to bring them up themselves, and then sent them into the free air of the fields—and the neighborhood of New York was admirably adapted to this sort of education. A few minutes walk brought the city youth out into green fields; under fresh shadows, to the brink of fair streams which, covered in the winter with thick ice, invited the skaters to rival the exploits of their Dutch ancestors. The city of New York possessed the most picturesque site ; Edinburgh alone, in Europe, could compare with it.

Now its rustic environs no longer exist; brick houses replace the verdure ; the mason has chased away the gardener ; a rail-road has destroyed even the fresh grots of Hoboken." What Irving has of inmost and truest, comes from these almost Dutch souvenirs of his childhood.

He went no farther than the flowery Isle of Manhattan or the neighboring shores ; his imagination was cradled in citizen and peaceful memories. Never had he dreamed of far forests ; nor of the plumes that fall from the golden-robed flamingo, nor of the desert flower, nor of the columns of wild rock which edge the Mississippi. What grace and nobleness he has belonged to this primitive and simple sphere. His youth was passed in the midst of an active, commercial population, nor had he longed for living brooks which murmur through the heart of antique woods, nor of the deer that crosses them, nor of the colonist's lodge, nor of lakes with gleaming waves. He early saw himself surrounded with small provincial rivalries, and his delicate observation, worthy of Teniers and of Wouvermans, was already in action.

" The city," says a cotemporary, " fifty years ago, exhibited the singular spectacle of various races distinct in origin, character, physiognomy, struggling for a puerile pre-eminence. Time has done justice to those very little quarrels, and showed us their innocent absurdities in relief: all those shades are now confounded into one—but in that day, the Dutch American stuck to his jargon as to a holy thing, his bitterness of a vanquished race, it is true, being much softened by his natural good temper. With the Dutch, mingled the French Protestants, banished by the edict of Nantes, and tempered the Dutch phlegm with Gallic vivacity. Then came the gentry and cavaliers of old England, proud of their genealogy and always citing their ancestors, who had come to the once Dutch colony and transformed it into a British province given by Charles II., to his brother the Duke of York. You remarked too, the New Englander, the real American, distinguished by his intelligent activity, and already beginning with the Batavian that strife which has terminated in the nearly total disappearance of the patronymics of old burgomasters from the commercial streets. Finally, the last, the least numerous of this population, but at the same time the most important by their acquired wealth and mercantile influence, the Scotch—formed a clan, canny, calculating, enterprising, and joining to their habits of worldly knowledge and economy, hospitable manners and a love of good eating."

The most loveable works of Irving, are those in which the delicate observation of his youth, is naïvely set forth. His satiric History of New York by Dietrich Knickerbocker, a parody on the Dutch minuteness, and the microscopic importance claimed for themselves by the very little—the Sketch Book, Bracebridge Hall, and the Tales of a Traveller—works which will remain and which, indeed, are refined continuations of the style of Addison—constitute what one may call Irving's first manner. Criticism had accused him of feebleness; he wished to rise higher, aad wrote the History of Christopher Columbus, and that of his companions—that of the Conquest of Grenada, and at last the Alhambra. In this second manner there is a little too high coloring and emphasis; but the research is conscientious and the style brilliant.

Returned among his compatriots, who had made him their ambassador to Spain, he undertook a voyage throughout the United States.

The Falls of Niagara, the Lakes of Champlain and Erie, the banks of the Ohio, the majestic course of the Missisippi, formed the theatre of his first excursions. Then, with a troop of mounted pioneers, he penetrated into the territories of the warlike Pawnees, explored the prairies and forests, chased the wild horse and the buffalo, slept in the open air by the camp-fire or in the Indian wigwam. This expedition inspired a charming book. The recent Life of Mahomet and his Successors is not a very clever production for so loveable and gracious a talent.

SECTION VIII.

The Novelist, Fennimore Cooper.

With Washington Irving appears the first light of vivid originality, which lends a halo to American literature.

This dawn will grow with Fennimore Cooper.

In his first romances, which awakened the attention of Europe, all is American, descriptions, inspirations, ideas, personages; he copies only translantic nature; certainly, he reproduces it minutely, long, without pause, without perspective, but he is always American. You find his pictures rather dry, fatiguing, by the fidelity of their details; the coldness of his coloring displeases; you accuse him of prolixity; the intrigue seems to be woven with a sufficient clumsiness; and the play of the passions reveals itself with a mechanical punctuality, and a scrupulous stiffness. Now, these Calvinistic and American defects are not without interest; the most rigid Quakerism seems to preside over Cooper's narration; his style is the style of an indictment. Others are prodigal of rich coloring, and shade with boldness, valueless stories and things; Cooper acts like the most conscientious of notaries; he gives an inventory and a description of the scene—a sheriff's officer levying, is less exact.

He describes with talent, and often in his detailed pictures, only one thing is wanting—life. While he rehearses the least circumstances attending an action, the action rests unaccomplished. This accumulation of small, particular facts, far from aiding the general effect of the picture, far from augmenting its interest, only seems to destroy it; the distracted and embarassed attention loses itself in this confused mass of minute particulars. Instead of disposing of his materials, arranging, commanding them as a master, he sometimes lets them get the better of him; he is their slave.

The author is as if in a jury-box, he tells the truth, and nothing but the truth. If two foemen fight with fierce rage upon the edge of a precipice, if there be between them issues of life and death, Cooper tells you the color of the rock; how many feet it rises above the level of the sea; whether it be of silex or granite; what plants grow there; what birds build there, its latitude. Another would be content to set forth the vicissitudes of the combat, the convulsions of suffering, the triumph, the agony. But this is not enough for Cooper. Every muscle of the combatants must be visible; he shows his subject not merely naked, but skinned.

If such a system were to prevail, a grain of sand or a butterfly's wing would serve as a text for volumes; there is no reason why authors should ever stop in their descriptions.

A savage comes upon the scene; you must describe his bow, his arrows, his tomahawk, his tobacco-pouch, and his pipe; the coarse sculpture with which these objects are adorned would fill more than one page; if, after that, you give to your reader, a biography of the child of the wilderness and of his forefathers, look where you will get to. Let a painter of style, Holbein or Mieris, be faithful in minutia, scrupulously exact, and I understand him; his art can seize but a moment, and he must compensate for this by not neglecting a single particular. The business of poetry, on the contrary, is motion; it takes an action, describes its course, reproduces its mobility, follows its rapid progress, developes its causes and results. It has its grand masses and its valueless circumstances; a lively impulse draws it along. If it were to strive to reproduce everything, after the manner of still-life painters, it would deprive itself of its most precious resources.

This is what happens to Cooper. There is a certain dryness in his finest pictures; half of what the romancer tells us, we are perfectly indifferent to: the outlines are stiff and full of mannerism. The author seems to trouble himself much less about his characters, and the incidents which occupy them, than about the circumstances which surround them and the little particulars which accompany them. So that characters well drawn and true, are often in want of grace and freshness. Compared with the characters whom we meet in the world, they are like what flowers preserved in an herbal are to the flowers of the meadow. There are the petals, the stamens, the corolla, the leaves, but where is the dew of heaven, the breath of morning and of night, which embalms the flower in its perfumes, the sap that circulates through the minutest pistil and the frail column which supports it. All this I look for in vain; Nature, so vivid, gay, animated; in which respires a soul so ardent, in whose silence there is so much eloquence; Nature with its eternal, inexhaustible power of life appears sterile and dead in the pictures drawn by Cooper. The more they ought to have savage grandeur and energy, the more is one astonished at the contrast between his manner and the objects which he describes.

These are the defects which the mighty talent of Cooper owes to the doctrinal severity and Calvinist rigidity inherent in the Anglo-American colonies. Yet, nevertheless, if Cooper be the slave of physical objects, that slavery has its power, he re-paints those objects with a dry sincerity. If he babble sometimes, he never lies. If he be prosaic, he is true. Read his *chef-d'œuvre*, the Pilot, a romance little understood, whose heroes are the ship and the sea. This work, admirable for its unity and its vigor, perfumed with odors of the deep, impregnated with foam and salt water, apotheosis of Man governing the Ocean as a cavalier his rebellious steed, could only have been written by an Anglo-American, passionate lover of the deep, fanatic for human industry, and its rudest triumphs.

No American writer before Cooper, had carried reproduction embellished by American thought and life so far. Irving himself, in rejuvenating the style and manner of Addison, had drawn too much from the antique and forgotten sources of English literature. Cooper's touch is more vigorous; there is a translantic freshness in his works.

This is an honor, a glory, a happiness, which few authors can enjoy. Rarely does one associate oneself so intimately with the civilization of his native land. And what a civilization! What a land! So vast and wild an aspect! So gigantic a nature! There is something strange in this strife of our industries, of our arts, of our ideas, transplanted to a new soil, forced to grapple with savage life, and to conquer it.

The genius of the artist has not yet penetrated into the solitudes of America; you look for him vainly in the cities. It is the genius of the artisan which founded this civilization and which sustains this Republic. You will find it in his romances; it is imprinted on his physiognomy.

Examine with attention this fine portrait which Madame de Mirbel has painted after nature. You perceive that this man, with his severe, vigilant eye, must observe physical objects with redoubtable attention and perseverance. An austere simplicity reigns in those features, drawn with hardness, animated by powerful genius, and without mobility. If there be any curved lines, they are separated from one another by hollows, by profound furrows or wrinkles; energy, promptitude, decision, firmness immovable, power of attention, perseverance, these are the characteristics of that essentially American face. Apply to this exterior and physiognomical examination the rules of Doctor Gall, and you find a high, singularly cut forehead, a positive phrenologic curiosity. On one hand, the organs of eventuality, locality, and individuality (most employed by the romance writer) start out, as it were, and detach themselves in bumps; on the other hand, the organs of causality, comparison of objects and gaiety, separated from the former by an austere line, form a projection no less prominent. The restless, piercing eye seems to be always in search of some new observation; the strange smile, sardonic and severe, announces a faculty of irony governed by an inflexible reason. The compression of the lips indicates a silent concentration of thought, without which there is no real talent. Cooper's stature is tall; his manners are frank and simple. The vigor of his mind, and the strength of his republican conviction, give to his whole face and outward man a strong, manly expression, which does not accord with the ideas of refinement and *recherché* grace which civilization usually attaches to the literary profession.

When Robinson Crusoe perceived the trace of Friday's steps upon the beach, he was not more astounded than the

European public at the moment of learning from Cooper's romances that one could live in New York, be born on the banks of the Delaware, imitate nobody and yet possess genius. For some time critics had decided that talent was irreconcileable with one's quality of American. A Dutch danseuse, an Esquimaux Venus de Medicis would not have been received with a profounder surprise, that a good novelist or poet, brought up in the United States,—that mercantile country, that nation insensible to art, give a rival to Walter Scott!

There were writers of Scottish history before the author of Old Mortality. Scottish superstitions and customs had furnished the subject of numerous and careful researches. Mrs. Grant, Burns, Allan Ramsay, Buchanan, Macpherson, had preceded Walter Scott. Cooper had no predecessor. Unworn paths presented themselves to him on every side. An inexhaustible variety of materials; scenes demanding a theatre; pictures demanding a frame; points of view asking for a painter; everywhere novelty, quaintness, marvels: a quite modern interest, a people hardly out of swaddling clothes and already mighty; a history whose first pages gleam with civilization, and speak of conquest; the singularity of calm, pious, persevering heroism; the names of Washington, Penn, Franklin; for background the forest of ages; for actors, the Apostles of the New World treating with the children of the wigwam and the calumet; the progress of European art in the midst of these masterless solitudes; the combat between son and father—of the oppressed with the oppressor; these demanding, those wishing to destroy liberty and tolerance: what do I know—perhaps a new social era is now born for the world and will issue from Philadelphia!

Cooper has seized with vigorous frankness the scattered elements which he found before him. He was careful not to corrupt their charm, or to change their purity, by an imitation of the Roman or the Greek; he has told, even in the language of the United States, the extraordinary adventures whose theatre was that vast continent or its surrounding seas.

Those who play in his drama, have come out from the hut of the colonist, the cabin of the savage, the shop of the tradesman; the gigantic nature of the land reflects itself in his books as in a mirror.

For his compatriots, Cooper was the Homer of their civilization; the bard who perpetuated their glory. To Europeans he gave a pleasure till then unknown.

I have not concealed his faults of manner. We can pardon them, in consideration of their intimate analogy with the author and his race.

Cooper is Calvinist; he tells a fact dryly, but with a profundity and truth which fascinate the hearer. He searches no éclat in his descriptions; he does not give colored or dark masses. He manages the whole so well, enriches it so exactly with its constituent elements, that you fancy you can distinguish each detail; be it a forest cabin; a vulgar hearthside, a wreck floating in the distance, he forces you to read, by his perfect exactitude, his extreme truth; and the description of a trivial object, without picturesque charms, will be to you more interesting than that of a magnificent site, a sublime spectacle, vaguely drawn or daubed with vivid colors. The women even, who always look for action and interest in a novel, have not the courage to skip the descriptions of Cooper. If you begin to read, you must devour all. Yet, he repeats himself; he goes over and over the portrait already sketched by his pencil. He will not omit one plank of the frigate, one tree of the wood. His diction is slow, sometimes even laborious and embarrassed; but it reproduces everything, green-gleaming savannahs, stretches of sand, old oaks and limitless deserts; lakes like the oceans—the shadows of those forests whose shadows are eternal.

Let him go upon the sea, and his enthusiasm becomes a religious passion. You would say that the waves were his, so beautiful in their terror, so sublime in their truth are his maritime pictures. He does not show you the phantom of a vessel or the phantom of an ocean; a painted ship upon a painted sea; but all, on his barks or around them, is action and life, character and poetry.

Enemy of the vague, never pleased with it, nor admitting it into his pictures, he surrounds you with accessories so numerous, so true, so detailed that even their insignificance adds to the truth of the whole. The sails swell, the cables rattle, the yards creak, the tar smokes, the sailors sing, the captain whistles, the billow foams, the wave strikes noisily the side of the ship. There is no more land, nor anything that recalls it. But when the land reappears, you find yourself cast upon a new shore, deserted, unknown.

He is the most positive novelist that ever existed. He anatomises without idealizing. Sometimes his portraits border on caricature; his defect is that he exaggerates and seeks out too curiously their characteristic traits. He is never false, but he dissects his model. Some of his personages are grotesque, others bizarre. There is every description of character in his works from baseness to heroism, from gaiety to terror; all stand out from the canvas, speak to the imagination, and having arrested the attention, are recognized as human, as beings who have lived, and who would still be alive if the narrator had not analyzed them to death. His portraits of women, however, exhibit an almost Shakspearian delicacy of observation. They are not women of the court, nor elegant women; they are not superhuman beings, but women. Goodness, sweetness, natural grace, and a naïve majesty surround them with a charming halo. Their beauty and devotion lighten and console the most inaccessible retreats, solace the sorrows of the man, and pour balm upon his wounds. Moral sentiment joined to their physical beauty, patience and serenity of soul constitute their characteristics. A good housekeeper, the wife of Heathcote in the Borderers, for instance, is far more charming than all oriental sylphs, or the brilliant princesses of Calprenede ; her exterior is not remarkable, her life is peaceable and humble ; well-being and repose are around her ; treasures of gentleness and charity are in her bosom. In a word it is a woman.

Among the numerous novels published by Cooper, that which is most characteristically original, is the "Last of the Mohicans." You would look vainly in the whole library of romance for its parallel. Smollett's or Fielding's sailors, or Scott's beggars have disappeared. The eternal family of heroes, who perpetuate themselves from fiction to fiction has vanished. You are in a new world where the original genius of the human race exists in its majesty. The child of the wilderness rises and paints himself before you. He has neither ornaments nor dress. He is alone, apart, a stranger to all civilization ; master of all around him, recognizing no master himself. King of his wilderness, he has no slaves. The passions, vices, virtues of society are to him unknown. Surrounding nature is grand, like himself. She has secret pleasures for him which the rest of the world ignore. This romance so full of magic and marvellous freshness, makes us live the life of primitive solitudes, and makes us the friend of man as they nurture him.

How remarkable and true are the characters of this drama. All bear the impression of the powerful hand which traced them. The old Indian and his son are symbols of the savage life. Still more do I admire Longue Carabine, a being placed between the wilderness and civilization; intermediate link between social industry and primitive independence. He is neither European nor wild Indian. The reflecting heroism which follows civilization, tempers the violent heroism which pervades it. If he have not quite lost the desire of vengeance and the stoicism of his fathers, he yet guesses instinctively the scrupulous demands of honor, and raises himself to a generosity whose grandeur he feels.

The *Prairie* contains characteristic and detailed descriptions; it is the most beautiful picture of the kind drawn by his pen. After having read it, you could fancy that you had lived on the banks of those streams, a thousand times crossed that prairie; questioned those charming scenes, and made them echo with your voice. We must add that this pleasure is purchased by an *ennui* caused by spinnings-out, and digressions and that this picture, so faithful, may be charged with prolixity.

The *Spy* has its partisans. Harvey Birch is a dramatic creation: to sacrifice to one's country not only life, but honor, is the greatest of sacrifices. How can one help admiring this hero of patriotism, who makes a glory of his infamy, and inwardly consoles himself for the opprobrium which covers him, by the sentiment of what he has done for his country. As to Washington, Cooper has idealized him with great talent; a no easy matter.

The interest of the *Borderers* is the most powerful. The *Red Rover* and the *Pilot* are greater as maritime pictures than as romances; nor does the *Water Witch* yield to these latter. Everything is picturesque, energetic and yet positive. The real and magnificent are mingled.

I love Tom Coffin, king of the deep, who cannot live on land, who breathes more freely on a lake, begins to enjoy existence on the Mediterranean, and finds himself in possession of all his faculties and all his happiness, only in ploughing with free keel, the vast floods of ocean. For this man there is no victory but that over the billows; no heroism save in the strife with them, no happiness but in this warfare. Coarse, barbarous, vulgar, he is yet great, for he represents the energy of humanity fighting with the energy of nature.

Cooper has his defects which we have not forgotten to indicate. Before him the world had never seen a novelist who was manufacturer, *industriel*, artisan. He materializes the interest of his best pages. If he launches a vessel, you will read a treatise on ship-building. If a rope break, you will learn how ropes are made, and by what mechanical means the accident might have been prevented. He says *all*, which is too much. He will not leave one detail unexplained, not a hatchway unanalyzed, nor a corner of the vessel without mentioning the wood of which she is built. Enemy of the ideal, he is like a chemist or mechanician—who must render a full account. He observes even men in this way, submitting them to a laborious and inexorable examination.

The history of his life is short. His family, originally from Buckinghamshire, England, moved to America about 1679. He was born at Burlington, on the Delaware, in 1789, and his education was commenced at Yale College, New Haven. At the age of thirteen, he entered the navy. This apprenticeship formed his spirit; here he collected the elements of those pictures so much admired. He married the daughter of Pierre de Lancy, quitted the service, and since that time has given himself up to the composition of his books.

Every year came a new one. Translated into German, French, Italian, they produced a vivid sensation in Europe.

He passed a good deal of his life in Europe, especially at Paris. In England, his frankness, austerity and clearly-expressed republicanism and his national pride displeased.

In America, the same puritan sincerity, his reprobation of democratic vices, in a word, his plain-speaking, of which he was proud, and which he pushed to excess; did not help to conciliate the love of his compatriots.

Inferior in art and style to the great European romancers, there is yet a vivid historical interest attached to his works, which philosophy will never read without curiosity. There, the pure Saxon race struggles with the savages, the solitude, the desert, hunger and nature. It is the same blood, cool and persevering valor, love of gain, industry, audacity, enterprize, which marked the old Norman conquests; it is the same force without vivacity; the same sagacity without frivolity, the same ferocity towards a fighting enemy, the same pardon for the conquered, and the same faith in human power.

This indestructible permanence of races, of their soul and genius, is a magnificent spectacle for the philosopher. The Gaul of the days of Brennus, the French Canadian or the Marquis under Louis XIV., are recognizable by indelible marks—the indomitable Caradoc, Hastings in India, and Cromwell's Puritan unite in the Last of the Saxons—the American Trapper!

SECTION IX.

PAULDING—THE BROTHER JONATHAN—DOCTOR CHANNING.

To those whose claims we have just examined, we might add Joel Barlow, author of the *Columbiad*, a poem which has both eloquence and vigor; and Paulding, whose *Dutchman's Fireside*, a pleasant elegy, is a soft and enfeebled imitation of the Vicar of Wakefield; and the biographer of *Brother Jonathan*, a cleverly puerile writer, for whom a mole-hill is a mountain, and a drop of milk, the ocean. The vigor of creation; the energy of original intelligence, are not to be found in any of these authors, in a sufficient measure to class them among men of genius, Cooper excepted. Doctor Channing, the most eloquent sacred writer of America, has a claim to our attention—the peculiar characteristics of his race and country are to be found in his works.

I doubt whether there be a quite impartial eloquence; yet, Dr. Channing tries to establish impartiality, equity, and balance of opinions. *This* is just and reasonable, but *that* may be equally so; these opinions may be sustained, yet the opposing ones have their probable and plausible side. Dr. Channing collects the most contradictory axioms which he strives to unite into a republic; to this barren labor, he applies an unequalled tact and diplomacy; he condemns, absolves, criticises, and praises; he is not only eclectic, but hospitable to every theory. Ancient prejudice has it merit, paradox its advantage. You may defend the one without warring against the other; can win approbation from all sides, and manage to win glory without belonging to any particular flag.

This cowardice of thought, this feeble terror of opinion, will disappear as more advanced civilization comes to the United States. The actual fashion of American institutions; the natural and necessary action of a people who use all their efforts for the material conquest of Nature and the creation of industry, causes all men to march in battalion and towards the same point. There is no more free opinion, no more hardiness of intellect. An inexorable ostracism, banishes all that passes a certain limit. Anathema on that thought which leaves the common hive!

Hence we have an universal complaisance, simple and easy, in received ideas. Now if everybody is to be like everybody else, common ideas will have the precedence, for they are the most general, and whosoever will dare attack them, will outrage the whole community and insult each of its members—then he will be treated like a general enemy. One does not like to commit *lèse-vulgaire;* one thinks like all the rest of the world; chokes one's fantasies, marches in the ranks and keeps step, and does not wish to become the black sheep of the flock. Political liberty ends by enslaving thought.

This can only be a temporary position. So soon as the material interests are satisfied, an opposition to the weight of opinion will soon be formed. Independence will be born; the free essays of intelligence will not be crimes, the popular inquisition will vanish and each *frater-familias* will cease to be what Cooper calls "a Familiar of the republican Holy Office."

This democratic sin, this wish to tickle the mob and to please everybody, is too easily recognized in the works of Dr. Channing. The tomb of Mahomet, suspended between heaven and earth does not vascillate in a more perilous position. The doctor loves liberty, but he does not deny that despotism has its advantages. He wants Europe to applaud him, but he must have also the praises of America. Looking at the same moment at the two worlds, trembling lest he lose popularity in either; bowing to all parties, flinging a bit of flattery to every sect, reserving a means of retreat and an asylum in all possible opinions; unitarian without exaggeration, he excuses the errors of the Catholic Church, at the moment that he confesses the merit and eloquence of the French philosophers accused of atheism; he loves the republic and defends the Bourbons; will not repulse the Jesuits but acknowledges their errors; insults Bonaparte without questioning his genius; is hostile neither to imagination nor cleverness, provided that they be moderate and serious; he is very fond of philosophical criticism but united to religion, and is devoted to the interests of the Faith, so long as it is tolerant. In a word, he has so much reserve in his predilections, so many modifica tions in his opinions, so many withdrawals, shades, conditions, amendments and amendments to amendments, that it is very difficult to find out what this republican soul is or desires. If he judge Milton or Bonaparte, he lacks the courage. Before such giants his pencil trembles; he understands only common ambitions. When, for instance, the doctor thunders against conquerors, and upholds the literary profession, it is like a pedagogue vaunting his grammar, elevating his own profession above all others, and considering himself as the equal of heroes. "I have known," says Fielding, "an excellent man, with but one absurdity. It was to consider a schoolmaster as the greatest man on earth, and himself as the greatest of schoolmasters. These two ideas could not have been driven out of his head, though Alexander himself, at the head of his armies, should have attempted it."

There are strong and beautiful pages in the works of Channing; though that eloquence sustained, elaborated and got up for effect recalls too much the declamations of Seneca the Rhetorician, or of Thomas the Academician. And thus, in spite of real talent and powerful solemnity, Channing takes no marked place among original writers.

Nations, like men, do not discover their proper originality until after long trials. Under the Puritans the literature of the United States is only a servile reproduction of the cross sermons of the Covenanters. With Franklin, and the *American* Cultivator, the American soul finds voice and accent, agreeable and graceful, but indistinct. Thus, in Irving, some pictures of American nature, or of Dutch households are gracefully and vigorously prominent. Fennimore Cooper follows them closely and pushes farther on the slow creation of a new literature.

In Cooper, nature is more than man. The interest of his romances is concentrated upon nature, upon the sea, on the prairies; and one sometimes regrets that he has spoken of anything but the waves or the forests, so much does man disappear in these vast solitudes.

There is a traveller, who, occupied exclusively with the birds, lakes, wild deer, the eagle and his haunts, and identifying himself with whatever is mighty in nature, has become a great writer, superior in our view, to the loveable Irving and to his vigorous successor.

SECTION X.

AUDUBON.

Had you visited the English drawing-rooms in 1832, you would have remarked in the midst of a philosophic crowd, speaking obscurely, and overthrowing without pity, the highest questions of metaphysics, a man very different from those around him.

The absurd and mean European dress could not disguise that simple and almost wild dignity which is found in the bosom of the solitude which nurses it. While men of letters, a vain and talking race, disputed, in the conversational arena the prize of epigram or the laurels of pedantry, the man of whom I speak remained standing, head erect, with free, proud eye, silent, modest, listening sometimes with disdainful though not caustic air, to the æsthetic tumult which seemed to astonish him. If he spoke, it was at an interval of repose; with one word he discovered an error, and brought back discussion to its principle and its object. A certain naïve and wild good sense animated his language, which was just, moderate and energetic. His long, black waving hair was parted naturally upon his smooth white forehead, upon a front capable of containing and guarding the fires of thought. In his whole dress, there was an air of singular neatness; you would have said that the waters of some brook, running through the untrodden forest, and bathing the roots of oaks, old as the world, had served him for mirror.

At the sight of that long hair, that bared throat, the independent manner, the manly elegance which characterized him, you would have said, "that man has not lived long in old Europe; our civilization, mother of the affected politeness so universal in courts, cities, and villages, and substituting symbols for true sentiments, had not left its common trace on him. He has not been crushed by its weight. The alloy, the falsity of society form no part of his character or his manners.

It is pleasant to encounter such a man in those loquacious and scientific assemblies, where so many talents and pretentions bore you. If you add to what we have already given, a frank, calm face, clearly cut features, an eye quick, ardent, penetrating and fixed as a falcon's, a foreign accent, unusual expressions, highly colored, and brief, picturesque and clever, without seeming to be so, you will have a tolerably exact portrait of the Historian of Birds, the American Audubon.

He has quitted his name and calls himself the "American Woodsman;" and it is the only title which would suit him. The wilderness was his study room. He has overrun thoroughly those great deserts peopled by wild animals. As he respired the air charged with emanations of the primitive vegetation, he drew in with it that dignified self-respect, that consciousness of human energy which has never quitted him.

Audubon was nurtured in love for nature. He passed his life in the open air, at the foot of a tree whose branches were the home of the feathered people whose habits he came to study and which he never lost sight of. The path which he chose, was that where the bird was hopping. The nest of the eagle whose throne was the peak of some inaccessible rock did not frighten him ; he gave to this study the patience of a Benedictine and the passion of an artist; he has pursued his task through every peril, and recommenced it with unequalled perseverance. His dreams were winged, and full of melodious songs and murmurs; the forms of his favorites haunted his thoughts.

Do not mistake nor accuse of singularity this vocation which Audubon has received from God. He was ornithologist from his cradle. He needed the winged race to paint, observe, describe and love, sweet woodland concerts to hearken to, brilliant plumage to reproduce, wandering pinions whose curves and spiral flights he might follow.

Let us see how he analyzes this instinct of solitary observation ; this devotion to an innocent study; this abnegation of all material cares, this intellectual force, which taught him, without a master, natural history in the depth of the forests, and made him alone complete an important branch of science which one had always despaired of completing.

"I received life and light in the New World. When I had hardly yet learned to walk, and to articulate those first words, always so endearing to parents, the productions of nature that lay spread all around, were constantly pointed out to me. They soon became my playmates; and before my ideas were sufficiently formed to enable me to estimate the difference between the azure tints of the sky, and the emerald hue of the bright foliage, I felt that an intimacy with them, not consisting of friendships merely, but bordering on frenzy, must accompany my steps through life ; and now, more than ever, am I persuaded of the power of those early impressions. They laid such hold upon me, that, when removed from the woods, prairies, and the brooks, or shut up from the view of the wide Atlantic, I experienced none of those pleasures most congenial to my mind. None but aerial companions suited my fancy. No roof seemed so secure to me as that formed of the dense foliage under which the feathered tribes were seen to resort, or the caves and fissures of the massy rocks to which the dark winged cormorant and the curlew retired to rest, or to protect themselves from the fury of the tempest. My father generally accompanied my steps, procured birds and flowers for me with great eagerness,—pointed out the elegant movements of the former, the beauty and softness of their plumage, the manifestations of their pleasure or sense of danger,—and the always perfect forms and splendid attire of the latter. My valued preceptor would then speak of the departure and the return of birds with the seasons, would describe their haunts, and, more wonderful than all, their change of livery; thus exciting me to study them, and to raise my mind toward their great Creator. A vivid pleasure shone upon those days of my early youth, attended with a calmness of feeling, that seldom failed to rivet my attention for hours, whilst I gazed in ecstacy upon the pearly and shining eggs, as they lay imbedded in the softest down, or among dried leaves and twigs, or were exposed upon the burning sand or weather-beaten rock of our Atlantic shores. I was taught to look upon them as flowers yet in the bud. I watched their opening, to see how nature had provided each different species with eyes, either open at birth, or closed for some time after; to trace the slow progress of the young birds toward perfection, or admire the celerity with which some of them, while yet unfledged, removed themselves from danger to security.

I grew up, and my wishes grew with my form. These wishes, kind reader, were for the entire possession of all that I saw. I was fervently desirous of becoming acquainted with nature. For many years, however, I was sadly disappointed, and for ever, doubtless, must I have desires that cannot be gratified. The moment a bird was dead, however beautiful it had been when in life, the pleasure arising from the possession of it became blunted; and although the greatest cares were bestowed on endeavors to preserve the appearance of nature, I looked upon its vesture as more than sullied, as requiring constant attention and repeated mendings, while, after all, it could no longer be said to be fresh from the hands of its Maker. I wished to possess all the productions of nature, but I wished life with them. This was impossible; then what was to be done? I turned to my father, and made known to him my disappointment and anxiety. He produced a book of *illustrations*. A new life ran in my veins. I turned over the leaves with avidity; and although what I saw was not what I longed for it gave me a desire to copy nature. To nature I went, and tried to imitate her, as in the days of my childhood. I had tried to raise myself from the ground and stand erect, before nature had imparted the vigor necessary for the success of such an undertaking. How sorely disappointed did I feel for many years, when I saw that my productions were worse than those which I ventured (perhaps in silence) to regard as bad, in the book given me by my father! My pencil gave birth to a family of cripples. So maimed were most of them, that they resembled the mangled corpses on a field of battle, compared with the integrity of living men. These difficulties and disappointments irritated me, but never for a moment destroyed the desire of obtaining perfect representations of nature. The worse my drawings were, the more beautiful did I see the originals. To have been torn from the study would have been as death to me. My time was entirely occupied with it.

"I produced hundreds of these rude sketches annually; and for a long time, at my request, they made bonfires on the anniversaries of my birth-day. Patiently, and with industry, did I apply myself to study, for, although I felt the impossibility of giving life to my productions, I did not abandon the idea of representing nature. Many plans were successfully adopted, many masters guided my hand. At the age of seventeen, when I returned from France, whither I had gone to receive the rudiments of my education, my drawings had assumed a form. David had guided my hand in tracing objects of large sizes, eyes and noses belonging to giants, and heads of horses represented in ancient sculpture, were my models. These, although fit subjects for men intent on pursuing the higher branches of the art, were immediately laid aside by me. I returned to the woods of the New World with fresh ardor, and commenced a collection of drawings which I henceforth continued, and which is now publishing, under the title of 'The Birds of America.' To these illustrations, I shall often refer you, good-natured reader, in the sequel, that you may judge of them yourself. Should you discover any merit in them, happy would the expression of your approbation render me, for I should feel that I had not spent my life in vain. You can best ascertain the truth of these delineations. I am persuaded that you love nature—that you admire and study her. Every individual possessed of a sound heart listens with delight to the love-notes of the woodland warblers. He never casts a glance upon their lovely forms without proposing to himself questions respecting them; nor does he look on the trees which they frequent, or the flowers over which they glide, without admiring their grandeur, or delighting in their sweet odors, or their brilliant tints.

"In Pennsylvania, a beautiful State, almost central on the line of our Atlantic shores, my father, in his desire of proving my friend through life, gave me what Americans call a "beautiful plantation," refreshed during the summer heats by the waters of the Schuylkill river, and traversed by a creek named Perkioming, its fine woodlands, its extensive fields, its hills crowned with evergreens, offered many subjects to my pencil. It was there that I commenced my simple and agreeable studies, with as little concern about the future as if the world had been made for me. My rambles invariably commenced at break of day; and to return wet with dew, and bearing a feathered prize, was, and ever will be, the highest employment for which I have been fitted. Yet think not, reader, that the enthusiasm which I felt for my favorite pursuits was a barrier opposed to the admission of gentler sentiments. Nature, which had turned my young mind towards the bird and the flower, soon proved her influence upon my heart. Be it enough to say, that the object of my passion has long since blessed me with the name of husband. And now let us return, for who cares to listen to the love-tale of a naturalist, whose feelings may be supposed to be as light as the feathers which he delineates!

"For a period of nearly twenty years, my life was a succession of vicissitudes. I tried various branches of commerce, but they all proved unprofitable, doubtless because my whole mind was ever filled with my passion for rambling and admiring those objects of nature from which alone I received the purest gratification. I had to struggle against the will of all who at that period called themselves my friends. I must here, however, except my wife and children. The remarks of my other friends irritated me beyond endurance, and breaking through all bounds, I gave myself entirely up to my pursuits. Any one acquainted with the extraordinary desire which I then felt of seeing and judging for myself, would doubtless have pronounced me callous to every sense of duty, and regardless of every interest. I undertook long and tedious journeys, ransacked the woods, the lakes, the prairies, and the shores of the Atlantic. Years were spent away from my family, yet, reader, will you believe it, I had no other object in view than simply to enjoy the sight of nature. Never for a moment did I conceive the hope of becoming in any degree useful to my kind, until I accidentally formed acquaintance with the Prince of Musignano at Philadelphia, to which place I went, with the view of proceeding eastward along the coast. I reached Philadelphia on the 5th April, 1824, just as the sun was sinking beneath the horizon. Excepting the good Dr. Mease, who had visited me in my younger days, I had scarcely a friend in the city; for I was then unacquainted with Harlem, Wetherell, Macmurtrie, Lesueur, or Sully. I called on him and showed him some of my drawings. He presented me to the celebrated Charles Lucian Bonaparte, who in his turn introduced me to the Natural History Society of Philadelphia. But the patronage which I so much needed I soon found myself compelled to seek elsewhere. I left Philadelphia, and visited New York, where I was received with a kindness well suited to elevate my depressed spirits; and afterwards, ascending that noble stream the Hudson, glided over our broad lakes, to seek the wildest solitudes of the pathless and gloomy forests.

"It was in these forests that, for the first time, I communed with myself as to the possible event of my visiting Europe again; and I began to fancy my work under the multiplying efforts of the graver. Happy days and nights of pleasing dreams; I read over the catalogue of my collections, and thought how it might be possible for an unconnected and unaided individual like myself to accomplish the grand scheme."

"I left the village of Henderson, in Kentucky, situated on the bank of Ohio, where I resided for several years, to proceed to Philadelphia on business. I looked to all my drawings before my departure, placed them carefully in a wooden box, and gave them in charge to a relative, with injunctions to see that no injury should happen to them. My absence was of several months; and when I returned, after having enjoyed the pleasure of home for a few days, I inquired after my box, and what I was pleased to call my treasure. The box was produced, and opened; but, reader, feel for me—a pair of Norway rats had taken possession of the whole, and had reared a young family amongst the gnawed bits of paper, which, but a few months before, represented nearly a thousand inhabitants of the air! The burning heat which instantly rushed through my brain was too great to be endured, without affecting the whole of my nervous system. I slept not for several nights, and the days passed like days of oblivion—until the animal powers being recalled into action, through the strength of my constitution, I took up my gun, my note book, and my pencils, and went forth to the woods as gaily as if nothing had happened. I felt pleased that I might now make much better drawings than before, and, ere a period not exceeding three years had elapsed, I had my portfolio filled again."

"I then sailed for the Old World, and as I approached the coast of England, and for the first time beheld her fertile shores, the dispondency of my spirits became very great. I knew no individual in the country; and, although I was the bearer of letters from American friends, and statesmen of great eminence, my situation appeared precarious in the extreme. I imagined that every individual whom I was about to meet, might be possessed of talents superior to those of any on our side of the Atlantic! Indeed, as I for the first time walked on the streets of Liverpool, my heart nearly failed me, for not a glance of sympathy did I meet in my wanderings for two days. To the woods I could not betake myself, for there were none near.

"But how soon did all around me assume a different aspect! How fresh is the recollection of the change! The very first letter which I tendered procured me a world of friends. The Rathbones, the Roscoes, the Trailes, the Chorleys, the Mellies, and others, took me by the hand; and so kind and beneficent, nay, so generously kind have they all been towards me, that I can never cancel the obligation. My drawings were publicly exhibited and publicly praised. Joy swelled my heart. The first difficulty was surmounted. Honors, which, on application being made through my friends, Philadelphia had refused, Liverpool freely accorded.

"I left that emporium of commerce with many a passport; bent upon visiting fair Edina, for I longed to see the men and the scenes immortalized by the fervid strains of Burns, and the glowing eloquence of Scott and Wilson. I arrived at Manchester; and here too, the Greggs, the Lloyds, the Sergeants, the Holmes, the Blackwalls, the Bentleys, and many others, rendered my visit as pleasing as it was profitable to me."

Such is the recital of Audubon himself; his ardent love of science, this heroic passion, have borne fruit which should immortalize his name. In the halls of the Edinburgh Royal Society, we have admired the exhibition of his colored designs executed in water colors. A magical power transported us to the forests so long inhabited by the man of genius. Wise and ignorant were equally struck by a spectacle which we will not try to describe.

Imagine an American landscape, trees, flowers, turf, the very tints of sky and water animated by a real, peculiar, transatlantic life. On these boughs, amid this foliage, on these shores, copied with such severe fidelity, live the ærial races of the New World, large as life, with their particular attitudes, their individuality, their singularity. These plumages gleam with nature's own coloring. You see the birds, in motion and repose, in their plays and wars, their angers and their loves, singing, brooding, sleeping, awake, cleaving the air, skimming the waters, tearing one another in their combats. It is a real and palpable vision of the New World, with its atmosphere, its glorious vegetation, and its tribes not yet submiss to a human yoke. The sun gleams through the glades; the swan floats suspended between a cloudless heaven and a sparkling water; strange and majestic figures mark the earth bright with mica. And this realization of an entire hemisphere; this picture of a nature so mighty, has come from the pencil of one obscure, unknown man; unheard of triumph of patient genius, over innumerable obstacles.

The lovers of art encouraged Audubon to have his great work engraved and published. It was temerity to do so. There were four hundred plates of the largest size, and two thousand colored figures. There was but one country in the world, where the author could find the necessary patronage—Great Britain. At last, thanks to the encouragements which he received, the movement was achieved.

It is the kingdom of birds, an unknown world, which lives in these beautiful engravings. The text is worthy of the plates; it is not a cold analysis nor a pompous description, but the romance of this winged people which the author has studied in their retreats. He communicates the love of birds to the reader. Audubon mingles his own history, with that of his favorites; he associates you in his adventures; he gives gratefully the names of all who helped him in his work. You cross with him those vast American landscapes. You follow the course of those gigantic streams, whose immense floods gather on their way the brooks of the same continent, and roll the mingled waters to the main. Sometimes Audubon travels alone; sometimes his wife and children accompany him. Let us hear him; or rather, travel with him.

"When my wife, my eldest son (then an infant); and myself were returning from Pennsylvania to Kentucky, we found it expedient, the waters being unusually low, to provide ourselves with a *skiff*, to enable us to proceed to our abode at Henderson. I purchased a large, commodious, and light boat of that denomination. We procured a mattress, and our friends furnished us with ready prepared viands. We had two stout negro rowers, and in this trim we left the village of Shippingport in expectation of reaching the place of our destination in a very few days. It was in the month of October. The autumnal tints already decorated the shores of that queen of rivers, the Ohio. Every tree was hung with long and flowing festoons of different species of vines, many loaded with clustered fruits of varied brilliancy, their rich bronzed carmine mingling beautifully with the yellow foliage, which now predominated over the yet green leaves, reflecting more lively tints from the clear stream than ever landscape painter portrayed or poet imagined. The days were yet warm. The sun had assumed the rich and glowing hue which at that season produces the singular phenomenon called there the 'Indian Summer.' The moon had rather passed the meridian of her grandeur. We glided down the river, meeting no other ripple of the water than that formed by the propulsion of our boat. Leisurely we moved along, gazing all day on the grandeur and beauty of the wild scenery around us. Now and then, a large cat-fish rose to the surface of the water in pursuit of a shoal of fry, which starting simultaneously from the liquid element, like so many silvery arrows, produced a shower of light, while the pursuer with open jaws seized the stragglers, and, with a splash of his tail, disappeared from our view. Other fishes we heard uttering beneath our bark a rumbling noise, the strange sounds of which we discovered to proceed from the white perch, for on casting our net from the bow we caught several of that species when the noise ceased for a time. Nature in her varied arrangements, seems to have felt a partiality towards this portion of our country. As the traveller ascends or descends the Ohio, he cannot help remarking that alternately, nearly the whole length of the river, the margin, on one side, is bounded by lofty hills and a rolling surface, while on the other, extensive plains of the richest alluvial land are seen as far as the eye can command view. Islands of varied size and form rise here and there from the bosom of the water, and the winding course of the stream frequently brings you to places where the idea of being on a river of great length changes to that of floating on a lake of moderate extent. Some of these islands are of considerable size and value; while others, small and insignificant, seem as if intended for contrast, and as serving to enhance the general interest of the scenery. These little islands are frequently overflowed during great *freshets* or floods, and receive at their heads prodigious heaps of drifted timber. We foresaw with great concern the alterations that cultivation would soon produce along those delightful banks.

"As night came, sinking in darkness the broader portions of the river, our minds became affected by strong emotions, and wandered far beyond the present moments. The tinkling of bells told us that the cattle which bore them were gently roving from valley to valley in search of food, or returning to their distant homes. The hooting of the great owl, or the muffled noise of its wings as it sailed smoothly over the stream were matters of interest to us; so was the sound of the boatman's horn, as it came winding more and more softly from afar. When daylight returned, many songsters burst forth with echoing notes, more and more mellow to the listening ear. Here and there the lonely cabin of a squatter struck the eye, giving note of commencing civilization. The crossing of the stream by a deer foretold how soon the hills would be covered with snow.

"Many sluggish flat boats we overtook and passed; some laden with produce from the different head waters of the small rivers that pour their tributary streams into the Ohio; others, of less dimensions, crowded with emigrants from distant parts in search of a new home. Purer pleasures I never felt; nor have you, reader, I ween, unless indeed you have felt the like, and in such company.

"The margins of the shores and of the river were at this season amply supplied with game. A wild turkey, a grouse, or a blue-winged teal, could be procured in a few moments; and we fared well, for whenever we pleased, we landed, struck up a fire, and provided as we were with the necessary utensils, procured a good repast. Several of these happy days passed and we neared our home, when one evening, not far from Pigeon Creek, (a small stream which runs into the Ohio from the State of Indiana), a loud and strange noise was heard, so like the yells of Indian warfare, that we pulled at our oars and made for the opposite side as fast and as quietly possible. The sounds increased, we imagined we heard cries of 'murder;' and we knew that some depredations had lately been committed in the country by dissatisfied parties of the aborigines. We felt for a while extremely uncomfortable.

Ere long, however, our minds became more calmed, and we plainly discovered that the singular uproar was produced by an enthusiastic set of Methodists who had wandered thus far out of the common way, for the purpose of holding one of their annual camp-meetings, under the shade of a beach forest. Without meeting with any other interruptions, we reached Henderson, distant from shipping-port by water, about two hundred miles.

"When I think of these times, and call back to my mind the grandeur and beauty of those almost uninhabited shores; when I picture to myself the dense and lofty summits of the forest that everywhere spread along the hills, and overhung the margins of the stream, unmolested by the axe of the settler; when I know how dearly purchased the safe navigation of that river has been, by the blood of many worthy Virginians; when I see that no longer any aborigines are to be found there, and that the vast herds of elks, deer, and buffaloes which once pastured on these hills and in these valleys, making for themselves great roads to the several salt springs, have ceased to exist; when I reflect that all this grand portion of our Union, instead of being in a state of nature, is now more or less covered with villages, farms, and towns, where the din of hammers and machinery is constantly heard; that the woods are fast disappearing under the axe by day and the fire by night; that hundreds of steam-boats are gliding to and fro, over the whole length of the majestic river, forcing commerce to take root and to prosper at every spot; when I see the surplus population of Europe coming to assist in the destruction of the forest, and transplanting civilization into its darkest recesses; when I remember that these extraordinary changes have all taken place in the short period of twenty years, I pause, wonder, and although I know all to be a fact, can scarcely believe its reality. Whether these changes are for the better or for the worse, I shall not pretend to say; but in whatever way my conclusions may incline, I feel with regret, that there are on record no satisfactory accounts of the state of that portion of the country, from the time when our people first settled in it. This has not been because no one in America is able to accomplish such an undertaking. Our Irvings and our Coopers have proved themselves fully competent for the task. It has more probably been because the changes have succeeded each other with such rapidity as almost to rival the movements of their pen. However, it is not too late yet; and I sincerely hope that either or both of them will ere long furnish the generations to come with those delightful descriptions which they are so well qualified to give, of the original state of a country that has been so rapidly forced to change her form and attire under the influence of increasing population. Yes, I hope to read, ere I close my earthly career, accounts from those delightful writers of the progress of civilization in our Western country. They will speak of the Clarks, the Croghans, the Boons, and many other men of great and daring enterprise; they will analyse, as it were, into each component part, the country as it once existed, and will render the picture, as it ought to be, immortal."

"Various portions of our country have at different periods suffered severely from the influence of violent storms of wind, some of which have been known to traverse nearly the whole extent of the United States, and to leave such deep impressions in their wake as will not easily be forgotten.

"Having witnessed one of these awful phenomena, in all its grandeur, I shall attempt to describe it for your sake, kind reader, and for your sake only, the recollection of that astonishing revolution of the ethereal element even now bringing with it so disagreeable a sensation, that I feel as if about to be afflicted by a sudden stoppage of the circulation of my blood."

We will not insult the reader by any comments upon these beautiful pages; they are animated by a true sentiment; this pure and vivid coloring, this simple and ardent tone; this inimitable conviction show the happiest genius. Audubon writes as he sees, under the dictates of his personal impressions. The fidelity of description is not less remarkable, in this description of a hurricane in North America.

"I had left the village of Shawaney, situated on the banks of the Ohio, on my return from Henderson, which is also situated on the banks of the same beautiful stream. The weather was pleasant, and I thought not warmer than usual at that season. My horse was jogging quietly along, and my thoughts were, for once at least in the course of my life, entirely engaged in commercial speculations. I had forded Highland Creek, and was on the eve of entering a tract of bottom land, or valley, that lay between it and Canoe Creek, when on a sudden, I remarked a great difference in the aspect of the heavens. A hazy thickness had overspread the country, and I for some time expected an earthquake, but my horse exhibited no propensity to stop and prepare for such an occurrence. I had nearly arrived at the verge of the valley, when I thought fit to stop near a brook, and dismounted to quench the thirst which had come upon me. I was leaning on my knees, with my lips about to touch the water, when, from my proximity to the earth, I heard a distant murmuring sound of an extraordinary nature. I drank, however, and as I rose on my feet, looked toward the south-west, where I observed a yellowish, oval spot, the appearance of which was quite new to me. Little time was left me for consideration, as the next moment a smart breeze began to agitate the taller trees. It increased to an unexpected height, and

4

already the smaller branches and twigs were seen falling in a slanting direction towards the ground. Two minutes had scarcely elapsed when the whole forest before me was in fearful motion. Here and there, where one tree pressed against another, a creaking noise was produced, similar to that occasioned by the violent gusts which sometimes sweep over the country. Turning instinctively toward the direction from which the wind blew, I saw, to my great astonishment, that the noblest trees of the forest bent their lofty heads for a while, and unable to stand against the blast, were falling into pieces. First the branches were broken off with a crackling noise; then went the upper part of the massy trunks; and in many places whole trees of gigantic size were falling entire to the ground. So rapid was the progress of the storm, that before I could think of taking measures to insure my safety, the hurricane was passing opposite the place where I stood. Never can I forget the scene which at that moment presented itself. The tops of the trees were seen moving in the strangest manner, in the central current of the tempest, which carried along with it a mingled mass of twigs and foliage, that completely obscured the view. Some of the largest trees were seen bending and writhing under the gale; others suddenly snapped across; and many, after a momentary resistance, fell uprooted to the earth. The mass of branches, twigs, foliage, and dust that moved through the air, was whirled onwards like a cloud of feathers, and on passing, disclosed a wide space filled with fallen trees, naked stumps, and heaps of shapeless ruins which marked the path of the tempest. This space was about a fourth of a mile in breadth, and to my imagination, resembled the dried up bed of the Mississippi, with its thousands of planters and sawyers, strewed in the sand, and inclined in various degrees. The horrible noise resembled that of the great cataracts of

Niagara, and as it howled along in the track of the desolating tempest, produced a feeling in my mind which it were impossible to describe.

"The principal force of the hurricane was now over, although millions of twigs and small branches, that had been brought from a great distance, were seen following the blast, as if drawn onwards by some mysterious power. They even floated in the air for some hours after, as if supported by the thick mass of dust that rose high above the ground. The sky had now a greenish, lurid hue, and an extremely disagreeable sulphureous odor was diffused in the atmosphere. I waited in amazement, having sustained no material injury, until nature at length resumed her wonted aspect. For some moments, I felt undetermined whether I should return to Morgantown, or attempt to force my way through the wrecks of the tempest. My business, however, being of an urgent nature, I ventured into the path of the storm, and after encountering innumerable difficulties, succeeded in crossing it. I was obliged to lead my horse by the bridle, to enable him to leap over the fallen trees, whilst I scrambled over or under them in the best way I could, at times so hemmed in by the broken tops and tangled branches, as almost to become desperate. On arriving at my house, I gave an account of what I had seen, when, to my surprise, I was told that there had been very little wind in the neighborhood, although in the streets and gardens, many branches and twigs had fallen in a manner which excited great surprise.

"Many wondrous accounts of the devastating effects of this hurricane were circulated in the country, after its occurrence. Some log houses, we were told, had been overturned, and their inmates destroyed. One person informed me that a wire-sifter had been conveyed by the gust to a distance of many miles. Another had found a cow lodged in the fork of a large, half-broken tree. But as I am disposed to relate only what I have myself seen, I shall not lead you into the region of romance, but shall content myself with saying that much damage was done by this awful visitation. The valley is yet a desolate place, overgrown with briars and bushes, thickly entangled amidst the tops and trunks of the fallen trees, and is the resort of ravenous animals, to which they betake themselves when pursued by man, or after they have committed their depredations on the farms of the surrounding district. I have crossed the path of the storm, at a distance of a hundred miles from the spot where I witnessed its fury, and, again, four hundred miles farther off, in the State of Ohio. Lastly, I observed traces of its ravages on the summits of the mountains connected with the Great Pine Forest of Pennsylvania, three hundred miles beyond the place last mentioned. In all these different parts, it appeared to me not to have exceeded a quarter of a mile in breadth."

During our Naturalist's long excursions, other dangers menace him, and the following recital would not be out of place in one of Cooper's novels:

"On my return from the Upper Mississippi, I found myself obliged to cross one of the wide prairies, which in that portion of the United States, vary the appearance of the country.

"The weather was fine, all around me was as fresh and blooming as if it had just issued from the bosom of nature. My knapsack, my gun, and my dog, were all I had for baggage and company. But, although well moccasined, I moved slowly along, attracted by the brilliancy of the flowers, and the gambols of the fawns around their dams, to all appearance as thoughtless of danger as I felt myself.

"My march was of long duration; I saw the sun sinking

beneath the horizon long before I could perceive any appearance of woodland, and nothing in the shape of man had I met with that day. The track which I followed was only an old Indian trace, and as darkness overshadowed the prairie, I felt some desire to reach at least a copse, in which I might lie down to rest. The night-hawks were skimming over and around me, attracted by the buzzing wings of the beetles which form their food, and the distant howling of wolves, gave me some hope that I should soon arrive at the skirts of some woodland.

"I did so, and almost at the same instant a fire-light attracting my eye, I moved towards it, full of confidence that it proceeded from the camp of some wandering Indians. I was mistaken;—I discovered by its glare that it was from the hearth of a small log cabin, and that a tall figure passed and repassed between it and me, as if busily engaged in household arrangements.

"I reached the spot, and presenting myself at the door, asked the tall figure, which proved to be a woman, if I might take shelter under her roof for the night. Her voice was gruff, and her attire negligently thrown about her. She answered in the affirmative. I walked in, took a wooden stool, and quietly seated myself by the fire. The next object that attracted my notice was a finely-formed young Indian, resting his head between his hands, with his elbows on his knees. A long bow rested against the log wall near him, while a quantity of arrows and two or three raccoon skins lay at his feet. He moved not; he apparently breathed not. Accustomed to the habits of the Indians, and knowing that they pay little attention to the approval of civilized strangers, (a circumstance which in some countries is considered as evincing the apathy of their character,) I addressed him in French, a language not unfrequently partially known to the people in that neighborhood. He raised his head, pointed to one of his eyes with his finger, and gave me a significant glance with the other. His face was covered with blood. The fact was, that an hour before this, as he was in the act of discharging an arrow at a raccoon in the top of a tree, the arrow had split upon the cord, and sprung back with such violence into his right eye as to destroy it for ever.

"Feeling hungry, I inquired what sort of fare I might expect. Such a thing as a bed was not to be seen, but many large untanned bear and buffalo hides lay piled in a corner. I drew a fine time-piece from my breast, and told the woman that it was late, and that I was fatigued. She had espied my watch, the richness of which seemed to operate upon her feelings with electric quickness. She told me that there was plenty of venison and jerked buffalo meat, and that on removing the ashes, I should find a cake. But my watch had struck her fancy, and her curiosity had to be gratified by an immediate sight of it. I took off the gold chain that secured it, from around my neck, and presented it to her. She was all ecstasy, spoke of its beauty, asked me its value, and put the chain around her brawny neck, saying how happy the possession of such a watch would make her. Thoughtless, and, as I fancied myself, in so retired a spot, secure, I paid little attention to her talk or her movements. I helped my dog to a good supper of venison, and was not long in satisfying the demands of my own appetite.

"The Indian rose from his seat, as if in extreme suffering. He passed and repassed me several times, and once pinched me on the side so violently, that the pain nearly brought forth an exclamation of anger. I looked at him. His eye met mine; but his look was so forbidding, that it struck a chill into the more nervous part of my system. He again seated himself, drew his butcher-knife from its greasy scabbard, examined its edge, as I would do that of a razor suspected dull, replaced it, and again taking his tomahawk from his back, filled the pipe of it with tobacco, and sent me expressive glances whenever our hostess chanced to have her back toward us.

"Never until that moment had my senses been awakened to the danger which I now suspected to be about me. I returned glance for glance to my companion, and rested well assured that, whatever enemies I might have, he was not of their number.

"I asked the woman for my watch, wound it up, and under pretence of wishing to see how the weather might probably be on the morrow, took up my gun, and walked out of the cabin. I slipped a ball into each barrel, scraped the edges of my flints, renewed the primings, and returning to the hut, gave a favorable account of my observations. I took a few bear-skins, made a pallet of them, and calling my faithful dog to my side, lay down, with my gun close to my body, and in a few minutes was, to all appearance, fast asleep.

"A short time had elapsed when some voices were heard, and from the corner of my eyes I saw two athletic youths making their entrance, bearing a dead stag on a pole. They disposed of their burden, and asking for whiskey, helped themselves freely to it. Observing me and the wounded Indian, they asked who I was, and why the devil that rascal (meaning the Indian, who, they knew understood not a word of English) was in the house. The mother, for so she proved to be, bade them speak less loudly, made mention of my watch, and took them to a corner, where a conversation took place, the purport of which it required little shrewdness in me to guess. I tapped my dog gently. He moved his tail, and with indescribable pleasure I saw his fine eyes alternately fixed on me and raised towards the trio in the corner. I felt that he perceived danger in my situation. The Indian exchanged a last glance with me.

"The lads had eaten and drunk themselves into such a condition, that I already looked upon them as *hors de combat;* and the frequent visits of the whiskey bottle to the ugly mouth of their dam I hoped would soon reduce her to a like state. Judge of my astonishment, reader, when I saw this incarnate fiend take a large carving-knife and go to the grindstone to whet its edge. I saw her pour the water on the turning machine, and watched her working away with the dangerous instrument, until the cold sweat covered every part of my body, in despite of my determination to defend myself to the last. Her task finished, she walked to her reeling sons, and said, 'There, that'll soon settle him! Boys, kill you —— and then for the watch!'

"I turned, cocked my gun-lock silently, touched my faithful companion, and lay ready to start up and shoot the first who might attempt my life. The moment was fast approaching, and that night might have been my last in this world, had not Providence made preparations for my rescue. All was ready.

"The infernal hag was advancing slowly, probably contemplating the best way of despatching me, whilst her sons should be engaged with the Indian. I was several times on the eve of rising, and shooting her on the spot;—but she was not to be punished thus. The door was suddenly opened, and there entered two stout travellers, each with a long rifle on his shoulder. I bounced up on my feet; and making them most heartily welcome, told them how well it was for me that they should have arrived at that moment.

"The tale was told in a minute. The drunken sons were secured, and the woman, in despite of her defence and vociferations, shared the same fate. The Indian fairly danced with joy, and gave us to understand that, as he could not sleep for pain, he would watch over us. You may suppose we slept much less than we talked. The two strangers gave me an account of their once having been themselves in a somewhat similar situation. Day came, fair and rosy, and with it the punishment of our captives.

"They were now quite sobered. Their feet were unbound, but their arms were still securely tied. We marched them into the woods off the road, and having used them as regulators were wont to use such delinquents, we set fire to the cabin, gave all the skins and implements to the young Indian warrior, and proceeded, well pleased, towards the settlements.

"During upwards of twenty-five years, when my wanderings extended to all parts of our country, this was the only time at which my life was in danger from my fellow creatures. Indeed, so little risk do travellers run in the United States, that no one born there ever dreams of any to be encountered on the road; and I can only account for this occurrence by supposing that the inhabitants of the cabin were not Americans.

"Will you believe, good-natured reader, that not many miles from the place where this adventure happened, and where fifteen years ago, no habitation belonging to civilized man was expected, and very few ever seen, large roads are now laid out, cultivation has converted the woods into fertile fields, taverns have been erected, and much of what we Americans call comfort is to be met with. So fast does improvement proceed in our abundant and free country."

Thus does this forest philosopher, this naturalist commissioned by God to observe and to paint His works, involuntarily enlarging his circle, copy and cause to live the manners, landscapes and scenes of the continent. He promised us birds only ; but he gives a panorama of North America ; he has perceived that these plains, trees and rivers, made as a home for the feathered, was the natural frame of his pictures. As to the history of the birds themselves, of their private life, of their loves, quarrels and customs, it is charming in its details; take for instance the biography of the mocking-bird, peculiar to America.

"It is where the great magnolia shoots up its majestic trunk, crowned with evergreen leaves, and decorated with a thousand beautiful flowers, that perfume the air around; where the forests and fields are adorned with blossoms of every hue; where the golden orange ornaments the gardens and groves; where bignonias of various kinds interlace their climbing stems around the white-flowered stuartia, and mounting still higher, cover the summits of the lofty trees around, accompanied with innumerable vines, that here and there festoon the dense foliage of the magnificent woods, lending to the vernal breeze a slight portion of the perfume of their clustered flowers; where a genial warmth seldom forsakes the atmosphere; where berries and fruits of all descriptions are met with at every step;—in a word, kind reader, it is where Nature seems to have paused, as she passed over the earth, and opening her stores, to have strewed with unsparing hand the diversified seeds from which have sprung all the beautiful and splendid forms which I should in vain attempt to describe, that the Mocking Bird should have fixed its abode; there only that its wondrous song should be heard.

"But where is that favored land? It is in that great continent to whose distant shores Europe has sent forth her adventurous sons, to wrest for themselves a habitation from the wild inhabitants of the forest, and to convert the neglected soil into fields of exuberant fertility. It is, reader, in Louisiana that these bounties of nature are in the greatest perfection. It is here that you should listen to the love song of the Mocking Bird, as I at this moment do. See how he flies round his mate, with motions as light as those of a butterfly! His tail is widely expanded, he mounts in the air to a small distance, describes a circle, and again alighting, approaches his beloved one, his eyes gleaming with delight, for she has already promised to be his and his only. His beautiful wings are gently raised, he bows to his love, and again bouncing upwards, opens his bill, and pours forth his melody, full of exultation at the conquest which he has made.

"They are not the soft sounds of the flute or of the hautboy that I hear, but the sweeter notes of nature's own music. The mellowness of the song, the varied modulations and gradations, the extent of its compass, the great brilliancy of execution, are unrivalled. There is probably no bird in the world that possesses all the musical qualifications of this king of song, who has derived all from nature's self. Yes, reader, all.

"No sooner has he again alighted, and the conjugal contract has been sealed, than, as if his breast was about to be rent with delight, he again pours forth his notes with more softness and richness than before. He now soars higher, glancing around with a vigilant eye, to assure himself that none has witnessed his bliss. When these love scenes, visible only to the ardent lover of nature, are over, he dances through the air, full of animation and delight, and, as if to convince his lovely mate that to enrich her hopes he has much more love in store, he that moment begins anew, and imitates all the notes which nature has imparted to the other songsters of the grove.

"For a while, each long day and pleasant night are thus spent; but at a peculiar note of the female he ceases his song, and attends to her wishes. A nest is to be prepared, and the choice of a place in which to lay it is to become a matter of mutual consideration. The orange, the fig, the pear-tree of the gardens are inspected; the thick briar patches are also visited. They appear all so well suited for the purpose in view, and so well does the bird know that man is not his most dangerous enemy, that instead of retiring from him, they at length fix their abode in his vicinity, perhaps in the nearest tree to his window. Dried twigs, leaves, grasses, cotton, flax, and other substances, are picked up, carried to a forked branch, and there arranged. The female has laid an egg, and the male redoubles his caresses. Five eggs are deposited in due time, when the male having little more to do than to sing his mate to repose, attunes his pipe anew. Every now and then he spies an insect on the ground, the taste of which he is sure will please his beloved one. He drops upon it, takes it in his bill, beats it against the earth, and flies to the nest to feed and receive the warm thanks of his devoted female. When a fortnight has elapsed, the young brood demand all their care and attention. No cat, no vile snake, no dreaded hawk, is likely to visit their habitation. Indeed, the inmates of the next house have by this time become quite attached to the lovely pair of mocking birds, and take pleasure in contributing to their safety. The dew-berries from the fields and many kinds of fruit from the gardens, mixed with insects, supply the young as well as the parents with food. The brood is soon seen emerging from the nest, and in another fortnight, being now able to fly with vigor, and to provide for themselves, they leave the parent birds, as many other species do."

We have many books upon Natural History wherein generalities and vague descriptions abound; here you have the finest touches of the pencil and the most delicate; there is an extreme precision in the details; a complete journal of the life of birds. Audubon destroys more than one popular prejudice. For instance, the opinions or rather the lugubrious metaphors which insult the owl as solemn and stupid. Men place him on tombs; chase him with stones when he appears in the day time; one says ordinarily, "sad as an owl, gloomy as an owl." Audubon teaches us that among the numerous kinds of owls, there is but one, the Black-beak, whose temperament and melancholy humors merit, not these reproaches and insults, but a charitable commiseration; the poor animal is nearly blind, and has a hereditary spleen. As to his brethren, Shakspeare knew them well, when he called them, "merry birds." The Athenians esteemed them greatly; and Audubon carried one, in his pocket, from New York to Philadelphia—it was the pleasantest sort of buffoon.

"Should you, kind reader, find it convenient or agreeable to visit the noble forests existing in the lower parts of the State of Louisiana, about the middle of October, when nature, on the eve of preparing for approaching night, permits useful dews to fall and rest on every plant, with the view of reviving its leaves, its fruits, or its lingering blossoms, ere the return of morn; when every night-insect rises on buzzing wings from the ground, and the fire-fly, amidst thousands of other species, appears as if purposely to guide their motions through the sombre atmosphere; at the moment when numerous reptiles and quadrupeds commence their nocturnal prowlings, and the fair moon, empress of the night, rises peacefully on the distant horizon, shooting her silvery rays over the heavens and the earth, and, like a watchful guardian, moving slowly, and majestically along; when the husbandmen, just returned to his home, after the labors of the day, is receiving the cheering gratulations of his family, and the wholesome repast is about to be spread out for master and servants alike; it is at this moment, kind reader, that were you, as I have said, to visit that happy country, your ear would suddenly be struck by the discordant screams of the Barred Owl.

Its *whah, whah, whah, whah-aa* is uttered loudly, and in so strange and ludicrous a manner, that I should not be surprised were you, kind reader, when you and I meet, to compare these sounds to the affected bursts of laughter which you may have heard from some of the fashionable members of our own species.

"How often, when snugly settled under the boughs of my temporary encampment, and preparing to roast a venison steak, or the body of a squirrel, on a wooden spit, have I been saluted with the exalted bursts of this mighty disturber of the peace, that had it not been for him, would have prevailed around me, as well as in my lonely retreat. How often have I seen this nocturnal marauder alight within a few yards of me, exposing his whole body to the glare of my fire, and eye me in such a curious manner that, had it been reasonable to do so, I would gladly have invited him to walk in and join me in my repast, that I might have enjoyed the pleasure of forming a better acquaintance with him. The liveliness of his motions, joined to their oddness, have often made me think that his society would be at least as agreeable as that of many of the buffoons we meet with in the world. But as such opportunities of forming acquaintance have not existed, be content, kind reader, with the imperfect information which I can give you of the habits of this Sancho Panza of our woods."

The following picture of the White-headed Eagle is as beautiful colored and more exact than Buffon.

"The figure of this noble bird is well known throughout the civilized world, emblazoned as it is on our national standard, which waves in the breeze of every clime, bearing to distant lands the remembrance of a great people living in a state of peaceful freedom. May that peaceful freedom last forever!

"The great strength, daring, and cool courage of the white-headed eagle, joined to his unequalled power of flight, render him highly conspicuous among his brethren. To these qualities did he add a generous disposition towards others, he might be looked up to as a model of nobility. The ferocious, overbearing, and tyrannical temper which is ever and anon displaying itself in his actions, is, nevertheless, best adapted to his state, and was wisely given him by the Creator to enable him to perform the office assigned to him.

"To give you, kind reader, some idea of the nature of this bird, permit me to place you on the Mississippi, on which you may float gently along, while approaching winter brings millions of water-fowl on whistling wings from the countries of the north, to seek a milder climate in which to sojourn for a season. The eagle is seen perched, in an erect attitude, on the highest summit of the tallest tree by the margin of the broad stream. His glistening, but stern eye, looks over the vast expanse. He listens attentively to every sound that comes to his quick ear from afar, glancing now and then on the earth beneath, lest even the light tread of the fawn may pass unheard. His mate is perched on the opposite side, and should all be tranquil and silent, warns him by a cry to continue patient. At this well-known call, the male partly opens his broad wings, inclines his body a little downwards, and answers to her voice in tones not unlike the laugh of a maniac. The next moment, he resumes his erect attitude, and again all around is silent. Ducks of many species, the teal, the wigeon, the mallard, and others, are seen passing with great rapidity, and following the course of the current; but the eagle heeds them not; they are at that time beneath his attention. The next moment, however, the wild trumpet-like sound of a yet distant but approaching swan is heard. A shriek from the female eagle comes across the stream, for, kind reader, she is fully as alert as her mate. The latter suddenly shakes the whole of his body, and with a few touches of his bill, aided by the action of his cuticular muscles, arranges his plumage in an instant. The snow-white bird is now in sight; her long neck is stretched forward, her eye is on the watch, vigilant as that of her enemy; her large wings seem with difficulty to support the weight of her body, although they flap incessantly. So irksome do her exertions seem, that her very legs are spread beneath her. tail, to aid her in her flight. She approaches, however. The eagle has marked her for his prey. As the swan is passing the dreaded pair, starts from his perch, in full preparation for the chase, the male bird, with an awful scream, that to the swan's ear brings more terror than the report of the large duck-gun.

"Now is the moment to witness the display of the eagle's powers. He glides through the air like a falling star, and, like a flash of lightning, comes upon the timorous quarry, which now, in agony and despair, seeks, by various manœuvres, to elude the grasp of his cruel talons. It mounts, doubles, and willingly would plunge into the stream, were it not prevented by the eagle, which, long possessed of the knowledge that by such a strategem the swan might escape him, forces it to remain in the air by attempting to strike it with his talons from beneath. The hope of escape is soon given up by the swan. It has already become much weakened, and its strength fails at the sight of the courage and swiftness of its antagonist. Its last gasp is about to escape, when the ferocious eagle strikes with his talons the under side of its wing, and with unresisted power forces the bird to fall in a slanting direction upon the nearest shore.

"It is then, reader, that you may see the cruel spirit of this dreaded enemy of the feathered race, whilst, exulting over his prey, he for the first time breathes at ease. He presses down his powerful feet, and drives his sharp claws deeper than ever into the heart of the dying swan. He shrieks with delight, as he feels the last convulsions of his prey, which has now sunk under his unceasing efforts to render death as painfully felt as it can possibly be. The female has watched every movement of her mate; and if she did not assist him in capturing the swan, it was not from want of will, but merely that she felt full assurance that the power and courage of her lord were quite sufficient for the deed. She now sails to the spot where he eagerly awaits her, and when she has arrived, they together turn the breast of the luckless swan upwards, and gorge themselves with gore."

Audubon has not neglected one detail in Ornithological annals; he has treated with peculiar care the loves of birds. Some men have sung the loves of angels—a most apocryphal history; others, chant the loves of poets, loves chimerical as those of Petrarch; symbolic as Dante's, or mad as Tasso's. We have had the conjugal mystery of flowers; the loves of the minerals, and at last of the Triangles. Who would not prefer to these absurdities, the ærial loves which our naturalist has so happily depicted.

The Carolinian Turtle-dove furnishes him with delicious pictures.

"I have tried, kind reader, to give you a faithful representation of two as gentle pairs of Turtles as ever cooed their loves in the green woods.

"I have placed them on a branch of Stuartia, which you see ornamented with a profusion of white blossoms, emblematic of purity and chastity.

"Look at the female, as she assiduously sits on her eggs,

embosomed among the thick foliage, receiving food from the bill of her mate, and listening with delight to his assurances of devoted affection. Nothing is wanting to render the moment as happy as could be desired by a couple on a similar occasion.

"On the branch above, a love scene is just commencing. The female, still coy and undetermined, seems doubtful of the truth of her lover, and virgin-like resolves to put his sincerity to the test, by delaying the gratification of his wishes. She has reached the extremity of the branch, her wings and tail are already opening, and she will fly off to some more sequestered spot, where, if her lover should follow her with the same assiduous devotion, they will doubtless, become as blessed as the pair beneath them.

"The Dove announces the approach of Spring. Nay, she does more :—she forces us to forget the chilling blasts of winter, by the soft and melancholy sound of her cooing. Her heart is already so warmed and so swollen by the ardor of her passion, that it feels as ready to expand as the buds on the trees are under the genial influence of returning heat

"The flight of this bird is extremely rapid, and of long duration. Whenever it starts from a tree or the ground, on being unexpectedly approached, its wings produce a whistling noise, heard at a considerable distance. On such occasions, it frequently makes several curious windings through the air, as if to prove its capability of efficient flight, it seldom rises far above the trees, and as seldom passes through dense woods or forests, but prefers following their margins, or flying about the fences and fields. Yet, during Spring, and particularly whilst the female is sitting on her eggs, the male rises as if about to ascend to a great height in the air, flapping his wings, but all of a sudden comes downwards again, describing a large circle, and sailing smoothly with wings and tail expanded, until in this manner he alights on the tree where his mate is, or on one very near it."

All birds are jealously inclined, save the golden-winged wood-pecker; this brilliant gentleman is the most amiable and sparkling of birds.

"It is generally agreeable to be in the company of individuals who are naturally animated and pleasant; for this reason, nothing can be more gratifying than the society of wood-peckers in the forests. To prove this to you, kind reader, I shall give you a full account of the habits of the golden-winged woodpecker.

"This species, which is usually called *pique-bois jaune* by the French settlers in Louisiana, and receives the name of high-holder, yucker, and *flicker* in other parts of the Union, being seldom or never graced with the epithet *golden-winged*, employed by naturalists, is one of the most lively of our birds, and is found over the whole of the United States.

"No sooner has spring called them to the pleasant duty of making love, as it is called, than their voice, which, by the way, is not at all disagreeable to the ear of man, is heard from the tops of high, decayed trees, proclaiming with delight the opening of the welcome season. Their note at this period is merriment itself; as it imitates a prolonged and jovial laugh, heard at a considerable distance. Several males pursue a female, reach her, and to prove the force and truth of their love, bow their heads, spread their tail, and move sidewise, backwards and forwards, performing such antics, as might induce any one witnessing them, if not of a morose temper, to join his laugh to theirs. The female flies to another tree, where she is closely followed by one, two, or even half a dozen of these gay suitors, and where again the same ceremonies are gone through. No fightings occur, no jealousies seem to exist among these beaux, until a marked preference is shown to some individual, when the rejected proceed in search of another female. In this manner, all the golden-winged woodpeckers are soon happily mated. Each pair immediately proceed to excavate a trunk of a tree, and finish a hole in it sufficient to contain themselves and their young. They both work with great industry and apparent pleasure. Should the male, for instance, be employed, the female is close to him, and congratulates him on the removal of every chip which his bill sends through the air. While he rests, he appears to be speaking to her on the most tender subjects, and when fatigued, is at once assisted by her. In this manner, by the alternate exertions of each, the hole is dug and finished. They caress each other on the branches, climb about and around the tree with apparent delight, rattle with their bill against the tops of the dead branches, chase all their cousins, the red-heads, defy the Purple Grackles to enter their nest, feed plentifully on ants, beetles, and larvæ, cackling at intervals, and ere two weeks have elapsed, the female lays either four or six eggs, the whiteness and transparency of which are doubtless the delight of their heart. If to raise a numerous progeny may contribute to happiness, these woodpeckers are in this respect happy enough, for they have two broods each season; and as this might induce you to imagine wood-peckers extremely abundant in America, I may at once tell you that they are so."

Such are the vivid, varied, naïve colors with which the pen of the Naturalist, picturesque as his pencil, comments on and explains the admirable plates which compose his work. So too do we understand science. Thanks to the progress of civilization, she contents herself no longer with a dry nomenclature; and shuts herself up no longer amid the dust of old books. Adieu forever to the symbolic and artificial classifications, which took the pla[illegible] of a study of the world; and substituted for harmonious nature, an indescribable skeleton whose erudite labels were the toys of the learned. Read those old monographs. What do you find there? titles and words, figures and eternal classifications which address neither the soul nor the thought. Is, O God! this thy living and eternal work, so full of animation! What puerile invention in the place of a grand whole!

Here is an eagle on a peak; you talk much about a class of birds, which, say you, have crooked beaks and feet armed with talons. What do I care for that? Insipid cicerone, why do you come between me and the spectacle for which my curiosity is seeking the causes—I want to know why that eagle is there; what interest has driven him from the plain where his prey abounds; why he chooses for throne and place of rest, that sharp rock, that sterile mass of broken ice; where is neither food nor shelter. I would know too, of what use are these arid, granite mountains bathed by the sea. If you tell me that the eagle, has need of a very lofty peak wherefrom to take his flight because of the spread and disposition of his pinions; if you prove by the conformation of the globe, the necessity of mountains for the elaboration of metals, or as reservoirs for streams and rivers, then you will indeed instruct me—then I could understand something of the harmony of nature; and could bow respectfully before that vast and thousand-chorded instrument formed by the eternal Author of all.

Audubon has not only understood this harmony, in the midst of which he has lived, and whereof the music has re-echoed in the very deeps of his soul; but he has reproduced it in a style admirable for its simplicity, full of savor, of sap, of eloquence, and of sobriety. It is his glory!

More varied than Irving; more brilliant and pure than Fennimore Cooper, with him ceases what we may call the first literary epoch of the United States.

CHAPTER II.

OF POPULAR LITERATURE, AND OF THE LITERATURE SO CALLED, IN ENGLAND AND IN THE UNITED STATES.

SECTION I.

INFANCY AND FUTURE OF AMERICA—AGE AND DESPAIR OF EUROPE—HOW AMERICA IS INCESSANTLY PEOPLED BY THE SUPERABUNDANT POPULATION OF EUROPE—EMIGRATION AND COLONIZATION.

There is no spectacle equal to that of which the thought has a presentiment now; of which the certainty does not rest upon hypothesis, but on the inevitable development of facts—the spectacle of that America, that new Europe, which occupies so vast a space, from sea to sea, from Greenland to the Antilles. All civilization moves towards the displacement of human destinies, and every effort which we make to sustain and prolong our lives, turns to the profit of that great heir of our wealth. The colonization of Canada, of which only a small part is occupied by the wrecks of French families, the wilds and forests of which are peopled by the British government with their poor, exported from Ireland and Scotland, will aid the advance of this new civilization. In less than a century, all the colonists of those regions will speak English, and feel that there is a closer connection between them and the inhabitants of Philadelphia, Washington, and Boston, more affinities of neighborhood, commerce, necessity, and situation, that exists between them and the citizens of London. All will be confounded—even the Southern republics—in that cluster of which Washington is the centre. The two colonizing nations will be represented there, Catholic Spain and Protestant England. France will have no representative if it be not in some unnoticed corner near Quebec or Montreal.

This is the chastisement of that careless violence, of that unpausing impetuosity which has made us neglect our colonies. There was even a grave fault—say what you will—in our helping the insurgent American colonies against their metropolis. The statesmen of that day thought only of revenging themselves upon their enemy and satisfying their anti-Britannic rancor. They saw not what is hardly visible even yet; that the question was about Europe's own self; and that it related rather to a continent (in spite of universal opinion) about to obtain an orbicular preponderance, than to a partial rebellion against an unjust mother-country. By her adhesion to the cause of America, France deserted the cause of Europe; and in playing the second role in the strife she lost her American colonies, without gaining the least advantage. This singular concurrence of human affairs, which none can deny, and none, save God, completely understand, has made that same American war sound not only the first victory-peal of the New World, but the first death-bell of the Old.

Then you saw the ancient institutions of Europe crumble, and the thrones were broken, yet the people could not build a durable habitation from the wreck ; all ideas and all systems erred as chance willed, till a man of genius by the force of conquest, succeeded in binding together for awhile the broken fasces.

What is still more strange, and what proves beyond contradiction, the future and inevitable dominion of that America, to which we will one day be what dying Egypt was to radiant Greece, is that American ideas invade, press us and every day usurp more space and power. They do not suit us. They have no analogy with our souvenirs, our life, our crowded populations, our rival cupidities. No matter, we cede to the logic of facts and antecedents, terrible necessity whose yoke we cannot break. Our hope of revival is by American ideas, as the Romans hoped for a moment to be revived by an Oriental infusion which ended by destroying them. These reflections, which belong only to the future and which cannot change the present, do not prevent the resolution of the British government and its efforts to people with poor families, Upper Canada, New Scotland, Cape Breton, New Brunswick, from being a good and useful measure. There is in those regions, some of which are fertile, room for some millions of workers. The city of Toronto alone supports 15,000 workmen who gain £2 per month, and their board. France has not yet reached this point, nor can she now make use of this grand remedy, emigration.

If we become Americans, let us carefully imitate their commercial energy, spirit of enterprize and active resolution. If we become English, let us try to employ, after their example, colonization and emigration to augment the resources and to heal the wounds of our country.

We know how much England is embarrassed by the development of her industry, commerce and wealth. Her pecuniary and moral force, her population, ambition and luxury have grown beyond measure; enclosed in the island which she occupies, she cannot enlarge its diameter, nor offer a theatre for labor proportionate to their need to these eager and famished avidities. Hence that furious competition, that excessive and vehement rivalry; that crowd which blocks up all the avenues of commerce and fortune; hence that difficulty of employing capital; that frightful pauperism; those poor laws which only aggravate the evil; that plethora which keeps up a permanent and burning fever in the veins of a vigorous body. Economists try a thousand means to counterbalance this movement, and to oppose a barrier to the progress of evil, which is, after all, only the progress of industry, of opulence and of commerce.

Mr. Malthus and Miss Martineau request the English not to marry any more, or at least very seldom, for the love of their country, since the increase of population is the evident source of the scourge. Other philosophers counsel the annual exportation of the poor to the American, Australian and even African colonies. While they offer an issue and means of decrease to this hungry crowd, permitting them to go work and die in some wild land far from their native one, England herself receives pauper crowds from Ireland, who not only replace the expatriated workmen, but lower, by their extreme misery and need, the price of labor, and increase the hardness of the lot of those who have not left the country. England, then, is like a vase, emptying itself at one end to be filled at another.

Ireland is a perpetual manufactory of poor-devil *sans-culottes*, who have no trade, and who, with three potatoes in their hand, cross the channel and go to demand work in England for the lowest possible wages. They get it, and then stretch themselves to sleep upon their rags. I wish that philanthropists and calculators would think of these things: they would see one of the many proofs that Europe cannot possibly long keep up its supremacy on the globe, and one of the gravest symptoms of that change, which is more interesting, than the revolutions of the Roman Empire; and which will undoubtedly give the sceptre of human destinies into the hands of those who are now in apprenticeship but who will soon be emancipated.

This far sight belongs only to philosophers. Statesmen in England act wisely in encouraging with all their power, the emigration of poor families, the foundation of new colonies, the extension of the old ones, and the employment of industry and national ambition outside of the small field offered by the mother country. There are now ten new Colonies which are beginning to flourish under the protection of the British government. I mention those in the Canadian Backwoods, and in Southern and Western Australia. The United States profit by the reception of immense numbers of Irish: workers, women, children, old men, throw themselves on board of vessels, cross the Atlantic, offer the feebleness or strength of their arms, are accepted, and die at the end of a few months or years, crushed by hard toil. They gain twice as much as they did at home, work six times as hard, and perish six times as soon. Their efforts are like combats. The American people in the course of its progress cares little for fatigue, nor for the existences devoured and absorbed by it. It walks or rather runs on; and be sure that it will not halt soon. Usurpation is easy to it, is necessary, almost *fatal*, in the sense of the Antique Destiny: we have seen with what facility, and irresistible motion Texas became part of the States.

English statesmen have a thousand motives for throwing their poor population into the woods of Canada, and to make of them an intervening rampart against the invasion of the American Confederation. They arm themselves against two enemies at a time; against the old French population of Canada, and the Republicans of the States, who know so well how to act for their own advantage. It is in order to favor and increase these emigrations that the British government has published and profusely distributed "Letters of certain indigent Persons who have emigrated to Canada." They contain the most seductive and brilliant picture of the happiness which attends future emigrants; they promise a land of Cocagne, whose rivers roll o'er sands of gold, with farm-houses already built, and swarms of young Canadian girls awaiting them with open arms. This little untruth, a common political hoax, is very pardonable. It is much better for the poor workmen of England, Scotland and Ireland, to clear, in the sweat of their brows, a wild domain on the great Canadian Lakes, than to rest famished or to become criminal in the streets of Glasgow, Birmingham or London.

Men have counted the victims of ancient conquerors; have they thought of those of modern industry, generations made meagre, intellects knotted and dulled, the *canuts* of Lyons, the *crazy men* of Birmingham. Since the year 1818, the weavers and hand-spinners of Scotland and Northern England petition incessantly for a means of gaining a living. Every year parliament treats them as Don Juan does M. Dimanche, puts them off until next year, and so the matter drops. Nevertheless, machine labor, gigantic rival of human toil, continues its progress, and crushes in its route all who resist. "Destroy the machines," cry some journals and pamphlets. "Favor emigration," say wiser politicians; it is the only remedy for exuberant population, for unemployed arms, for overstocked professions. Found colonies in good situations, fertile, peaceable; the money consecrated to that will be placed at heavy interest; the more your colonists are satisfied, the more will others be attracted; the more will you lighten the burden of the metropolis. These advices are excellent. Colonies are admirable *exutoires*, useful to the metropolis even at the moment that they separate from it. Unfortunately, France has only been able to discover for others a proper territory for colonization without herself founding colonies.

We will not return to that sad old malady of our France which seems always destined to sow the seed of progress, but never to reap. England, on the contrary, is essentially a colonizing country. She *must* continue that work which created the United States, and carry it on with redoubled energy, activity and perseverance. She is notified of this necessity by facts hideously distinct.

There are three standing armies of paupers, Irish cotters, Sussex laborers, and Glasgow weavers; and these three form a mass of thirty thousand men, without any means of existence, without knowing where to get daily bread. You see, say the parliamentary reports, troops of thirty or forty workmen, who go from one end of England to the other, looking for work, asking alms on the road, picked up by the police officers, and happy to get the black bread of the parish workhouse.

While the English political economists struggle against this population, the American of the United States, and the inhabitants of Canada demand loudly hands for the cultivation of the soil. "All the world," says a Canadian journal, "knows that population is wealth." Thus, for one country, that population is riches, which makes the poverty of another. And in these two axioms, placed in juxtaposition, one can see the future of Europe and America; here rivalries, unsatisfied ambitions in the midst of great industrial prosperity, the decline and the pressure of famished men, of which China offers an example; there, continuous, rapid, onward, inevitable progress.

These emigrations, which should be favored by England and by France, augment and precipitate the progress of North America. It is not probable that the anglo-Canadian colonies, and the British possessions bordering on the United States, will long remain insensible to the near and contagious example of independence and self-government. When their cities shall have been built, their fields cleared, their forests thinned, their commercial relations established, they will separate, one by one, from the parent stock, and affiliate themselves to that formidable group of republics which borders the Atlantic, and is stretching towards the Pacific.

SECTION II.

POPULAR MOVEMENT IN FRANCE AND ENGLAND—EDUCATION OF THE MASSES.

The despair of old Europe, fatigued by labors, exhausted by pleasure, enervated by desire, manifests itself especially in England, France, and Germany. The chartist movements which have recently alarmed Great Britain, are but the powerless, yet mad aspiration after necessary well-being; the roar of the popular lion agitated in his den. In France, it is more mingled with self-love, envy, and jealous hatred; with our neighbors, there is more hunger, thirst and sorrow. The insurrection of vanities is not less terrible than that of hunger. Here, and on the other side of the channel, the masses seek to employ their power. You cannot oppose the fact, nor strive against what exists. All good politics, worthy of the name, takes situations as it finds them, and strives to direct them.

At present there is a difficult and fearful question in England. Would popular education have prevented these sorrows?

Popular education, its distribution, the control which it should exercise, and the choice of men to whom to confide it, occupies to-day the minds of Great Britain, or rather, all the thoughtful minds of Europe. It is not a simple question. It is allowed that the people must be enlightened; it is not agreed, either as to the degree of instruction, or the means of education, or the relative proportion of moral and religious teaching. The clergy declare that the intellectual direction of humanity belongs to them alone; the enemies of the clergy accuse them of wishing to revive fanaticism for their own profit. Some philosophers see with terror an immoral education going on in the people; others assert that moral light always accompanies intellectual, and that there can be no risk in enlightening men.

"Alas, you deceive yourselves," reply some clear-seeing men to these latter. "All the ambitions awakened by an equalized education would render a government impossible. Men crowd already to the professions called liberal, and which constitute the aristocracy of to-day. You will soon have twenty-five doctors to one patient, and sixty lawyers for a single suit. Prepare workmen to exercise mechanic arts, which are certainly as useful as the babble of tongue or pen. Keep them far from a literary education which will make them bad men of letters, indifferent artists, and painters of screens and Swiss watches."

To this the partisans of equality answer, that it is infamous to establish a hierarchy of education and instruction, that the University is a feudal institution, behind the age, opposed to progress, and which ought to be destroyed. On the other hand, the clergy continue to fulfil their task ; philanthropists print little volumes, and every year prizes are given for pretty treatises on popular morality, of which the people never read a line, but which profit two persons, the author and the printer.

We have spoken of France. England is exposed to greater dangers ; forced to continue her colossal industry, her universal commerce, and her gigantic exportations. She assembles in several parts of her territory, thousands of men vowed to the manual labor made necessary by her industry. They are the servitors of the temple ; poor souls, they are its sacrifices ! Every time that a new invention advances the car, as the poets say, a thousand existences are crushed beneath the wheel of this Juggernaut. I do not say this to calumniate industry, but because, unfortunately I love truth, and will write it. In a season of calm, when there are no revolutions, no riots, no new machine to replace by a copper piston two hundred vigorous human arms ; when all goes well for the workman, look at his life at Manchester, Birmingham, Leeds, Liverpool, Sheffield, London or Edinburgh. He and his wife rise early, because they must arrive as early as the others. The workmen are so numerous and pressing that a little laziness would lose both place and bread. The wife confides to a paid, yet careless nurse, her little child, sallow, diminutive, thin or ricketty ; one of those frightful children, found only at Lyons or Liverpool, and which will also, one day become a laborer. Then, the husband and wife go to their toil. No duties, no domestic pleasures, no motion of the intelligence, nothing which can awaken in these materialized creatures, the soul, the mind, the spark of divinity. In speaking of this horrid use of humanity, one must restrain one's self, and not give way to declamation. As living is dear in these great cities of industry, a child not yet grown becomes useful in proportion to his strength. They use his little arm as soon as it can move a wheel or lift a hammer. He has not one moment free for instruction or pleasure; all his minutes are occupied. The great thing is to live; one moment lost is a mouthful of bread lost. When all days and hours pass thus, what of Sunday? and of Monday? Those who know man, and the eternal laws of his organization, know that these unfortunate slaves require pleasure and violent distraction. They take it. The limbs fatigued with labor, or stiffened by a week without exercise, are distended and bathed in drunkenness and coarse joy. To the abominable torpor, the frightful lassitudes succeeds twenty-four or forty-eight hours of orgies. Then the man re-becomes a beast of burden, takes up again his weekly yoke, and so goes on till he dies.

You will acknowledge that none need education more than this man; but how to give it! what education to give him!

The workmen in manufactories are employed before they grow up. His physical force, as it grows, strangles the intellectual. He has no time to think; he knows or can do but two things, act and enjoy. The brute faculties develope themselves, without his possessing the happy instincts of conservative wisdom which Providence has given to the animals. Every day he does the same work in the same way. He acts like a lever; a pulley, a hammer; he loses his manhood; he is a bit of brass or of iron. Are these observations a calumnious attack upon industry? No. We seek, completely disinterested, the truth, the reality, the facts, the evils, and the remedies. The father of political economy, Adam Smith, a really eloquent man, like all profound and sincere writers, foresaw these results; he declared that the division of labor would produce necessarily and fatally, an epoch where the cleverness and strength of every workman would be concentrated in a very simple and purely material operation. No idea can germinate in the brain of a man who has cut a thread, turned a spindle, or unscrewed a nut two thousand times a day, for three hundred and fifty days a year. The composer in a printing office, obliged to reflect while he works, and to accomplish a variety of complicated and delicate operations, is nearly always a smart, intelligent fellow; "but," says Smith, "the greater portion of workmen in the factories have no occasion to exercise their intelligence. They lose the habit of thinking, and grow stupid and ignorant. Their mental torpor hinders them, not only from taking part in a reasonable conversation, but from understanding a tender or generous sentiment, and consequently, from forming a solid and equitable judgment on the duties of private life. How can such a man associate himself with the great interests of the country? The uniformity of his stationary life corrupts the courage of his soul, and even the activity of his body. He buys his partial dexterity at the price of all his intellectual, social, and moral virtues. If the governments do not take some measures to correct the degradation, this will be the miserable condition to which it will reduce the poor workmen of all civilized society, that is, the large majority of the population.

The recent movements of the Chartists have proved that the great economist was right. Uneducated masses, worn out by toil and want, broke suddenly forth. At the voice of certain leaders they seized upon spade and mattock, and descended like avalanches upon the peaceable cities. One was obliged to give battle to these Cyclops, and when they were beaten on one side, they were likely to rise up again on the other. They have immense physical force; they have no principle, no light nor bridle; they are habituated to every fatigue and privation; they want more bread, more leisure, and less toil. How to answer them! A new Agrarian law even would not satisfy them. Understanding no economy, no moderation, no virtue, they would dissipate in a few days, the riches of pillaged provinces, for incapacity to make profitable use of well-being and repose is the frighful result of a material and brutal existence. Thus civilization has created new scourges; industry has given birth to unheard of monsters. Utopians dream vainly; the promisers of destiny vainly rock humanity in their hammocks woven of silken phrases; our original misery exhibits itself always, exacting from us vigilant care, attentive prudence, and forcing us constantly to repair the bark of civilization which is no doubt triumphant, but triumphant only by courage and labor. To show the bright side of things only; to issue to the people bulletins of victory as false as those of conquerors are; to affirm that certain magic words are enough for social happiness; thus to dupe the ears of men by that flattering song which pleases the weaknesses of Hope, is perhaps a lucrative business, but it is also a dangerous and an alarming one. Let us not seduce a civilization grown old by a wretched and perpetual caress; nor resemble the courtizan, who turns to her profit the shameless passions, and grows rich by the profusions and follies which she encourages.

Every epoch has its diseases; every new epoch sends out its unknown diseases which we cannot study, but must guess at. You need not be a pessimist because you are a physician; you do not assassinate the man whose wound you probe. There are minds, at once thoughtful and practical, which see all the consequences of a situation: Do not call them misanthropic. Misanthropic! Bacon, Montesquieu, Machiavel, Pitt, minds of the same order, did not desire to be esteemed dupes by their century, and they were right. They saw that advantages have their inconvenience, and a conquest its perils; and they were right! They would have told you of the dangers of an enormous increase of the material forces of society; they would have recommended you, above all, to elevate the moral and intellectual condition of the masses; which serve as blind instruments to a new civilization. They would have told you that it is alway from the bosom of Force and Life that Death is developed; that war was the enemy of Rome; that feudality perished by the inequality of the powers upon which it was based;—in a word, that instead of worshipping herself, the reigning Industry of to-day, should take precautions and guarantee herself against the results of her conquests. Under the protection of the great names which I have cited, these useful counsels would obtain some attention; would escape at least the hollow accusation of pessimism and bad-humor.

The social crisis in which we live, in which all Europe is more or less plunged, is simply an ascending movement of the inferior classes, who covet the power and riches of the class immediately above them. This covetous movement is peculiarly felt in large cities where interests come in collision, where passions ferment, where a luminous and ardent atmosphere envelops every thing, where ambition is in the vital air, where, before the eyes is a dazzling luxury, the pleasures of the rich, and the delights which civilization reserves for its favorites. The Birmingham workman, wanting bread if he should miss one week's labor, imprisoned in a garret six feet square, inflamed by the preaching of street-orators, would not certainly be any more content, nor more peaceful, should a half education enable him to read Cobbett's pamphlets, or even to translate the theories of Rousseau. The light which you would give him would only make him seize his arms, by showing to him the hideous wretchedness and iniquity of his position.

According to late statistics there are in Manchester, Salford, Liverpool, Bury, and York, alone, 80,000 children growing up to be Chartists. The first measures, to be taken are at once the most simple and the most difficult: it relates to the giving of bread and well-being to these people. I am not sure that a wise and extended legislation would not oppose all excessive agglomeration of workmen and manufactories at the same point. First, well being; then morality—instruction will come afterwards. Popular instruction would leave to the working generations, a self-respect and attachment for society if they could feel themselves to be its esteemed supports and not its victims.

What England shall do, will be a lesson for all Europe; for all Europe treads the same path. All Europe must struggle against the same dangers born of the progress of industry and of the blind force which industry employs, inflames and exalts. According to us, the first duty of prudent politics will be to provide for the urgent necessity of these unfortunate populations, then to elevate them gradually to the moral level of their minds, and at last to make them to participate in that instruction which will be the last and greatest benefit. What now occupies the Chartists is wages, bread, drink, and covering; the problem of the moment is to increase their wages, not their light. Educate their children, and let the state encourage those parents who are moral and intelligent enough to send their offspring to school. England, always prudent in her ameliorations, faithful to her personal traditions, and always opposed to the scabrous experience of empirical politics, will unquestionably follow, the gentlest and least violent way; the surest, not the noisiest; not the most democratic, the most flattering to vulgar passions, but the most benevolent, the most useful to those who suffer to-day, as to those who will pay to-morrow the sufferings of their fellow creatures.

SECTION III.

POETRY OF VENGEANCE AND OF POPULAR WRATH IN EUROPE.

Such a position should find a poetic expression.

The first in date, the chief of these poets is Crabbe. Before him the Saxon and domestic tendencies were revealed, but with less violence and harshness. It is easy to go back from Crabbe and Burns to Goldsmith, whose "Deserted Village" is a popular and social elegy, or to Gray's "Elegy in a country Church-yard." This popular view is ancient; long interrupted by Puritanism or by Italian and French influence, it is to be found even in the middle ages, and appears in the Vision of Pierce Plowman, the roturier and Saxon reclamation of a peasant against the abuse of Norman Sovereignty.

In America, the poetry of vengeance could not arise. The primitive liberty of nature, the great struggle of the Puritans with the elements, the waves, the soil, the wind, did not permit the domestic muse to take this fearful and bitter flight, nor to become hateful and violent. The earliest of American literateurs, Franklin, Audubon, Cooper, are amiable and human writers, that is popular in the true sense of the word. They write for all the world like Shakspeare, Montague, Cervantes. But in England, in the midst of an old and refined society, is produced another falsely-popular literature, vindicative and furious, destined exclusively for workmen, peasants, and men without property or civil rights. Strange, that while democratic America fostered a literature graceful and elegant, full of fine and delicate shading, aristocratic and natural, old, weary Europe gave birth to a brood of tragic poets, dithyrambic and academic in the dress of the penniless;—false men of the people who speak loudly and boldly, and roughly, and lyingly.

Hierarchic, feudal England gave the first impulse. Crabbe is the primary instigator. Robert Burns, a peasant, followed him closely. Robert Bloomfield, and Southey, in his youth, trod the same path.

Among these prose and poet-workmen, some have really issued from the inferior classes. Two are men of genius, Robert Burns, and the Sheffield Blacksmith. The latter, Ebenezer Elliot, Saxon and Puritan by his Christian name, has been powerfully reviewed by Carlyle.*

As an artist, Elliot is far from being perfect. Epic without knowing it, he tries to be lyric, and does not always succeed. His poetry is Crabbe, Wordsworth, Cowper, exaggerated. His energy would be more valuable if he contained it more; if his flame were not mingled with whirlpools of smoke, such as float over the furnaces of Birmingham. He throws out his poetry in ardent puffs, somewhat like Savage, the cotemporary of Johnson; and the incoherence of his words, mingled with his perpetual cry of fury, pain and hunger, produces a painful sensation. Yet sometimes he forgets his political mission, ceases to speak against taxes, the dearness of bread and proprietors, seeks the shadows of the wood,

* Here Mr. Chasles gives the review of the Corn Law Rhymes by Carlyle, too well known here to be reprinted in this volume.

climbs the mountains, and then his accents penetrate, born as they are of religious sentiment and the view of Nature.

Yet he might have expressed in prose what he has said in verse; the lesson would not have been less striking. One can live in prose. The Koran, half the works of Goethe, the Emile of Rousseau, and the novels of Scott, are in prose. Perhaps even, the thought of Elliot would have been more vigorously developed, if he had not wished to be a versifier; if he had not mounted that often restive, often lame steed, which the ancients called Pegasus, and we Rhyme.

Thomas Cooper has written a savage poem, called the Purgatory of Suicides; the idea of which is as follows: Society, down to our day, has been a hell which noble souls hasten to flee from. By destroying the frame of government, and crushing religion and existing institutions, human force will regain its normal development; the triumph of our race over material force, already more than half conquered, will pursue its inevitable course, and assure an universal well-being.

To these must be added in their measure, "Ernest, or Social Regeneration," "Nights of a Workingman," edited by Dickens, "Rhymes and Recollections of a Hand-loom Weaver," by Thom; and Leonard Addison's "Tenant of Creation." Then there are autobiographies in the same taste: Thom's, Mary Ann Wellington's, Mary Catchpole's, and others.

Now, America, the latest in the road to civilization, has no taste for these memoirs of penniless people and working men. But she delights in the recital of adventures, violent narratives, strange odysseys, full of sudden changes of fortune, of motion, and of novelty. Sometimes, after the English fashion, they are apocryphal confessions. The heroes, therefore, if they have no great moral valor, have at least a piquant singularity.

For instance, there is now at Charleston a poor negro, who

has a little mercer-shop, and attends the Methodist Church with great assiduity. He gets along well with his wife, also an African, and the little establishment is much esteemed in the neighborhood. How can a noisy glory attach itself to so humble, so retired a household. By what literary alchemy change this poor man into a hero, and his life into a romance? We will see.

One night, a Protestant minister, no doubt in search of a call, enters and sits down by the counter of Zamba. As he listens to his half-African jargon, confused ideas of speculation, philanthropy and literature arise in the mind of the visitor. The negro, freed by the kindness of his master, recounts his adventures, which are those of all his race; he he says that he was a king in his own land; king like those petty chiefs who, on the shores of African rivers, adorned with old small-clothes, remnant of European frippery, and an ancient uniform coat, bought from a sailor, rule over two hundred poor people, annually decimate their people and so provide for the slave trade. The story of Zamba, his lion hunts, the burning of a neighboring village, the voyage on board an American ship, and the peculiar position of a king who, in trying to sell his subjects, gets sold himself, interest the visitor. He thinks that Zamba's narrative may be worked up; and as the American market is not very favorable to these writings, he prints at London, "The Life and Adventures of Zamba, a Negro King, and Recollections of his Captivity in South Carolina; written by himself." This work had some run; and occupies even a prominent place in the literature of fraudulent confessions and false individuality. In the two hundred and fifty pages which form the volume, the author has imitated Paul and Virginia, borrowed from Raynal, copied the negrophilists, and used the worn-out literature of Europe. You find here, the eternal recriminations in favor of human liberty and fraternity; a thousand hunting stories and adventures copied from travel-books; and at last, the picture already over-painted by Mrs. Trolloppe, Miss Martineau, and twenty others, of the tyranny exercised by the Southern planters. In this individual confession all that is lacking is an individuality; out of the recital of Zamba, but one thing is left—Zamba.

There is far more interest and talent in certain American Autobiographies, among others the "Memoirs of Jonathan Sharp." The "Sojourn of two Americans at Noukahiva," and the "Return of the American Sailor to the United States." The "Sojourn, etc.," was much read and sold well, because of the singularity of the hero's adventures; the author then found it natural to plough in the furrow which had procured so good a crop; and thus he did it.

The hero was taken captive by the inhabitants of the Isles of Marquesas, and recounts how his savage hosts carried off, one fine day, the sailor who served him for domestic—he even lets you see how much he fears that this *fidus Achates* had been eaten by the savages with great pomp. In a more recent autobiography this Sancho Panza revives; he was not eaten, but came very near it. From cataract to abyss; from promontory to valley; from wigwam to wigwam, he got at last to New York; where he published his Odyssey, the most gasconading and amusing of the fictions of which I speak. Here at least there is warmth, action, noise, and when analysed, much interest in the narrative in which the author seems quietly to make fun of the public. I love his effrontery when I compare it with the Puritan pretensions of Zamba, etc. Since quackery there is to be, give me that which marches hand on hip, like Callot's footmen, and not that which plays the hypocrite, adopts a sanctified air, and affects an ingenuous coarseness.

The life of Jonathan Sharp contains also facts new to Europe. It is the history of a convert to the dogmata of the singular sect founded by Joseph Smith, a sect whose outward practices are strangely bizarre, and conceal, says the writer, very important ulterior designs.

"I was dreaming in my shop," he says, "on the point of bankruptcy, a very common and natural event in our country, when I saw coming in a large muscular man, who took his hat off with politeness and sate down; I had never seen him before. It was Smith. From what I had heard of him, I regarded him as one of those numerous American speculators, people who mingle pious fraud with vulgar trickery, and so cheat humanity in two ways.

"'I am Joseph Smith,' he said, 'I will not employ any oratorical precautions with you; I know that you have imagination, intelligence, resources, and also that you are on the brink of ruin. I offer you a support; profit by it. The ignorant detest me, the foolish fear me. The mass never sees anything but the exterior, which makes it stupid; it neither looks for the causes, nor examines into their consequences. What is now certain is that I am now master of twenty-five hundred men, whom I have taught, who believe in me; for whom my word is law, whose customs seem singular and who therefore are more attached to these customs. Can any one reproach me with having employed mysticism, fanaticism, incantations, hallucinations or magnetism, to attain my object. Will you, like an idiot, laugh at my dances in church, my religious waltzes? The Dervises do the same. I have mastered minds, and conquered souls by these means. Without my inflexible energy, I could not have bound, in the same chain, all these men, some wild and uncultivated, other civilized and perfidious. I come to you because I know that you can understand me; because in your present situation you can do nothing better than come with me. My dogmata are for the vulgar crowd; it is amused by my rites, and my grotesque ceremonies help to pass the time. To superior intellects, and to men of a certain order I have to offer a more precise and elevated object.'

"I looked at him attentively, while his small, deep-set, black eye, penetrated me, and seemed to look into my very soul. Flattery, stratagem, resolution, suppleness and ferocity were the unmistakable characteristics of that Jewish face, with its nose crooked like the beak of a bird of prey, its forehead high as a wall. He seemed to be studying the effect which he had produced on me. His brows were raised, and the quick gleam of his fiery eye betrayed the secret fire of withheld thought. We kept silence for a while.

"Life is a struggle," said he. "The strongest will win. Till now I have been the strongest. If you do not know my history I will tell it you. Nurtured on alms, born in a street of New-Orleans, apprentice, hawker, small tradesman, I was thrown among the masses, and lived and suffered like them. The first fact which I recognized was the folly with which the so-called *free* men of our American Republics, so proud of their institutions, strive to destroy each other, and consider each other as devouring, or to be devoured. From these inimical atoms, these individual egotisms, these quarreling appetites, there was nothing to hope for but perpetual war and destruction without end. These men have not even the instincts of self-preservation, by which the animals unite to defend themselves against a common enemy.

"This I understood, and an idea struck me, to unite these wills by the force of a superior will. The folly of the opinions, or of the ideas by which men are united under the same standard, are of little importance, provided that the battalion be formed. I set myself to work, therefore, and I succeeded. My first efforts were limited to a small district in Pennsylvania. Soon, nearly all Ohio was mine. I realized anew the miracles of the first Christian monasteries. Among my many adepts, some brought me fortune, others credit, and all power. Our force was in union, and every day, our group, grown more compact, contrasted more with the feebleness and enervation which surrounded us. Now, I am master of nearly all Missouri, and I form vast plans. On the very edge of the wilderness there are Mormons, men whose hearts beat in union with mine. I have given them unity, discipline, zeal, habits of order; now, all that we want to be strong is persecution—one single persecution, and the number of my followers will be centupled. You do not know how much liberty of action weighs upon the majority of men; how necessary despotism is to them. It is one of the great causes of my success. Few have the courage to begin; few know how to use their independence. I am a despot, and all obey me. The territory which separates us from Mexico is filled with savage tribes, which only want to be rallied. The Irish laborers, who suffer and die of hunger; the European exiles, of whom there are more every year, will come to me; the Comanches, the Patagonians, the mingled races which live on the borders of civilization, will one day be mine. I have harmony and order for me. I unite the divided elements; the future must be mine. While democracy isolates individuals, I group them; and sooner or later you will see me raising the cupolas and domes of my capital city above the forests which surround us.

"There is a future empire in the still little civilized provinces of Wisconsin, Illinois, Iowa, Michigan, and Indiana. Would you know why I address myself to you? Your uncle commands the miners of this district, is the principal magistrate, and one of the richest proprietors. Do you and he come with us, and our power is assured. We will pass the northern lakes, and go even to the Pacific. You see that the words liberty and equality are but words; no men are equal; the rest is political fraud. I will not treat you as I do my vulgar subjects. I tell you the truth; I do not hide my ambition. Come then with me."

If the popular books published by certain Americans are badly written; if the form be imperfect and the diction careless or insufficient; at least they interest by the facts which they give and the experience which they teach.

CHAPTER III.

SECTION I.

HERMAN MELVILLE AND HIS REAL VOYAGES.

Mr. Melville lived for four months, absolutely like a primitive man, in Noukahiva, a Polynesian island, and it is his adventures while there that form the subject of his first books, the narratives of his actual voyages. He lived in an unknown valley in one of the Marquesas Isles, in the midst of an inland tribe, scarcely visited by the missionary, and which has not yet undergone that half-civilization which is imposed upon the savages of the coast by their contact with Europeans. These latter have, as we know, become strange samples of pretentious barbarism, and coquettish ignorance. Mr. Melville, who lived very little among the half-civilized, knew well the savages who ate up his comrade, and intended to eat him.

Unfortunately, Mr. Melville's style is so ornate, his Rubens-like tints are so vivid and warm, and he has so strong a predilection for dramatic effects, that one does not know exactly how much confidence to repose in his narrative. We do not take except *cum grano salis*, his florid descriptions.

Like all travellers, he is an enthusiast for Noukahiva. Since Doctor Saaverde described these scenes, down to the aphrodisiac narratives of Bougainville, these latitudes have had the singular property of warming the traveller's pen. Mr. Melville has felt the same influence; he writes like his predecessors, except that Don Christoval Saaverde de Figueroa was more mystic, that is, more a man of his age; Cook more simply, naïve, and sailor-like; Bougainville more ornate, more eighteenth-century-like and refined; while our cotemporary, Mr. Melville, is hardy, violent, and brusque, with a tendency to the terrible, the interesting, the unforeseen. It is, however, for him, not for us, to answer for the truth of his story.

Certainly he tells rather romantic stories; but the violence of his coloring, natural in a sailor, takes its source from the force and variety of his impressions. The sailor does not proceed gently and gradually from one degree of latitude to a neighboring one; there are no shades for him; nothing prepares his imagination to receive the shock of those energetic oppositions which shake it incessantly; he passes without preparation from the activity of a European port, Liverpool or Brest, to the flowering and silent solitudes of Noukahiva; from the charms of Mexico to the Polar ices which beat his ship and imprison it in their silent desolation. Thus no one can more closely resemble an Arabian Night's story-teller, than a genuine sailor. Mr. Herman Melville, endowed with a strong taste for the marvellous, found himself on board of the Dolly; he does not say in what rank; perhaps he was making for his special diversion one of those voyages to which Americans willingly consecrate their pocket-money.

Be it as it may, he had accompanied the Dolly in her previous voyages. Turn by turn, with her, he had visited the icy coasts of the Atlantic regions, the scenes of mad cannibalism at the Viti Islands, the Spanish Tertullias and Alamedas at Manilla, strange strand, where the guitar of Seville resounds beneath the fingers of women, barely clothed; and finally he he had seen the lake festivals of Soulou, draped in muslin and leading the indolent life of a Rajah of Hindostan.

Then the Dolly carried Mr. Melville to New South Wales, whose ferocious tribes made the crew associate in their war-ceremonial and their death-dances. The Dolly's relaxation at Noukahiva succeeded to so many and various impressions and emotions, to six months of danger and fatigue.

[*Note.*—This is followed in the original by the complete substance of Typee, which we do not of course reproduce here, but give only the criticism of Mr. Chasles.]

Taipee is a work in which we find most abundant details, new and circumstantial of the Pacific archipelago, a world held in reserve for future civilization. In reading it, one cannot avoid being surprised at the immensity of the margin still left for the development of the human race.

A fiftieth part of the globe is nearly civilized. Already we see, in certain groups, in the zones of which we speak, some germs, rather grotesque, of imitation of Europe; by the side of the entirely savage chiefs of Ambao, the king of the Sandwich Isles, Kamehameha III., in his capital of Honolula, wears the slight Spanish moustache, the uniform à la française, the beard close shaved, yellow gloves, and no shoes nor stockings. The Kanakas of Sandwich, and the habitants of Tahiti, the most advanced in their social education, are amusing models of an incomplete sociality. As for the Typees of Noukahiva, among whom Mr. Melville has lived, they preserve the ancient characteristics of their race; they are very lazy, simple, and limited of intellect, adroit with their hands, voluptuous and fond of eating their fellow creatures—in other respects, the best fellows in the world.

What may be doubted by the readers of the Taipee is that human races are elevated only slowly and with difficulty; that the progress of their education is the work of time and circumstances, and the ideal type of physical and moral beauty is no more found upon the shores of unknown seas, nor in virgin forests than the hundred-leaved rose, or the savory peach in the pampas of America or the primitive shadows of Australia. I have always suspected that MM. de Bougainville, Maupertuis, Rousseau and Diderot did not tell us the truth; that one was of powerful imagination, and that another embellished the facts, covered them with an agreeable warmth and gave us false pictures of savage life.

Virtue for virtue Malesherbes is much greater than Tongatabou or the Great Black-snake; pleasure for pleasure, the ballet at the Opera is finer than the naïve dances and graceful entwinings of the Hamadryads of Otaheite. The work of our American proves this. If he exaggerate his coloring and strive after effect, still you see that he is a truthful man, who will have sensation, at any price; excitement gives him life, he must have its seasoning even at the peril of death. Curious as a child, adventurous as a savage, he goes head foremost into objectless enterprises and executes them bravely. What he begins in the blundering headlong way of a beetle, he achieves with the courage of a man.

It is the same spirit of violence, enterprise, and disdain for the consequences, which the Americans have borrowed from their Saxon ancestors and from the savage tribes indigenous to the land which they inhabit; it is the same thirst for emotions which is shown in their commercial and industrial speculations—which makes them prefer national bankruptcy to the ennui of economical repose—which urges them forward on the inclined plane of amelioration, and which exhibits to amazed travellers, those thousand leagues of rail-road, those immense streams covered with steamers which jostle each other on the route, sink one another, or take unexpected leaps into the air.

SECTION II.

ARE MR. MELVILLE'S VOYAGES APOCRYPHAL?

I took these voyages for a reality. The English critics said that I deceived myself; that Herman Melville was but a *nom de plume*, and that his romance-travels merely showed a vigorous power of imagination, and a great skill in drawing the long-bow.

I was not of the same mind as the English critics. Certainly he has told a thousand very strange stories; he spoke of erotic and savage nymphs, idylic cannibals, temples hidden in forests and perched upon rocks of Noukahiva, handsome *morais* in the valleys and anthropophogy mixed with sentimental dances; but nearly all this may be found in de Bougainville, Ongas, Ellis, and Earle. He had too a stamp of verity, a savor of unknown and primitive nature, and a vivacity of impression which struck me. The shades appeared to me real, even if rather warm and for effect; and to me, the romantic adventures of the author were given with a sufficient air of truth.

Still they obstinately laughed at my credulous eulogies, and took the book for a hoax of the largest calibre. The style, without being pure and elegant, had vivacity and interest. You were astonished to see so imaginative and so *gascon* an American, but you admired him. The Americans understand pleasantry, except when it touches the national pride;

they like it also, nor is it repugnant even when of very high flavor. They say very singular things to each other in their legislative assemblies. Some serious and estimable journals announce their column of marriage under the vignette and title of "The Matrimonial Mouse-trap." Besides, it was an old English custom, used with remarkable dexterity by Daniel Defoe, to catch the public by fictions which seemed true. One can still remember the "Death-bed Revelations of Mrs. Veal," sold in the streets of London in 1688, and which deceived many good Calvinists. The pleasantry displeased no one, and Mr. Melville passed for a very amusing and very original *story*-teller.

Nevertheless, an austere review, the New York Evangelist, had some scruples, showed in high relief the romantic inventions of Mr. Melville, accused him of improper jesting, and of having spoken lightly and slanderously of the missionaries of Tahiti and the Marquesas. It was not the affair of the author to be treated thus. He answered nothing; but suddenly, in January, 1846, one saw in a distant provincial journal, (Buffalo Commercial Advertiser,) a letter from the valet-de-chambre sailor, Toby, accompanied by a note from the editor, who said that he had himself seen Toby. "His father is a good farmer of the village of Darien, Genesee County: Toby lives in our city, and is a house-painter: He affirms that the adventures told by Herman Melville are generally, and in all that is essential, true. Nor is there any cause to doubt the assertion of Toby, who is a very honest man."

Then comes Toby's own letter, "whose name is Richard Green, and who was not eaten, though he came very near it. On his forehead is still a scar, remaining from a blow given him by a Noukahiva chief. He wants very much to find his old master and comrade in misfortune, Melville, and begs the editor to print his letter, which he hopes will be copied by Albany, Boston, and New York papers, so that he may find Mr. Melville."

Toby's letter did not persuade anybody; no doubt it was all arranged beforehand. How, indeed, could you put the matter to the proof, and verify the names, facts, and dates? Toby swears for Melville, and Melville for Toby, and the Buffalo editor for both; whereupon, he too, receives a brevet of veracity. Mascarille answers for Jodelet, and Jodelet for Mascarille. The affair became complicated, and the galleries were very much amused; there was something there for the Americans to *guess, speculate, conjecture, calculate* about. The chances of betting and the hazard of the stocks had gotten into literature. Mr. Herman Melville pushed his point like a true child of the United States, he *went a-head* according to the sacramental word. The *go-a-head* system, the enterprise, the *en-avant* is everything now with the most *going*, most *active* people on the globe, the *smartest nation in all creation.* "Our mothers," says a clever American, "make haste to get us into the world; we are in a hurry to live; they are in a hurry to bring us up. We make our fortune by a turn of the hand, to lose it again in the twinkling of an eye. Our body goes ten leagues an hour; our spirit is high-pressure; our life goes like a shooting star; our death is like a thunder-clap."

Mr. Herman Melville was then in a hurry to profit by his first success. He produced a sequel to Typee, told how Toby had escaped being eaten, and called this sequel Omoo. About the same may be said of this book as of the others. It had success enough, and the reputation of the teller was made. Every body allowed that Mr. Melville had an infinite imagination; that he invented the most curious possible extravaganzas, and that, like Cyrano de Bergerac, he excelled in serious mystification.

After reading Typee and Omoo, I had, as I have said, much doubt as to the justice of the general English and American opinion, which one finds in the majority of the journals and reviews, wherein the "romances" of Mr. Melville are discussed. The freshness and depth of the impressions produced by these books amazed me. I saw a writer, not so capable of amusing himself with a dream, or of playing with a cloud, as oppressed by a powerful memory which beset him. Type of the present anglo-American, living for and by sensation, I found that Mr. Herman Melville had described himself. Yet, I was content to hesitate, when chance brought me in contact with one of the worthiest citizens of the United States, a clever and instructed man, well versed in the intellectual affairs of his race.

"Will you," said I, "tell me the true name of the singular writer who calls himself Herman Melville, and who has published Omoo and Typee?"

"You are," he replied, "much too subtile. You look for deceit everywhere. Mr. Herman Melville's name is Herman Melville. He is the son of one of our old secretaries of legation at the Court of St. James. Fiery and ardent in his temperament, he early went to sea, and, as we say, *followed the sea*. Were he in the Navy, or in a privateer; what adventures marked his stormy and unclassical studies he only can tell; and if you will visit Massachusetts, where he married and lives, I would recommend you to ask him. He is an athletic man, still young, naturally hardy and enterprising; one of those men all nerve and muscle, who love to struggle with wind and wave, men and seasons. He married the daughter of Judge Shaw, one of the most distinguished magistrates of New England, and now lives a calm, domestic life, surrounded by a just and singular celebrity, which he accepts, although somewhat equivocal; for he is regarded as a maker of clever, but useless fables. His family, who know that his adventures, as told by him, are true, are not flattered by the eulogium accorded to his imagination, at the expense of his morality. His cousin, with whom I passed last summer, said much about the obstinate refusal of readers to believe in the truth of Typee and Omoo. Said he, 'my cousin writes very well, especially when he re-produces exactly what he has felt; not having studied in the usual way, he preserves the freshness of his impressions. It is precisely because his young life was passed in the midst of savages, that he has an air of reality, and such brilliant coloring. He could not invent the scenes which he describes. Charmed by his improvised reputation, he would be vexed, I think, to lose his reputation as an inventor. The re-appearance of his companion Toby or Richard Green, a real personage, annoyed him to some degree. It made him descend from the pedestal of a romance to the level of a mere narrator.'

"For me, who know Melville, his wild disposition, and the history of his youth—who have actually read his *rough notes*, now in the hands of his father-in-law, and who have talked twenty times with Richard Green, his *fidus Achates*, I laugh at the pre-occupation of a public accustomed to see a lie where no lie is, the truth where all is a lie. Read Typee again, I do not speak of Omoo, a pale second impression—read the first of these books, not as a romance, but as a simple picture of Polynesian manners. The new traveller is more truthful than Bougainville, who has changed the groves of Tahiti into Pompadour saloons; than Diderot who takes the voluptuous narratives of Bougainville to embellish and color his sensual materialism; than Ellis or Earle who busied themselves in justifying the English missionaries, and who lack both strength and style. To be sure Melville's coloring is too violent, but that is not astonishing. At his age, when the first sap of life lends a passionate force to ideas, he must have received emotions, vivid, exaggerated, if you will, from the novelty of the scenes, the singularity of the perils. His style is exuberant; his colors Rubens-like, and his predilection for dramatic effect in bad taste. Nevertheless, there are as many romantic details in the old Spanish doctor, Saaverde de Figueroa, who first described these voluptuous isles. Like all his predecessors, Figueroa, Cook, Bougainville, Melville wrote under the power of an intoxication produced by the prestiges of Nature and the strangeness of customs.

SECTION III.

NEW VOYAGES OF MELVILLE—OF HOW, NOT HAVING BEEN EATEN, HE THROWS HIMSELF INTO THE REGION OF CHIMERA. SYMBOLS.

The real value of the two books aforesaid consists in the vivacity of their impressions, and the lightness of the pencil. Seduced by his first success, the author tried to write a new and singular book "Mardi, and a Voyage thither." Oppressed by the reputation of inventor which men had given him, he determined to merit it: he strove to exhibit all those treasures of imagination which were attributed to him. Let us see how he succeeded.

In the first place, like a good merchant, not wishing to lose the credit that his first affair in the isle of Tior had procured, he stuck to Polynesia—fault the first. Then he tried to be absolutely original—fault the second. Is one original at will?

We must not reproach the Americans with want of originality in the arts; originality is not to be commanded, and comes late; nations and individuals begin by imitation. Originality is a quality of ripe minds, of such as know thoroughly their own depth and extent; childhood is never original. This excessive pretention to novelty has, of course, ended in a mournful mixture of grotesque comedy and fantastic grandeur, to be found in no other book. There is nothing so wretched as pomposity in what is vulgar, common-place in the unintelligible, an accumulation of catastrophes with emphatically slow description. These vagaries, ornaments, graces; this flowery style, so festooned and scolloped, is like the arabesques of certain writing masters, one cannot read the text.

A humoristic book, a voyage without compass upon a limitless sea, is the rarest product of art: Sterne, Jean Paul, and Cervantes—men of genius—have alone succeeded. What study, reflection, toil, knowledge of style, what power of combination and progress of civilization was necessary to create Rabelais, Swift, Cervantes!

Mr. Melville begins with faery, to continue by romantic fiction and then essays symbolical irony. We are not astonished then that Mardi has all the defects of the infant Anglo-American literature. We observe the curious development of a nationality of the second creation; and we must remember that there are diseases peculiar to growth, and that men and races do not develope themselves by their virtues alone but also by their vices.

Americans, like all people who have not yet a personal literature, see vulgarity in simplicity. Hyperbole is the common vice of a commencing as of a decaying literature. To this is joined the incorrectness consequent upon too rapid labor. Mr. Melville does not use the English with wise ease like Longfellow, nor with somewhat timid grace like Bryant, another remarkable poet. He breaks vocables, upsets periods, creates unknown adjectives, invents absurd elipses, and composes unusual words, against the laws of the antique Anglo-Germanic tongue—" unshadow," " tireless," " fadeless," and other such monsters.

Nevertheless, and in despite of an unheard-of style, the sea emotions are admirably given. Sometimes he represents it as a mighty but rebellious courser, conquered by industry, patience and knowledge: at other times as a Herculean Force which plays with man as the wind with a plume.

The first part of Mardi, if we except the incessant effort of the author to be eloquent, ingenious, and original, is charmingly life-like. There is much interest and vigor in the maritime scenes, the pictures of calm and storm, and of the brigantine taken and abandoned. You hope for truthful or true adventures. Nothing like them. Hardly has the author entered those lagoons, where spring-time is eternal, and the night luminous as the day, when he renounces reality, and faery and somnambulism begin.

A double bark, bearing on one of its prows a dais, covered with flowers and precious stuffs, and rowed by twelve Polynesians who seem to obey an old, white-bearded man, covered with ornaments, draws nigh. Our hero and his comrades go to meet it. A combat ensues; the priest, who attacks Melville and the others with fury, is killed; his accolytes flee, and a young girl, hidden under the dais, fair as a European, transparent as mother-of-pearl, with eyes blue as an iris flower, becomes the prize of the travellers. It is a *tulla*, or white maiden, such as are sometimes seen here; her name is Aylla; the priest was carrying her, with great pomp, to a neighboring island, there to be sacrificed to the evil spirit. Melville

6*

is taken with Aylla, who has nothing to recommend her but her beauty ; you cannot imagine a heroine more insignificant, a divinity more insupportable.

As well as the somnambulism of this portion will permit one to guess the intention of the author, Aylla is Human Happiness, sacrificed by the priests, for Melville has a lurking rancor against the clergy since the N. Y. Evangelist accused him of irreverence.

Here begins the strange symbolical Odyssey—a clumsy imitation of Rabelais, and which will introduce us to a world of extravagant phantoms.

Turn by turn, the adventurer visits the chiefs of the smaller islands, each of which has a signification. Barabolla the gourmand, is modern epicureanism ; Maranna is religion or superstition ; Donjalolo is the poetic world ; the antiquary Oh-oh, symbolizes learning. One chapter appears given to Spanish etiquette, another to Italian art, a third to French mobility. The Isle of Piminie is, I fancy, the gay world, whose society Mr. Melville satirizes in a way piquant enough.

Young America mocks old Europe ; nor do we object to receive from the young, precocious and robust child some lessons of which our decrepitude stands in need We play very mournful comedies ; but Mr. Melville is mistaken in his manner. What to us are the excursions of Melville, Sancoah, and Jarl ? What have we to do with King Prello and King Xipho, who represent feudalism and military glory ?

At last a Queen Hautia (pleasure, we suppose,) determined to carry off Melville, with whom she has fallen in love ; sends him symbolical flowers, which he rejects, and so forth. Amid this chaos, the old theories of Holbach, the superannuated dogmata of Hegel, the pantheistic algebra of Spinosa, twist and jumble themselves into inextricable confusion. The philosophic common-places of the infidel school wear veils of many symbolical folds, and the author seems to fancy that he is yet very bold.

The second volume is given to an obscure satire against European belief, and to pantheistic scepticism. Our travellers have lost Happiness, (Aylla) and will not accept Pleasure (Hautia) as a compensation. So they leave Mardi, a cloud-land:—and so we pass from metaphysical symbolism to transparent Allegory.

Mardi is the modern political world. We are curious to see how a republican of the United States will judge of present and future civilization, and how explain the obscure problem of our destinies. Let us pass the strange names given to modern countries. England is Dominora; France, Franko; Spain, Ibiria; Rome, Romara; Germany, Apsburga; Canada, Kaneda. This is too much like our Rabelais, so fertile in appellation, whose mere sound can provoke pantagruelic titillation. Mr. Melville is by no means a magician of this kind. He has good sense and sagacity, and wishes to be humorous. It is more difficult.

The fantastic vessel bearing a poet, a philosopher, Mr. Melville and other fabulous persons, visits the shores of Europe or Porpheero—star of the morning; and of America, or Vivenza, Land of Life. They visit Germany, England, Spain, Italy, France. The author speaks of Great Britain with a profound and filial respect, and of Ireland with a severe pity quite Anglo-Saxon. At last he sees France—just as the year 1848 is about to begin.

"Gliding away from Verdanna at the turn of the tide, we cleared the strait, and gaining the more open lagoon, pointed our prows for Porpheero, from whose magnificent monarchs my lord Media promised himself a glorious reception.

"'They are one and all demi-gods,' he cried, 'and have

the old demi-god feeling. We have seen no great valleys like theirs:—their sceptres are long as our spears; to their sumptuous palaces, Donjalolo's are but inns:—their banqueting halls are as vistas; no generations run parallel to theirs: —their pedigrees reach back into chaos.

"'Babbalanja! here you will find food for philosophy:—the whole land checkered with nations, side by side, contrasting in costume, manners, and mind. Here you will find science and sages; manuscripts in miles; bards singing in choirs.

"'Mohi! here you will flag over your page; in Porpheero the ages have hived all their treasures: like a pyramid, the past shadows over the land.

"'Yoomy! here you will find stuff for your songs;—blue rivers flowing through forest arches, and vineyards; velvet meads, soft as ottomans; bright maidens braiding the golden locks of the harvest; and a background of mountains, that seem the end of the world. Or if nature will not content you, then turn to the landscapes of art. See! mosaic walls, tattooed like our faces; paintings, vast as horizons; and into which, you feel you could rush: See! statues to which you could off turban; cities of columns standing thick as mankind; and firmament domes forever shedding their sunsets of gilding: See! spire behind spire, as if the land were the ocean, and all Bello's great navy were riding at anchor.

"'Noble Taji! you seek for your Yillah; give over despair! Porpheero's such a scene of enchantment, that there, the lost maiden must lurk.'

"'A glorious picture!' cried Babbalanja, 'but turn the medal, my lord;—what says the reverse?'

"'Cynic! have done.—But bravo! we'll ere long be in

Franko, the goodliest vale of them all; how I long to take her old king by the hand!'

"The sun was now sitting behind us, lighting up the white cliffs of Dominora, and the green capes of Verdanna; while in deep shade lay before us the long winding shores of Porpheero.

"It was a sunset serene.

"'How the winds lowly warble in the dying day's ear,' murmured Yoomy.

"'A mild, bright night, we'll have,' said Media.

"'See you not those clouds over Franko, my lord,' said Mohi, shaking his head.

"'Ah, aged and weather-wise as ever, sir chronicler;—I predict a fair night, and many to follow.'

"'Patience needs no prophet,' said Babbalanja. 'The night is at hand.'

"Hitherto the lagoon had been smooth: but anon, it grew black, and stirred; and out of the thick darkness came clamorous sounds. Soon, there shot into the air a vivid meteor, which bursting at the zenith, radiated down the firmament in fiery showers, leaving treble darkness behind.

"Then, as all held their breath, from Franko there spouted an eruption, which seemed to plant all Mardi in the foreground.

"As when Vesuvius lights her torch, and in the blaze, the storm-swept surges in Naples' bay rear and plunge toward it; so now, showed Franko's multitudes, as they stormed the summit where their monarch's palace blazed, fast by the burning mountain.

"'By my eternal throne!' cried Media, starting, 'the old volcano has burst forth again!'

"'But a new vent, my lord,' said Babbalanja.

"'More fierce this, than the eruption which happened

in my youth,' said Mohi—'methinks that Franko's end has come.'

"'You look pale, my lord,' said Babbalanja, 'while all other faces glow;—Yoomy, doff that halo in the presence of a king.'

"Over the waters came a rumbling sound, mixed with the din of warfare, and thwarted by showers of embers that fall not, for the whirling blasts.

"'Off shore! off shore!' cried Media; and with all haste we gained a place of safety.

"Down the valley now poured Rhines and Rhones of lava. a fire-freshet, flooding the forests from their fastnesses, and leaping with them into the seething sea.

"The shore was lined with multitudes pushing off wildly in canoes.

"Meantime, the fiery storm from Franko, kindled new flames in the distant valleys of Porpheero; while driven over from Verdanna came frantic shouts, and direful jubilees. Upon Dominora a baleful glare was resting.

"'Thrice cursed flames!' cried Media. 'Is Mardi to be one conflagration? How it crackles, forks, and roars!—Is this our funeral pyre?'

"'Recline, recline, my lord,' said Babbalanja. 'Fierce flames are ever brief—a song, sweet Yoomy! Your pipe, old Mohi! Greater fires than this have ere now blazed in Mardi. Let us be calm;—the isles were made to burn; —Braid-Beard! hereafter, in some quiet cell, of this whole scene you will but make one chapter;—come, digest it now.'

"'My face is scorched,' cried Media.

"'The last, last day!' cried Mohi.

"'Not so, old man,' said Babbalanja, 'when that day dawns, 'twill dawn serene. Be calm, be calm, my potent lord.'

"'Talk not of calm brows in storm-time!' cried Media fiercely. 'See how the flames blow over upon Dominora!'

"'Yet the fires they kindle there are soon extinguished,' said Babbalanja. 'No, no; Dominora ne'er can burn with Franko's fires; only those of her own kindling may consume her.'

"'Away! Away!' cried Media. 'We may not touch Porpheero now.—Up sails! and westward be our course.'

"So dead before the blast, we scudded.

"Morning broke, showing no sign of land.

"'Hard must it go with Franko's king, said Media, 'when his people rise against him with the red volcanoes. Oh, for a foot to crush them! Hard, too, with all who rule in broad Porpheero. And may she we seek, survive this conflagration!'

"'My lord,' said Babbalanja, 'where'er she hide, ne'er yet did Yillah lurk in this Porpheero; nor have we missed the maiden, noble Taji! in not touching at its shores.'

"'This fire must make a desert of the land,' said Mohi; 'burn up and bury all her tilth.'

"Yet, Mohi, vineyards flourish over buried villages,' murmured Yoomy.

"'True, minstrel,' said Babbalanja, 'and prairies are purified by fire. Ashes breed loam. Nor can any skill make the same surface forever fruitful. In all times past, things have been overlaid; and though the first fruits of the marl are wild and poisonous, the palms at last spring forth; and once again the tribes repose in shade. My lord, if calms breed storms, so storms calms; and all this dire commotion must eventuate in peace.'"

The author talks very coolly of our wretchedness; but his calm philosophy disappears when he sees America.

Her bower is not of the vine,
But the wild, wild eglantine!
Not climbing a moldering arch,
But upheld by the fir-green larch.
Old ruins she flies:
To new valleys she hies;—
Not the hoar, moss-wood,
Ivied trees each a rood—
Not in Maramma she dwells,
Hollow with hermit cells.

'Tis a new, new isle!
An infant's its smile,
Soft-rocked by the sea.
Its bloom all in bud;
No tide at its flood,
In that fresh-born sea!

Spring! Spring! where she dwells
In her sycamore dells,
Where Mardi is young and new:
Its verdure all eyes with dew.
There, there! in the bright, balmy morns,
The young deer sprout their horns,
Deep-tangled in new-branching groves,
Where the Red-Rover Robin roves,—

Stooping his crest,
To his molting breast—
Rekindling the flambeau there!
Spring! Spring! where she dwells,
In her sycamore dells;
Where, fulfilling their fates,
All creatures seek mates—
The thrush, the doe, and the hare!

This is a very fine lyric; the poet is true in his own emotion, and in what he expresses. What will this America become, when each year such varied masses of men seek her shores to unite themselves to the Puritan and Calvinistic germ of the Anglo-Saxon colonies! What will be the genius of this new-born world?

It is a curious subject for speculation and conjecture. What may be said, is, that America has not yet reached her necessary development; and that she will attain to proportions which will throw Europe into the shade. Europeans are too much disposed to think that their civilization contains both the Past and the Future of the world. The zones of light change; the march of civilization is indubitable, and this upward progress alone is in conformity with the Divine Love.

Mr. Melville predicts the transformation of the whole American Continent into a renewed Europe.

"Canada," he says, "must become independent, like the United States. An event not desirable but inevitable. Great Britain cannot preserve all the nations which she protected and fostered; the eternal vicissitude of things render it impossible. The East peopled the West, which will one day re-people the East: 'tis the everlasting ebb and flow. Who can say, that from the shores of America, now scarce inhabited, armies of young men will not one day go to regenerate deserted Europe, her ruined cities and her sterile fields."

Despite this patriotism, Mr. Melville tells his fellow-citizens some truths, veiled it is true, yet worth hearing.

"Sovereign-kings of Vivenza! it is fit you should hearken to wisdom. But well aware, that you give ear to little wisdom except of your own; and that as freemen, you are free to hunt down him who dissents from your majesties; I deem it proper to address you anonymously.

"And if it please, you may ascribe this voice to the gods: for never will you trace it to man.

"It is not unknown, sovereign-kings! that in these boisterous days, the lessons of history are almost discarded, as superseded by present experiences. And that while Mr. Mardi's Present has grown out of its Past, it is becoming obsolete to refer to what has been. Yet, peradventure, the Past is an apostle.

"The grand error of this age, sovereign-kings! is the general supposition, that the very special Diabolus is abroad; whereas, the very special Diabolus has been abroad ever since Mardi began.

"And the grand error of your nation, sovereign-kings! seems this:—The conceit that Mardi is now in the last scene of the last act of her drama; and that all preceding events were ordained, to bring about the catastrophe you believe to be at hand,—a universal and permanent Republic.

"May it please you, those who hold to these things are fools, and not wise.

"Time is made up of various ages; and each thinks its own a novelty. But imbedded in the walls of the pyramids, which outrun all chronologies, sculptured stones are found, belonging to yet older fabrics. And as in the mound-building period of yore, so every age thinks its erections will forever endure. But as your forests grow apace, sovereign kings! overrunning the tumuli in your western vales; so, while deriving their substance from the past, succeeding generations overgrew it; but in time, themselves decay..

"Oro decrees these vicissitudes.

"In chronicles of old, you read, sovereign-kings! that an eagle from the clouds presaged royalty to the fugitive Taquinoo; and a king, Taquinoo reigned; No end to my dynasty, thought he.

"But another omen descended, foreshadowing the fall of Zooperbi, his son; and Zooperbi returning from his camp, found his country a fortress against him. No more kings would she have. And for five hundred twelve-moons the Regifugium or King's-flight, was annually celebrated like your own jubilee day. And rampant young orators stormed out destestation of kings; and augurs swore that their birds presaged immortality to freedom.

"Then, Romara's free eagles flew over all Mardi, and perched on the topmost diadems of the east.

"Ever thus must it be.

"For, mostly, monarchs are as gemmed bridles upon the world, checking the plungings of a steed from the Pampas. And republics are as vast reservoirs, draining down all streams to one level; and so, breeding a fulness which can not remain full, without overflowing. And thus, Romara flooded all Mardi, till scarce an Ararat was left of the lofty kingdoms which had been.

"Thus, also, did Franko, fifty twelve-moons ago. Thus may she do again. And though not yet, have you, sovereign-kings! in any large degree done likewise, it is because you overflow your redundancies within your own mighty borders; having a wild western waste, which many shepherds with their flocks could not overrun in a day. Yet overrun at last it will be; and then, the recoil must come.

"And, may it please you, that thus far your chronicles had narrated a very different story, had your population been pressed and packed, like that of your old sire-land Dominora. Then, your great experiment might have proved an explosion; like the chemist's who, stirring his mixture, was blown by it into the air.

"For though crossed, and recrossed by many brave quarterings, and boasting the great Bull in your pedigree; yet, sovereign-kings! you are not meditative philosophers like the people of a small republic of old; nor enduring stoics, like their neighbors. Pent up, like them, may it please you, your thirteen original tribes have proved more turbulent, than so many mutinous legions. Free horses need wide prairies; and fortunate for you, sovereign-kings! that you have room enough, wherein to be free.

"And, may it please you, you are free, partly, because you are young. Your nation is like a fine, florid youth, full of fiery impulses, and hard to restrain; his strong hand nobly championing his heart. On all sides, freely he gives, and still seeks to acquire. The breath of his nostrils is like smoke in spring air; every tendon is electric with generous resolves. The oppressor he defies to his beard; the high walls of old opinions he scales with a bound. In the future he sees all the domes of the East.

"But years elapse, and this bold boy is transformed. His eyes open not as of yore; his heart is shut up as a vice. He yields not a groat; and seeking no more acquisitions, is only bent on preserving his hoard. The maxims once trampled under foot, are now printed on his front; and he who hated oppressors, is become an oppressor himself.

"Thus, often, with men; thus, often, with nations. Then marvel not, sovereign-kings! that old states are different from yours; and think not, your own must forever remain liberal as now.

"Each age thinks its own is eternal. But though for five hundred twelve-moons, all Romara, by courtesy of history, was republican; yet, at last, her terrible king-tigers came, and spotted themselves with gore.

"And time was, when Dominora was republican, down to her sturdy back-bone. The son of an absolute monarch became the man Karolus; and his crown and head, both rolled in the dust. And Dominora had her patriots by thousands; and lusty Defenses, and glorious Areopagiticas were written, not since surpassed; and no turban was doffed save in homage of Oro.

"Yet, may it please you, to the sound of pipe and tabor, the second King Karolus returned in good time; and was hailed gracious majesty by high and low.

"Throughout all eternity, the parts of the past are but parts of the future reversed. In the old foot-prints, up and down, you mortals go, eternally travelling to Sierras. And not more infallible the ponderings of the Calculating Machine than the deductions from the decimals of history.

"In nations, sovereign-kings! there is a transmigration of souls; in you, is a marvelous destiny. The eagle of Romara revives in your own mountain bird, and once more is plumed for her flight. Her screams are answered by the vauntful cries of a hawk; his red comb yet reeking with slaughter. And one East, one West, those bold birds may fly, till they lock pinions in the midmost beyond.

"But, soaring in the sky over the nations that shall gather their broods under their wings, that bloody hawk may hereafter be taken for the eagle.

"And though crimson republics may rise in constellations, like fiery Aldebarans, speeding to their culminations; yet, down must they sink at last, and leave the old sultan-sun in the sky; in time, again to be deposed.

"For little longer, may it please you, can republics subsist now, than in days gone by. For, assuming that Mardi is wiser than of old; nevertheless, though all men approached sages in intelligence, some would yet be more wise than others; and so, the old degrees be preserved. And no exemption would an equality of knowledge furnish, from the inbred servility of mortal to mortal; from all the organic causes, which inevitably divide mankind into brigades and battalions, with captains at their head.

"Civilization has not ever been the brother of equality. Freedom was born among the wild eyries in the mountains; and barbarous tribes have sheltered under her wings, when the enlightened people of the plain have nestled under different pinions.

"Though, thus far, for you, sovereign-kings! your republic has been fruitful of blessings; yet, in themselves, monarchies are not utterly evil. For many nations, they are better than republics; for many, they will ever so remain. And better, on all hands, that peace should rule with a sceptre, than that the tribunes of the people should brandish their broadswords. Better be the subject of a king, upright and just, than a freeman in Franko, with the executioner's axe at every corner.

"It is not the prime end, and chief blessing, to be politically free. And freedom is only good as a means; is no end in itself. Nor, did man fight it out against his masters to the haft, not then, would he uncollar his neck from the yoke. A born thrall to the last, yelping out his liberty, he still remains a slave unto Oro; and well is it for the universe, that Oro's sceptre is absolute.

"World-old the saying, that it is easier to govern others, than oneself. And that all men should govern themselves as nations, needs that all men be better, and wiser, than the wisest of one-man rulers. But in no stable democracy do all men govern themselves. Though an army be all volunteers, martial law must prevail. Delegate your power, you leagued mortals must. The hazard you must stand. And though unlike King Bello of Dominora, your great chieftain, sovereign-kings! may not declare war of himself; nevertheless, has he done a still more imperial thing:—gone to war without declaring intentions. You yourselves were precipitated upon a neighboring nation, ere you knew your spears were in your hands.

"But, as in stars you have written it on the welkin, sovereign-kings! you are a great and glorious people. And verily, yours is the best and happiest land under the sun. But not wholly, because you, in your wisdom, decreed it: your origin and geography necessitated it. Nor, in their germ, are all your blessings to be ascribed to the noble sires, who of yore fought in your behalf, sovereign-kings! Your nation enjoyed no little independence before your Declaration declared it. Your ancient pilgrims fathered your liberty; and your wild woods harbored the nursling. For the state that to-day is made up of slaves, can not to-morrow transmute her bond into free; though lawlessness may transform them into brutes. Freedom is the name for a thing that is *not* freedom; this, a lesson never learned in an hour or an age. By some tribes it will never be learned.

"Yet, if it please you, there may be such a thing as being free under Cæsar. Ages ago, there were as many vital freemen, as breathe vital air to-day.

"Names make not distinctions; some despots rule without swaying sceptres. Though King Bello's palace was not put together by yoked men; your federal temple of freedom, sovereign-kings! was the handiwork of slaves.

"It is not gildings, and gold maces, and crown-jewels alone, that make a people servile. There is much bowing and cringing among you yourselves, sovereign-kings! Poverty is abased before riches, all Mardi over; any where, it is hard to be a debtor; any where, the wise will lord it over fools; every where, suffering is found.

"Thus, freedom is more social than political. And its real felicity is not to be shared. *That* is of a man's own individual getting and holding. It is not, who rules the state, but who rules me. Better be secure under one king, than exposed to violence from twenty millions of monarchs, though oneself be of the number.

"But superstitious notions you harbor, sovereign-kings! Did you visit Dominora, you would not be marched straight into a dungeon. And though you would behold sundry sights displeasing, you would start to inhale such liberal breezes; and hear crowds boasting of their privileges; as you, of yours. Nor has the wine of Dominora a monarchical flavor.

"Now, though far and wide, to keep equal pace with the times, great reforms of a verity, be needed; no where are bloody revolutions required. Though it be the most certain of remedies, no prudent invalid opens his veins, to let out his disease with his life. And though all evils may be assuaged; all evils can not be done away. For evil is the chronic malady of the universe; and checked in one place, breaks forth in another.

"Of late, on this head, some wild dreams have departed.

"There are many, who erewhile believed that the age of pikes and javelins was passed; that after a heady and blustering youth, old Mardi was at last settling down into a serene old age; and that the Indian summer, first discovered in your land, sovereign-kings! was the hazy vapor emitted from its tranquil pipe. But it has not so proved. Mardi's peaces are but truces. Long absent, at last the red comets have returned. And return they must, though their periods be ages. And should Mardi endure till mountain melt into mountain, and all the isles form one table-land; yet, would it but expand the old battle-plain.

"Students of history are horror-struck at the massacres of old; but in the shambles, men are being murdered to-day.

Could time be reversed, and the future change places with the past, the past would cry out against us and our future, full as loudly, as we against the ages foregone. All the Ages are his children, calling each other names.

"Hark ye, sovereign-kings! cheer not on the yelping pack too furiously. Hunters have been torn by their hounds. Be advised; wash your hands. Hold aloof. Oro has poured out an ocean for an everlasting barrier between you and the worst folly which other republics have perpetrated. That barrier hold sacred. And swear never to cross over to Porpheero, by manifesto or army, unless you traverse dry land.

"And be not too grasping nearer home. It is not freedom to filch. Expand not your area too widely, now. Seek you proselytes? Neighboring nations may be free, without coming under your banner. . And if you can not lay your ambition, know this: that it is best served, by waiting events.

"Time, but Time only, may enable you to cross the equator; and give you the Arctic Circles for your boundaries."

When Mr. Melville has well visited and criticised Europe and America, he goes back to the metaphysical cloud-land, where he admires, without being able to inhabit the realms of Alma, and Serenia (Christ and His Kingdom.) Aylla, or Human Happiness, is lost forever: Mr. Melville is resigned to do without her.

Such is the colossal machine invented by Mr. Herman Melville. It is not unlike the gigantic American Panorama, thus advertised on the London walls.

"GIGANTIC, ORIGINAL AMERICAN PANORAMA. *In the great American saloon, can be seen the prodigious moving*

Panorama of the Gulf of Mexico, the Falls of St. Anthony and the Mississippi, painted by J. R. Smith, *the great American artist, covering four miles of canvass, and representing nearly four thousand miles of American Landscape.*

CHAPTER IV.

AMERICANS IN EUROPE—EUROPEANS IN THE UNITED STATES.

SECTION I.

ANGLO-AMERICAN TRAVELLERS.

Many citizens of the United States have visited Europe and communicated their reflections to the public. Willis has given his "Pencillings by the Way;" Cooper, his "Recollections of Europe: England, Italy, Excursions in Switzerland, Residence in France, Homeward Bound;" six volumes of criticism, or rather of prejudice. We have Sanderson's "American in Paris," and "Sketches of Paris;" J. D. Franklin's "Letters from Paris;" C. S. Stewart's "Sketches of Society in Great Britain."

Willis has spirit and fun, without good taste or good breeding: Cooper has bad humor changed into philosophy. The rest are not above mediocrity.

Americans have written a good deal about their own country; Cooper, whose "Democrat" greatly irritated his fellow-citizens; Channing, eloquent adversary of Slavery; George Waterton and Nicholas Biddle Van Zandt, good editors of Statistic Tables; the author of "A Voice from America," a pamphlet remarkable for the justice and courage of its ideas; Sanderson, author of "America;" Jack Downing's Letters, by Davis, a raillery at the political manners of the Union; Washington Irving; James Hall's "Sketches of the West;" "Dr. Reid's Tour;" and above all, Audubon, painter of the immense forests and their inhabitants. Three Germans, Prince Puckler Muskau, F. Lieber and J. Grundt follow, the work of the last, as badly composed as written, tries to prove the reign of Aristocracy in the United States.

As for the English who have visited the United States to growl or mock, their name is legion. Mrs. Trolloppe, Fanny Kemble, Tyrone Power, Basil Hall, Hamilton, Miss Martineau, Marryatt, and Dickens, who has printed his voyage under the title "Notes for general circulation."

These works, so various, written with intolerable diffusion and carelessness, full of the pre-occupations and interests of their authors, compose one side of the process now pleading between the old and new civilization; between feudal Europe, who is losing her Past, and the United States, which have not yet gained their Future. Every year, fresh British travellers cross the ocean, to see the progress of their grand-children. These latter, in their turn, pass the Atlantic, when they can get leisure from their speculations, clearings, or bankruptcies, look closely at their old mother, and hope to avenge themselves on her, and to find in her, faults, vices and absurdities. Each does his work. The aristocrats try to prove that the democracy is vicious and *vice versa:* the young vainly battles with the old; Marryatt, Hall, Martineau, Trolloppe, Dickens, have fired upon Americans; Cooper, Willis, and others return it. Irving, the man of taste, treats his English fathers with filial kindness.

Thanks to these sixty odd volumes, one can see America without going there, without quitting one's fireside. We borrow the spectacles of twenty people from different nations, Americans included. We listen, without taking all for Gospel, and we compare the reports. How can any phase of North America escape you, helped as you are by a German doctor, a Swedish diplomatist, an American novelist, a priest, a historian, a writer of statistics, not to mention a lady novellist, a sailor, a cavalry Captain, a writer on manners and a playwright. Points of view, epochs and localities are all diverse. The cleverest of all these, Charles Dickens, does not pique himself upon his philosophy or eloquence; he is gay and funny. He brought back from his travels a dozen of sketches, done with rapid pencil, without bad humor or pretension. Compare his sketches with the bitter caricature of Mrs. Trolloppe; the clumsy justifications of Miss Martineau, and the caustic accusations of Marryatt, who was hung in effigy by his hosts, and who in revenge has skinned and crucified them in his book, and you will obtain a curious result. This way of verifying the history of nations and of facts has always appeared to me infallible. Rectify one by the other, and you will get right; balance contradictory opinions and you will arrive at the truth. Amid these violent contradictions all the facts which continue to exist, are sure.

Nothing shows more clearly the bottom of the American character, and the social condition of the Union, than the singular aspect which our European countries present to these travellers of the United States, and their manner of judging us. They have incredible admirations, and unreasonable angers. They fall on their knees before a Vaudeville, and take no notice either of our great events or of our great men. The most distinguished member of this still swaddled society, scarcely comprehends the social phœnix of our world, which, since 1790, writhes upon its pyre, hoping one day to be born again. Willis, in England, watches how people eat;

Fennimore Cooper, in France, observes the manner of giving one's arm to a lady. This childishness provokes a smile; we fancy that it is a little girl, playing with the jewels, patch-box and *toilette* of her great-grandmother, without understanding them.

Fennimore Cooper's blindness in the midst of our émeutes, is singular. He sees only the Garde Nationale running about the streets, and the boys who shout. He is especially pleasant, when, after having painted the émeute in very amiable colors, and after being caught by it in the streets of Paris, he puts himself under the protection of a body-guard and exclaims, " For once in my life, I have thought the juste-milieu the best." We know Cooper's talent for narration, and we supposed that so picturesque a story-teller, should have found in Paris, in 1830, materials worthy of his pen. No ; this observer passed 1830, 1831, 1832, the years of the cholera and of St. Mery, among us, without seeing anything. This happened to Mr. Cooper. One is frightened by this absence of observation in a man of genius, who *can* not see. Dickens, a man of charming sagacity and good humor, at least amuses and distracts us, when he speaks of the States, but Cooper at Paris, remarking only that the Tuilleries were built by Catharine di Medicis, and that a National Guard who passes him has a big corporation, afflicts us: of what use his talent and his glory!

Cooper, in revenge makes curious revelations about his native land. He alleges facts whose future value and importance are enormous. He values at 500,000, the annual increase of population, comprising emigration. One single State already is more thickly peopled than the kingdoms of Hanover, Wirtemburg and Denmark. Dissertations on the *soupe au lait*, on its identity with the pap given to infants; on casements and their origin; on Parisian gardens, and the good *bourgeois* who like to dine in them ; this is what he has gathered in our world so old, so filled with young desires, this reservoir of mutually destructive ambitions, and of follies which betray wisdom—in Paris.

His political opinions and precepts are marked with a stamp peculiar and often profound. He wrote, in 1835, that the best government for France would be Henri V., at the head of a republic. An absolute monarch, son of absolute monarchs, commanding an all-powerful democracy, did not astonish him. One night, at the Tuilleries, during the fire-works, he met an old man who predicted that the revolution would recommence in 1840 ; it recommenced, or rather continued in 1848.

Another day he fell into raptures about a negro, a spy by trade, whom he found in an anti-chamber, dignified by the double virtue of blacking boots, and of having lied all his life. Some people love fraud for fraud's sake, and such was this negro, yet Cooper praises him highly, so much are his notions of probity altered by his political opinions. Harris had served as double spy, for the English under Cornwallis, for the Americans under the Marquis de Lafayette. When Cornwallis surrendered, he found in his conqueror's anti-chamber, on paying a visit there, this nigger traitor cleaning the boots of the Marquis.

"Bah," cried the British General," is it you, Harris ! I did not expect to find you here !"

"Oh," said the spy, "one must do something for one's country."

And this false nigger, who had no other country than the purse of the two adversaries, nor patriotism than his shameful cupidity, has probably served as model for Cooper's Spy.

To read eight or ten American travellers in Europe is

rather piquant for a Frenchman. The absurdity of our pretensions, the illogical character of our habits and manners seldom escape them. Cooper has well remarked in France that dangerous mixture of facts resulting from old despotism, and laws or desires born of young democracy. "Centralise is to despotise," said Napoleon after Louis XIV. "Individualise and scatter," says the liberty of the journals, and the books repeat it. Absurd union of contradictory terms! A government is not a juxtaposition of contraries, but a fertile strife of interests, each of which yields a little in order to gain more. In France, the habits come from extreme servitude; they tend towards extreme liberty.

Our old world, in its struggle to grow young again, necessarily resembles, at least in intention, that young and scarcely formed world, which desires to aid it. The France of Mirabeau and Voltaire strives to identify itself with the new republic made by Washington and Locke. We coincide in several points with this new, strange creation, born of English Puritanism, a democratic egg, laid in the world in the seventeenth century, and hatched in the eighteenth, by Voltarian philosophy. You must read the sixty travellers among whom I have named the chief, to recognise how much of actual France there is in North America, how much of the United States in France. They start from the same principle, march towards the same goal; believe in the equality of men, which is dangerous, and in the natural goodness of man, as if he had neither passions nor interests, which is madness. They regard material and industrial labor as an all-sufficient panacea—which is false.

But, at least, this exclusive preponderance of industry and commerce, dangerous for advanced states, is beneficial to the United States. North America is not yet a country, it is a sketch; nor a government, but a trial; nor a people, but a thousand peoples. There, to the eye of the philosopher, all is transformed, like the substances mixed in a vase when the chemist's eyes watches and sees the change. This civilization which developes itself on so enormous a scale, merits an attentive contemplation. It is not yet far advanced; the laboratory is a *bizarre* as vast, and no philosopher could find a worthier subject.

SECTION II.

ENGLISH TRAVELLERS IN AMERICA.

Unfortunately, the majority of visitors to the States are not philosophers. Mrs. Butler, a distinguished and clever actress, describes very well the singularity of manners, and the vivid impressions produced by the great landscape upon a sensitive and feminine mind. Captain Hamilton appreciates nicely the diplomatic relations and political tendencies of the Union. The German Prince, Puckler Muskau, is light like a Dutchman who tries to be light, i. e., too much so. The other German, Grundt, a sort of paradoxical doctor, mixes up all ideas into a confused assemblage of European souvenirs and philosophic affectations. Audubon, the poet and the friend of birds, bothers himself little about men, cities, or villages. Miss Martineau, quitting England with a firm resolution to admire the States, according to the laws of æsthetics and political economy, is quite surprised at being obliged to moderate her admiration; and the shadows of involuntary blame, which her preconceived enthusiasm, produce an amusing effect. Marryatt, bringing to the New

World his English prejudices, avenges himself by epigrams for the ennui he feels in the land of material ameliorations. Dickens takes his part bravely; and his amiable pleasantry shows a graceful light upon some particulars of private life in America.

Tyrone Power is an actor. His style is vivid, supple, easy, hazardous and discursive as that of a mimic who runs over the world. He has seen the Americans in their best light, and he judges them with the most sympathetic indulgence; they applauded him, he likes them for it. Nobody is more democratic than an actor. The habitude of a crowd: the subservience to the mass, the apparent worship which bends the knee of the noblest and worthiest—of Talma, Garrick, Kemble, are all essentially democratic. You must oppose Power to Hall and Marryatt to learn the merits and qualities of the citizens of America, generally too severely judged by the English.

Captain Basil Hall is of that race, now perishing in England, which could only be produced on an island, and which we see in the earliest British civilization; a race which loves to see for the mere pleasure of seeing, to "see-sights," an exclusively English expression. "Since my infancy," said the Captain, "I determined to see certain curiosities, and I have seen them." These curiosities were Japan, America, Egypt, and Polynesia. If all have badly understood and so superficially judged the United States, at least the parallel study of their narratives is important, they contradict and so explain one another.

The democratic element, detaching itself from the other elements of the British Constitution, took refuge in the 17th century in America. There, it does its work alone, and exhibits the singular spectacle at which we are looking. As the same element, in the 18th century, became extravagant in France and produced moral effects by which we are still governed, it happened that on two sides of the Atlantic, the country of Franklin and that of Mirabeau and Camille Desmoulins walked in the same road. How can America not insult England? She represents the puritan, rebellious, democratic portion, which would not live at peace with the British aristocracy How could France help becoming fevered by hatred and ancient vengeance? She represents the Third estate, so long time in servitude, and now triumphant with a heart full of bitterest gall. The American Democracy must cross the ocean to confront the old enemy; France need not go so far. In many things, especially in the least worthy, the two countries are alike.

The most of our defects are American. In that country as in ours words are large and phrases grandiloquent. We call an apothecary a *pharmacien*; we have no more grocers, but in gilt letters on a red sign, we read "Universal Commerce of Colonial Products." The Americans, like us have two or three thousand men of genius in prose and verse; they speak proudly of their *three hundred best poets.* They despise, insult and manage each other as we do, like us they mutually fear and compliment each other. They have the inconveniences as well as the advantages of democracy of which they have too the reality—what for them is a cradle will be for us a tomb, if we be not careful.

There are some singular resemblances in pronunciation. The English say *tchivalry*, the French, *chevalerie*, the Americans *shivalry.* The identity of results prove that the identity of institutions merits close observation. Tyrone Power arrived at New York, fancied himself on some unknown portion of the Boulevard. All that we fear for France manifests itself already, in North America; levelling of capacities; reign of money; boasting; deterioration of products to remedy deterioration of price; neglect of women, honored and set aside; habit of doing nothing for the future; improvisation, rapidity, lightness; singular vices, which you would not have believed possible in a Saxon people, but the influence of political institutions is inevitable.

Between America and us is all the distance which separates extreme youth from extreme age. We are embarrassed by our Past, the Americans because they have none. We sweep clean our ruins, they dig foundations in a virgin soil. Our history is a drama, ever growing more complicated, with its numberless springs. America is a prologue. We have too many souvenirs and acquisitions; there is something provisional and incomplete in that immense and ever active fabric called the United States; for it is so much a work-shop, a furnace, a laboratory for the future manufacture of a yet unknown civilization; so little a finished country, complete, possessing all the results of definitive societies, that no sooner have they made a fortune there, than they come to enjoy it in Europe. Sanderson reproaches the *elite* of his fellow-citizens with their taste for Europe, "where it became daily more and more the habit to go and live." The Americans could reply that that preparatory and restless life, that existence of harassed and wandering artisan, that breathless race after fortune and enterprize, offer few charms to the philosopher, few leisures to the meditative man. A society in its infancy marches much and blunderingly, loves action and exercise for themselves, eats and goes rapidly, knows no Past, nor knows how to educate women, give them their place, elevate their minds, refine their manners.

Thus North America is plunged in admiration before the sex, admiration without discernment, instinct rather than preference. This position of women in America has greatly occupied travellers. They are honored and isolated; amiable and without influence ; read much and have few ideas—even Miss Martineau cannot explain this enigma.

SECTION III.

JUDGMENT OF ENGLISH TRAVELLERS IN AMERICA—WOMAN—BLUÉ LAWS—PURITAN AUSTERITY—JUDICIARY ANECDOTES.

The condition of woman is, in every country, the certain sign of the degree of civilization to which that country has arrived. Woman is nothing to the savage; a slave at the outset of civilization, she acquires her rights and her value, as she passes the successive degrees, which efface the tyranny of physical force and give supremacy to the intellectual. Not to crush the feebler being ; to give her her share of the sun-light, to recognize her privileges and assign her an influence, is the symptom of a highly-perfected society which recognizes that the law of the body is the law of the brute. There comes a moment when civilization is ruined by excess, degrades itself by over-refinement, till one is not content to protect the feeble creature, but teaches her to make up for her feebleness by voluptuousness. This epoch of gallantry and decadence attains, at last, the same result as the savage life, to wit, degradation of woman, promiscuous mingling of the sexes, and confusion of duties. The beautiful time, the sane and glorious epoch, is when, according to the condition of each society, everything takes its natural place ; when the woman is no more a mere nurse or slave, or faithful guardian of the house; when she is not yet transformed into the arbiter of temporary folly, or distributor of the world's favor. In our day she has wanted more; she has asked for her feeble hands the plough, the sword, the axe, the helm of the vessel, the port-folio of the minister, and the painful government of society.

That powerful sketch of civilization, which is called North America, gives to woman an intermediate position. There she tries vainly to imitate the aristocratic manners of Europe, to acquire the elegance, the *recherché*, the *bon ton*, to which old society is accustomed—unsuccessful imitation! A young and mercantile society has only the time to dispose of its bales of cotton, and to clear its forests.*

America must wait. When she has time, she will create a literature and arts, and the woman of the world, exquisite and singular production of an extreme civilization, will at last appear. Men have a great deal to say against the lazy, the unproductive, the men of leisure. Without this leisure, without this laziness, there can be no poetry, nor style, nor art, nor elegance, nor even meditation and thought. These flowers blow only in perfect abstraction from material cares.

I may affirm, that the grand artistic beauty of Greek civilization, developed itself with so much force and éclat, with such fertile and easy splendor, only because of the leisure of Epaminondas, and Socrates and Plato, and Praxiteles—they were gentlemen. All the material and inferior part of life was for their slaves to take care of; they were to grind or weave; the business of the masters was to become great men, brilliant writers, sublime artists. In spite of the law of Polytheism, which made the woman the first slave, one saw Aspasia and Sappho appear in the bosom of this singular

* See last chapter in this work.

civilization of which we have no idea, and share the crown of Pindar, of Anacreon, of Tyrtœus.

Present America, born of the Christian element, has reached a much higher pitch of civilization; but comparatively speaking, she is not nearly so far advanced as antique Greece. Miss Martineau, philosophical woman, who hoped to find in America the paradise of philosophy, and republican independence, was very much astonished to see in how narrow a circle the Americans *embark* and enclose feminine force and intellect.

The anglo-American colonies had not the chivalric Catholic spirit to start from, a spirit favorable to woman; but the Calvinistic spirit, profoundedly rigid, and governed by the terror of the dogma of predestination. The honoring of the Virgin Mary was renounced; separation of the sexes became a law. This inhuman rigidity of the Calvinistic belief has not yet lost all its influence—it has left profound traces in Connecticut. Theatres are not tolerated there. In 1840, an equestrian troupe were obliged to halt on the borders of the State, after having played in the neighboring provinces. The Government of Connecticut sent them the useful and frank notice, not to hazard themselves within the limits of the State, if they would not expose themselves to the confiscation of their horses. The neighboring inhabitants do not lose the opportunity of saying, that the severity of Connecticut is pure hypocrisy, and that its people are secretly addicted to the most odious vices.

The fundamental and creative spirit of the United States, modified since its commencement by the more tolerant philosophy of Locke, is only to be found in that old Puritan code called the *blue* laws, but which should have been named the *black* laws. "If," says the 13th chapter of this Draconian code, "a child, or children above the age of sixteen, and possessing intelligence, strike, or curse their father or mother, they shall be put to death, according to Exodus xxi. 17, and Levit. xx." "If," says chapter xiv., "there be a son rebellious and stubborn, of competent age and intelligence, who harkeneth not to the voice of his mother, his parents shall lay hands upon him, carry him before the judge, proving that he is stiffnecked, stubborn, and rebellious, and yieldeth not to their voice, nor to their chastisements, but liveth in sin—then that son shall be put to death."

Lying is punished with stripes, blasphemy with the pillory; and the use of tobacco is rigidly prohibited. "No man shall use tobacco, without having exhibited to the magistrate, a certificate signed by a physician, setting forth that the use of tobacco is necessary for him. Then he shall receive a license and may smoke. It is forbidden to all inhabitants of this colony to use tobacco upon the highways, etc., etc." Extracts from the judicial records, at the period when the blue laws, were in vogue, offer more comical details, and are of so indecent a prudery that our pen refuses to reproduce more than an idea of these incredible details.

In 1660, during the brilliant reign of Louis XIV., and the debauched reign of Charles II., was registered thus:

"May 1st, 1660,—Jacob Macmurline and Sarah Tuttle were called before the court for the following reasons: On the marriage day of John Potter, Sarah Tuttle visited Mrs. Macmurline to ask for some thread. Mrs. M., sent her into the room of her daughters, where she found John Potter and his wife, both of whom were lame, and in speaking to them she made use of very improper expressions. Then came in Jacob Potter, brother of John Potter, and Sarah Tuttle having let fall her gloves, Jacob picked them up. Sarah asking for them, he refused unless she would give him a kiss, whereupon both sate down, Sarah Tuttle with her arm on Jacob's shoulder, and his about her waist; they remained thus nearly half-an-hour, before Mary Ann and Susan, who testify also that Jacob did give a kiss unto Sarah." Here comes in the testimony as to where were the arms, foreheads, lips, analyzing that kiss with a vigor beyond all criticism, and filling three pages with more astonishing, prudish, immodest, severe, and in a word licentious writing, than can be found in any novel. Jacob and Sarah are both admonished and fined, the court declaring "that is a singular and ever to be deplored thing that young people should have such ideas and should thus mutually corrupt each other." Sarah is of unjustifiable corruption in word and speech, and Jacob's conduct and manner are "uncivil, immodest, corrupt, blasphemous, and devilish," he must go to prison and pay a fine.

For getting tipsy, poor Isaiah, servant of Captain Turner, pays £5, which may be something like Fcs. 300 to-day. The servant Ruth Acie, is whipped for lying and for having received a visit from William Harding, the Don Juan of the Colony. Martha Malbon, has the same chastisement for having supped with this bandit of a Harding. Goodman Hunt is banished for having baked a pie for the said Harding, and his wife both whipped and banished for giving or receiving a kiss.

All these executions, which relate to pies and kisses, date from January, 1643. Our Don Juan Harding pursues his career until 1631; in December of which year we find him—but he has exhausted the indulgence of all. He is condemned to pay £5 to Mr. Malbon; £5 to Mr. Andrews, to quit the colony and to be very severely whipped. Poor Don Juan!

Such was the Puritan legislation which civilized and prepared the United States. Several articles of the Blue Laws are terrible in their terseness. "No Quaker shall receive nourishment or lodging. Whosoever shall turn Quaker shall be banished, and if he return be hanged." "Art. xvii. No one shall *run* on the Lord's day, nor walk in his garden nor elsewhere, but shall only walk to and from church with gravity." "Art. xviii. No one shall travel, nor cook, nor make the beds, nor sweep the house, nor cut hair, nor shave on the Lord's day." "Art. xxxi. All are forbidden to read the English Liturgy, to keep Christmas, to make *mince* pies, to dance, to play upon any instrument except the drum, the trumpet, or the *jewsharp*."

This is clearly not the civilization which would institute courts of love. The cruelty of the Blue Laws, which considered it very evil for the young people to have *such ideas*, was gradually mitigated, yet its influence still exists. To day the American woman, physically so well treated, is morally kept down. One stands before her, lowers the voice, is careful not to wound nor displease her; she has the best place at table or in a public coach, and possesses neither influence, confidence, nor sympathy. She is disposed of as something incomplete, yet necessary and to be honored, since the existence of humanity is confided to her; to be cared for, because from her deterioration comes that of races; but not as a partaker of the intellectual and moral rights of man. Sunday's sermon, the newspaper's common-place, the talk with a neighbor, shopping, these are the only episodes which give variety to her restrained and monotonous existence. As there is not in the air of society any of those elements of intellectual curiosity with which Europe is filled; and as the men think only of eating, drinking, and becoming millionaires or bankrupts, so the women think only of getting married as soon as possible, bring up numerous children, and die with a mind enfeebled by a constant repetition of the same half-servile duties, and the same objectless amusements. Such are the fruits of that austere severity, which, recognizing woman as the type of pleasure and of grace, condemns her because she is so.

In the American puritanic moral, the woman, it is true, ceases to be an object of barter—a material thing—but she is passive, timidly docile, without resource, without motive. She is tolerated rather than accepted, and if humanity could continue to exist without her, one could do without her well enough.

In the South and West, girls are married very young. One sometimes finds a woman of twenty-three a widow for the second time. Neither is rare to find double or even triple divorces. All the laws and customs tend to the relaxation of the bond between the sexes, or to the rendering them independent of one another. It is enough that the woman show some moral danger to her judges to be relieved of the bond which galls her. "Her husband is a gambler, or too lazy to support his children, or he gives them a bad example and evil precepts." So marriages are broken.

So an independence is established which maintains the woman in her inferior rights, the man in his hard superiority. Hence comes a cold liberty, a mutual indifference, and an almost entire destruction of vivid affections and durable attachments. I know not if morality gain by it; Miss Martineau thinks not. If we are to believe her, American marriages are mercenary, founded upon interest, which would induce secret corruption, passionless, pleasureless. In New England the majority of women are married to men who might be their fathers; everywhere speculation chokes the sentiments of the heart; everything is immolated to the rules of arithmetic. Miss Martineau, with her woman ardor calls it legal prostitution, and speaks bitterly of the "sanctity of marriage being profaned by interest." I do not blindly adopt the romantic vehemence of this lady-philanthropist ; I merely report an accusation which I will examine hereafter.

A collateral result of this space existing between the two sexes, the destruction of household and family. They go to live at a hotel ; the husband goes to his business, the woman remains in her boudoir. They dine at *table d'hôte*, and this common life, without home, domicile, or domestic hearth, this wandering life displeases no one. These hotels contain sometimes fifty households, if we may use that word, for the accidental re-union of a husband and wife, who see each other twice a-day, at dinner and at breakfast. One can imagine the education of young persons who pass their lives in these crowded parlors, at these tables so variously attended ; the life of a hotel must produce the same effect upon them as bar-room or club-life upon men. Besides, it is hard to have a household where servants are so rare.

The word is not in use. The person whom you employ, and whom you call your *help*, will dress as well as her mistress, in silk, with plumed hat, or will stand behind her chair at dinner, with her hair dressed with flowers or a golden comb. "I saw one," says Miss Martineau, "who, to her other charms of dress, added a pair of green spectacles." For the least word, these helps will threaten you with the magistrate, and make their employers their slaves. Therefore, they prefer the hotel waiter, who is active, obedient, and ready.

The American woman then attaches herself to nothing ; has no house to keep, nobody to talk to, and her pretensions to originality of thought would be rather a source of irritation and discontent to others, than of honor to herself. In household, the husband goes to market, perhaps by economy.

These are the pictures drawn by the travellers whom I have cited, and of which I by no means accept the personal responsibility. According to them, American women read much and reflect little. They know generally several languages, though they lack activity of thought; the faculty which they most cultivate is the humblest of all—memory. Pretty, fresh, delicate, and showy in youth, endowed with finesse, and with all that goodness and gracefulness which God has given to their sex, with leisure to cultivate their minds and to elevate their souls, and with wealth to surround themselves with elegance—what more do they want? A society less absorbed by commerce, more chivalric, more impetuous, more in love with the ideal, less concentrated upon interest. They want judges to stimulate, to recompense them.

The Old World, in spite of its democratic bearings, differs from young America. It owes the intellectual culture and the exquisite delicacy of women to the ineffaceable traces of its ancient institutions, mixtures of vice and greatness, light and shade, incomplete, irregular, and often evil, as all that is human is. To-day, the American institutions which repulse chivalry and encourage personal interest, produce contrary effects.

After all, the future of this novice nation is so vast, and its situation so evidently transitory, that it would be unjust to believe all that the British travellers say. They judge a growing country as though it were ripe and formed. They do not see that the most amiable and appreciated qualities of the Old World would be vices and dangers in the New. They say that American women are more instructed and polite than their brothers and husbands. How could it be otherwise? What need have the Americans of to-day of refinement and politeness? Of what use to them a Danté, a Raphael, a Molierè? They have something harder to do. For them, rude ambition, ardent and pitiless trade. If individuals lose, the country gains.

Unfortunately, exaggerated activity brutalizes. Repose, revery, forgetfulness of daily care, give birth to graces and delicacies. Hope not for poetry from that pivot of hot iron called a business-man, rolling eternally in a circle of egotist activity ; if you get in the way of his interest, he will tear you to rags.

SECTION III.

POLITENESS OF THE DEMOCRACY—"YES, SIR"—CONVERSATION BETWEEN TWO HATS.

Some coteries in New York and Philadelphia endeavor to model their customs upon those of London and Paris ; it is that portion of American manners, which Mr. Grundt has noticed well enough, but a little grossly. As to Dickens, much more sly, his portraits are distinguished by a fineness and gaiety often profound. He is not foolishly angry with the democracy, but he picks out their good points, and the benevolent germs which they develope, and sets them in full relief. Among the qualities which the American institutions have evidently protected, are activity, patience, mutual complaisance and gentleness. The crowd is a grand master of philosophy. This blind mass, sightless and mute by instinct, compels the community not to exaggerate its own value, and to esteem a fellow-creature. Therefore, they help one another, and endure each other's neighborhood.

The democratic habit has produced among the Americans a sort of empty politeness, a complaisant habit of assent which becomes insipid. Everybody agrees with everybody else, and common-place becomes a refuge for all.

Dickens has written deliciously about this. According to him, the basis of American language is "Yes, sir," words which wound nobody, and which the citizens of the United States, repeat at every moment with diverse inflections. "I have heard this 'Yes, sir,'" he says, "more than two thousand times a day. It rings like a bell, and like a bell expresses all emotions, fills up gaps in the conversation, understanding and leisure.

"Whenever the coach stops, and you can hear the voices of the inside passengers; or whenever any bystander addresses them, or any one among them, or they address each other, you will hear one phrase repeated over and over, and over again, to the most extraordinary extent. It is an ordinary and unpromising phrase enough, being neither more nor less than "Yes, sir;" but it is adapted to every variety of circumstance, and fills up every pause in the conversation. Thus:

"The time is one o'clock at noon. The scene, a place where we are to stay to dine, on this journey. The coach drives up to the door of an inn. The day is warm, and there are several idlers lingering about the tavern, and waiting for the public dinner. Among them is a stout gentleman in a brown hat, swinging himself to and fro in a rocking-chair on the pavement.

"As the coach stops, a gentleman in a straw hat looks out of the window.

Straw Hat. (To the stout gentleman in the rocking-chair). I reckon that's Judge Jefferson, a'nt it?

"*Brown Hat.* (Still swinging, speaking very slowly, and without any emotion whatever). Yes, sir.

"*Straw Hat.* Warm weather, Judge.

"*Brown Hat.* Yes, sir.

"*Straw Hat.* There was a snap of cold last week.

"*Brown Hat.* Yes, sir.

" *Straw Hat.* Yes, sir.

" A pause. They look at each other very seriously.

Straw Hat. I calculate you'll have got through that case of the corporation, Judge, by this time, now?

" *Brown Hat.* Yes, sir.

" *Straw Hat.* How did the verdict go, sir?

" *Brown Hat.* For the defendant, sir.

" *Straw Hat.* (Interrogatively). Yes, sir?

" *Brown Hat.* (Affirmatively). Yes, sir.

" *Both.* (Musingly, as each gazes down the street). Yes, sir.

" Another pause. They look at each other again, still more seriously than before.

" *Brown Hat.* This coach is rather behind its time to-day, I guess.

" *Straw Hat.* (Doubtingly). Yes, sir.

" *Brown Hat.* (Looking at his watch). Yes, sir, nigh upon two hours.

" *Straw Hat.* (Raising his eyebrows in very great surprise). Yes, sir.

" *Brown Hat.* (Decisively, as he puts up his watch). Yes, sir.

" *All the other Inside Passengers.* (Among themselves). Yes, sir.

" *Coachman.* (In a very surly tone). No it a'nt.

" *Straw Hat.* (To the coachman). Well, I don't know, sir. We were a pretty tall time coming the last fifteen mile. That's a fact.

" The coachman making no reply, and plainly declining to enter into any controversy on a subject so far removed from his sympathies and feelings, another passenger says, ' Yes, sir;' and the gentleman in the straw hat, in acknowledgment of his courtesy, says ' Yes, sir,' to him, in return. The straw hat then inquires of the brown hat, whether that coach in which, he (the straw hat) then sits, is not a new one ; to which the brown hat again makes answer, 'Yes, sir.'

" *Straw Hat.* I thought so. Pretty loud smell of varnish, sir ?

" *Brown Hat.* Yes, sir.

" *All the other Inside Passengers.* Yes, sir.

" *Brown Hat.* (To the company in general). Yes, sir.

" The conversational powers of the company having been by this time pretty heavily taxed, straw hat opens the door, and gets out, and all the rest alight also. We dine soon afterward with the boarders in the house, and have nothing to drink but tea and coffee."

SECTION V.

ENGLISH EXAGGERATION—DIALECT—NEW CITIES.

This feebleness of individual character, this fear of wounding any one ; this apathy in conversation, this perpetual and insignificant consent ought to make American society lukewarm and fatiguing. One is gentle, hospitable, one dissembles, annoys oneself, yields individual right to the rights of all. Thus with the roughness and sharpness of natural character, one loses the wild naïveté, the originality and the piquant variety which result from contrasts. Miss Martineau, who never tires of praising her dear republic, is astonished that the Americans should thus pass their lives in flattering one another, and the disgust which this inspires, dictates a comparison somewhat hardy for an English woman. " I am less disgusted," she says, "at the filthy habit of smoking and spitting everywhere, in parlor, boudoir, or Congress. The father flatters the son; the son the father. Hence comes a contempt for well merited praise, since praise is thus commonly awarded. Does a wretched bankrupt fraudulent and suspected of forgery, die, some one will preach a eulogy at his funeral. The journals are full of panegyrics on worthless books. Orators flatter the people, people the orator. The pastor praises his flock, the flock are amazed at the superiority of their pastor: professors admire their pupils, and these immeasurably exaggerate the merits of the professor. All this is puerile, vulgar, and what is worse, egoist. Everybody in this free country lavishes the small change of praise, to purchase for himself the praise of another. They pitch into the maw of a cross Cerberus, a bit of eulogy which prevents his biting.

It is not only Miss Martineau, and the sailor Marryat who thus accuse America of lacking sincerity and liberty. In 1835 appeared at Boston a small volume entitled "Sober Thoughts on the state of the Times," from which we borrow the following passage. "The foolish vanity of our journals is incessantly repeating that we are the freest people on the earth; that with us, liberty of thought and opinion is complete. Well, I defy any observer to point out one state in which thought or opinion are free. On the contrary it is a deplorable fact, that intelligence is nowhere so enslaved as here. Never was there so hard and so crushing a despotism, as public opinion, with us; surrounded with darkness, a monarch more than Asiatic, illegitimate in its source, tyrant which cannot be impeached nor dethroned; irresistible when it would strangle reason, repress action, silence conviction, and beat down timid souls, to make them perhaps leap up in admiration of the merest impostor. Be a cheat, get in your favor the popular prejudice, and you will make the wise flee to hide themselves until the moment when some new trickster comes and dethrones you. Such is the moral and intellectual position of America, the least free, in reality, of any region on the globe."

In the singular dialogue, quoted from Dickens, you may have remarked certain words singularly applied: *I guess*, *I calculate*, *I reckon*. These are locutions peculiar to the anglo-American dialect. They are worth noticing. *Calculate* takes the place of the words *think* and *suppose*; *guess* is used for *believe*, *imagine*. Instead of saying *directly*, they say *right away*. America, in preserving the language of the mother country, has changed the signification of some words; as Italy has changed the meaning of *virtu*, which now means the science of the arts; and Greece the sense of the word τιμη (timé) which once meant "*honor*," but now means "*money*?" What may appear singular is, that this people of the future and of expectation, instead of saying, *I conjecture*, or *I imagine*, say, *I expect*—"*expect*, *guess*, *calculate*"—these are the sacramental words.

Says Dickens:

"In a railroad car, you are pretty sure to be accosted somewhat as follows:

"'I expect that the English railroads are like ours?'

"You reply 'No.'

"The American says interrogatively:

"'Yes? and what is the difference?'

"You tell him, and at each pause of your explanation, he says:

"'Yes?' and continues,

"'I guess you don't go any faster in England?'

"'Pardon me,' you say.

"'Yes?' he says, and then is politely silent, being persuaded that you have lied. For ten minutes he bites the head of his cane, and then addressing it, rather than you, says,

"'The Americans are reckoned to be a people who go ahead.'

"'You cannot help saying, interrogatively, 'Yes?' and he answers very vigorously,

"'Yes.'"

These familiar circumstances show the true leanings of a nation. This nation is still too young, and already too powerful, too incomplete, yet too rich, to escape the susceptibility, weakness, and morbid sensitiveness and follies of the *parvenu*. All travellers find in the Americans a suffering and nervous sensitiveness which hides the best part of the national character. Seeing only the timid side, the English are pitiless; they note the defects, and forget that these are effaced by good qualities.

Upon this Miss Martineau has endless dissertations, Basil Hall chatters, Dickens jokes, and Marryatt flies into a passion. We do not much heed an author's passion: nevertheless that is the moving power, the wind that drives the bark. English rancor is blind with reference to America. They pick out and present before us the worst points of view: but what cannot be said of a country which contains everything! which is made up of all materials, is always changing, always getting larger, has no natural limits save the two oceans, does not itself know what it is, what it *can*, what it *should*, or what it will be; which has neither Past nor Present, but only a boundless Future. Paint in divers colors, the *squatters* who struggle with the desert; the fanatics who howl in the forests; the travelling traders, and all these isolated pictures will be inexact. United and grouped, they will give a just idea of the American Democracy, a gigantic embryo, a heap of wandering particles, which will one day form one colossal mass.

It would appear that the climate of North America, aids in making the sons of the Puritans somewhat like the aboriginal inhabitants of the forest. The predilection for vast images, and grand metaphors; the love of a wandering life, coldness in the relation between the two sexes, coldness mingled with dignity, appear to be characteristics borrowed from the Indian; whether the temperature have modified the Anglo-Saxon race, or that the example of the red-skins has been contagious. In the most remarkable novels of Cooper, the savage and the squatter resemble each other almost to identity.

The ancient sap of the race mingles with the action of a a new climate, with the philosophy of the 18th century, with the democratic spirit, and finally with the puritan spirit, the traces of which are, as we have said above, not yet effaced. Several scenes reported by Marryatt and Dickens recall the times of Cromwell, you fancy yourself to be reading a page of Butler or of Scott. Take this sketch from Dickens.

"The only preacher I heard in Boston was Mr. Taylor, who addresses himself peculiarly to seamen, and who was once a mariner himself. I found his chapel down among the shipping, in one of the narrow, old, water-side streets, with a gay blue flag waving freely from its roof. Sometimes, when much excited with his subject, he had an odd way—compounded of John Bunyan and Balfour of Burley—of taking his great quarto Bible under his arm and pacing up and down the pulpit with it; looking steadily down, meantime into midst of the congregation. Thus, when he applied his text to this first assemblage of his hearers, and pictured the wonder of the church at their presumption in forming a congregation among themselves, he stopped short with his Bible under his arm in the manner I have described, and pursued his discourse after this manner:

"'Who are these—who are they—who are these fellows? where do they come from? where are they going to? Come from! What's the answer?' leaning out of the pulpit, and pointing downward with his right hand: 'From below!' starting back again, and looking at the sailors before him: 'From below, my brethren. From under the hatches of sin, battened down above you by the evil one. That's where you came from!' a walk up and down the pulpit: 'and where are you going'—stopping abruptly, 'where are you going? Aloft!'—very softly, and pointing upward: 'Aloft!'—louder: 'aloft!'—louder still: 'That's where you are going—with a fair wind—all taught and trim, steering direct for Heaven in its glory, where there are no storms or foul weather, and where the wicked cease from troubling, and the weary are at rest.' Another walk: 'That's where you're going to, my friends. That's it. That's the place. That's the port. That's the haven. It's a blessed harbor—still water there, in all changes of the winds and tides; no driving ashore upon the rocks, or slipping your cables and running out to sea, there. Peace—peace—peace—all peace!'—Another walk, and patting the Bible under his left arm.'"

In so vast a country there is room for all, Past and Present; English eccentricities, French novelties, and specimens of antiquated manners are all at their ease there. The increase of population is in proportion to the immensity of the land. The single city of Rochester which in 1815 counted 331 inhabitants now counts 15,000. They have more than tripled in three years; and eleven years have been enough to multiply its population by twenty five. When one thinks that these things are going on all over America without being noticed, one recognizes the force of this infant, giant society. It goes so rapidly and so powerfully that we cannot demand elegant attitudes from it.

It has its puerilities, and buries our Europe before she is dead. It has villages called Paris, and towns called Rome. There is something comic about this renewing of the Old World, this dressing of it in masquerade clothes. Syracuse after Orleans, Chartres and Memphis, Canton and Venice. The old globe is mirrored here, upon this young unknown hemisphere. You cross Troy to get to Pontoise; thence you go to Mondaga, or Tchecktawasaga; you find yourself in Corinth, and from thence you go to Madrid, passing on your road Thebes, Tripoli, Schenectady, Tomkins, Babylon, London, Sullivan, and Naples. What is remarkable is the progress of all these places. Where Captain Basil Hall saw two shops and a church, Hamilton found a town; three years afterward, Miss Martineau saw here a small city, and two years later Charles Dickens admires its hotels, its theatre, its promenade, its port, its quai.

'Tis a miraculous rapidity of growth. Everything grows like mushrooms. How then can you ask a finished society from a people in so great a hurry! A nation so soon successful *(parvenue)*, has the faults of parvenues, susceptibility, ostentation, vanity, love of rule, anxiety about public opinion. One is not astonished, one does not try to enjoy perfect pleasure in a house which is being built, where the hammer is sounding, where flames sparkle and cyclops toil regardless of aught else but their toil. Why impute, to them, as a crime, the intense activity which is both their strength and their greatness.

SECTION VI.

SUPERSTITIOUS REGARD FOR PUBLIC OPINION—THE AMERICAN PRESS AND ITS EXCESSES—HELPS.

Public opinion, and the press, its minister and slave, have made extraordinary ravages and accomplished incredible usurpation in the United States. It appears that every people have need of a tyrant, and that the laws of humanity require it to submit to power, as the law of power seems to require abuse. The Americans, professors of democratic principles, have created a power of opinion to which they submit. This power is abused. As the nation chooses it, she also encourages it. Armed with a journal, that is, with a battery of opinion, you can pillage and assassinate with impunity. For instance, the horrible case of the murderer Colt, who was several times reprieved by journal-influence and at last committed suicide.

Some citizens of the States who have had the courage to tell the truth have incurred real danger. "Where," cries an American, "shall the free thinker take refuge? To speak unreservedly of any country, must we establish a press in some desert island? or beside the Pole? The facility and rapidity of communication seem to have repressed rather than encouraged the independence of ideas, and soon one will recognize with astonishment that typography, that second Word of humanity, has been, like speech, given but to conceal thought." The independent thinkers who have dared to write thus, true heroes of moral courage Clay, Webster, Channing, Cooper, and Garrison, should be cited with honor.

Garrison has sustained the rights of the slave at the peril of his life; had he possessed the power, slavery would not now exist. But in the Carolinas where no one will serve, how can one get on without slaves? Bells are banished, their use being humiliating. The servants or rather the *helps*, as there are no servants, let you wait for hours.

This chapter is, as we have already said, abundant in original adventures. A lady expected some friends to supper, they came late, and the dishes were placed in one of those portable stoves intended to preserve the heat and kept in the eating room. When the guests entered, they saw a help sitting at table and demolishing a fine bird. When reproached the answer was, "Well, nobody came, and everything was getting cold." "Another lackey," says Miss Martineau, "received orders from his mistress to say and do nothing, but to see that every guest had sugar and milk for their tea. For two hours he performed this service well and then opened the door and went out. But remorse seized him and half opening the door he cried to a company occupying a sofa, 'Say! you! have you got sugar enough?'"

Nor is it only in this article that destruction of class is felt. There, as in France, commerce and production lower each other. The buyers are no longer a class; consumers are on the same footing with furnishers; makers and sellers are on the same level. They manufacture quick and well enough to secure a sale, at race-course speed, and hence results a general mediocrity of products.

Germans, Spaniards, Irish, Scottish, French, fall at once into the Anglo-Saxon and Dutch mass, the ancient basis of the colony, and produce a curious result; the hostile colors are neutralized and lost, as the fusion of all the colors on a painter's palette results in a grey and nameless tint.

Yet there are terrible dramas there. Near the Rocky

Mountains, and in parts of the South, the life of the settlers is frightfully wild. There law is silent or powerless; in those solitudes take place the most horrible and incredible things. We were much amased in Europe at the Hindoo association of Thugs and Phansigars, who strangled travellers so scientifically, and formed a religious sect. The little volume published in Boston, called the Life and Confessions of Murel, prove that the same sort of association, submitted to more refined laws (as was proper for the children of the old European civilization) can exist in the United States. There was the same concord of evil for money, the same cupidity, the same secret and cautious regularity in the execution of murders. It is only necessary to read the trials in the public papers to form an idea of these horrors. It is generally on the banks of the Mississippi that they occur; muddy and blood-stained stream, whose waters, says an American, has engulfed more corpses, and whose banks have concealed more crime than we will ever know. A clever writer could make much of the life of Murel or of Mike; or even of the newspaper recitations of the loss of the *Home* or the *Moselle*.

Still, in all this, the ancient nationalities may be traced, the enterprising energy and patient audacity of the Saxon, the indomitable temerity of the Norman, the exaggerated cockneyism and vulgarity of Wapping, the calm sterility and *cipher*-egotism of Leadenhall Street, the adventurous smartness of the blackleg, the outward and formal rigor of the Puritan. The Old English nationality has not yet had the time to get quiet and refined, nor to transform itself thoroughly; but this will take place, and soon one will no longer recognise its source. Every day furthers the metamorphosis, and few see what is going on under their very eyes.

Precisely as in 1666, the germs of a republic filled America without attracting notice; so now a colossal Europe is being formed there, and no one sees it. What will become of the Puritan civilization submitted to a mathematical education? It is the first time that the experiment has been made, and that philanthropy, the arts, religion herself, are formulised by cube-roots and cosines. Captain Hall says that the pupils of the Military School at West Point lose their names and are numbered. How will it work, this reduction of men to figures? We will know hereafter. Marryatt gives another illustration of this reign of figures, two young women speaking, in a stage-coach, about their new bonnets, do so mathematically.

Such a social organization is not favorable to literature, and does not need it. This nation of laborious ants, of busy bees, of human beings forever at work, who do not take time to eat, who despise leisure, who abhor repose, is in the most detestable position—for the cultivation of art and poesy. Yet there are political orators, Webster, Clay, Everett, Cass:—historians, as Bancroft, Schoolcraft, Butler, Carey, Pitkins, Prescott, Sparks—miscellaneous writers as Neal, Stevens, Child, Leslie, Sedgewick, Sanderson, Willis, Hall, Fay, Washington Irving, Herman Melville;—novelists, Paulding, Ingraham, Kennedy, Bird;—poets, Drake, Longfellow, Bryant, Sigourney, Hallock; —legists, Kent, Story, Hall—but above all that courageous man, who has revealed to the Americans their danger, who has pointed out the reefs upon which their prosperity may suffer shipwreck, FENNIMORE COOPER.

It is strange that the government of masses do not develop mental liberty; it strangles it and for a mathematical reason. When all have rights over us, he who detaches himself from the mass offends all. You cannot unite originality with equality. Elegance, exactitude, magniloquence, affectation may get along with such a position, but humor and liberty, never.

They are trying now in America that stimulating and caustic literature which still exists in France. Our dramatic representations, have not yet attained to the exciting intensity of a recent drama called "*The Infernal Regions.*" The author does not bother himself about the dialogue: but his piece is filled with the damned and the hanged; with cauldrons, tortures, skinnings, and flames, howlings, gnashing of teeth; a darkness illumined by streaks of lurid light, seas of blood, plaintive wails, unfortunates plunged in boiling pitch, and devils tearing off with their pincers, long shreds of human flesh. All this replaces, with advantage, Æschylus and Sophocles, Shakspeare and Corneille.

CHAPTER V.

OF SOME ANGLO-AMERICAN POETS.

SECTION I.

JOEL BARLOW, DWIGHT, COLTON—WASHINGTON, A HEROIC POEM—ROBERT PAYNE AND CHARLES SPRAGUE—DANA, DRAKE AND PIERREPONT—WOMEN-POETS—STREET AND HALLECK.

In a certain American Collection, the editor, apropos to the very innocent novels of Frederika Bremer, writes six pages against fiction in general and the novel in particular. "Positive and practical life," quoth he, "is enough for man; imagination is dangerous; arts are evil." Let the Americans be tranquil. They are not in the slightest danger of ruin from imagination and refinement. In another part of the same work, philosophy is treated in the same way. In a word the highest faculties of the mind are anathematized; and what would frighten us, were it not for the reparation of the Future, is that European civilization appears to be sinking into this hollow of thick materialism opposed to the progress of human destiny.

American civilization, born of prose, built upon prose, struggling with matter, and only esteeming matter when made useful to the body, has neverthelesss its poets; has a crowd indeed of them, and naturally enough; Poetry costs them nothing; they make their verses in their lost moments, as one plays ninepins or billiards, on Sunday, after a long and laboriously industrious week. Mr. Rufus W. Griswold has been pleased to collect in an enormous volume, equal to twelve common ones, the colossal mass of American poetry. An historical introduction serves as Propylœum to these redoubtable five hundred pages, where gleam the names of more than one hundred indigenous poets. The distinctive sign of all the specimens is common-place; they are all made with a shoemaker's punch. Take off your hats to these epithets, salute these images, they are from the *Gradus ad Parnassum*. The worn-out forms of Europe make fortunes in the States, as bonnets of passed fashion do in the colonies. The figures are stereotyped; the lake is ever blue, the forest ever trembling, the eagle invariably sublime. The bad Spanish poets did not write more rapidly *stantes pede in uno*, their wretched rhymes, that the modern American verse-makers, bankers, settlers, merchants, clerks and tavern-keepers, their epics and their odes.

In the way of counterfeiting, they are quite at ease. One redoes the Giaour, another the Dunciad. Mr. Charles Fenno Hoffman repeats the songs of Thomas Moore; Mr Sprague models after Pope and Collins. One takes the Byronic stanza, another appropriates the cadence and images of Wordsworth. Mrs. Hemans, Tennyson, Milnes, all find imitators. Once the consecration of the British public given, the American counterfeit soon appears.

Why should a decrepit and provincial Muse seat herself at the foot of the Alleghanies. I have said above, this nation is too young. The freshness of those gulfs of foliage, old as the world, and sunlight breaking into rainbows over immense cascades, cannot yet bring forth a poesy which possesses the elements of its work, but not the force to accomplish it.

The majority of the poets boasted by Mr. Griswold, offer discolored reflections of the metropolis, enfeebled echoes of the British nationality. With most, rapidity of execution and incorrectness of language is strangely joined with a descriptive exaggeration, and a flood of vague, enormous metaphors which express nothing. Some renounce even the grammar, and forget the proper formation of English words. Poet Payne says *fadeless*, *tireless*, which are frightful barbarisms, compositions foreign to Anglo-Saxon grammar and analogy. The primitive *less*, the Gothic *laus*, the German *los*, meaning "exempt from," "free of," "deprived of," cannot evidently be united to anything but a substantive, *houseless*, *colorless*. This is a simple rule, strictly observed by the Germans, who say *ehrlos*, *furchtlos*, but not *ehrlich-los*, *furchtbar-los* any more than we say *sans honorable*, *sans rédoubtable*, instead of *sans honneur*, *sans crainte*.* Now the true poet never destroys the elements of a language but uses them with a wise freedom which makes them more abundant.

Faithful to their commercial probity, the American poets generally give good measure, yea, whole tons of mediocre verses; the quantity is to make amends for the quality. The *Columbiad* by Joel Barlow, *Conquest of Canaan* by Dwight, *Tecumseh* by Colton, epics, colossi of cotton and papier maché form a mass of about ten thousand verses which, however, yield the palm of absurdity to the epic entitled "*Washington*," printed in Boston, 1843.

Channing had accused the United States of possessing no

* We fear that Mr. Chasles' difficulty is somewhat like the oft-cited Irish *flea*: *when you put your finger on it, it is not there.* Neither Mr. Payne, nor any other American man known to us ever said *honorable-less*, or *fearful-less*.

national Literature. "This struck me," says the author in his preface, "and I formed a resolution to present my country with an epic." Alas, the honest man had a shop to take care of, and how could one attend to the counter and the necessities of an epic poem. "I had the prudence," says he, "to put off the fabrication of my poem, until I should have made a fortune." It would have been a shame to have spoiled a good merchant without making a good poet. I therefore arranged my affairs, and then retired to the solitude with my imagination. Once comfortably settled in the "solitude with his imagination," the American poet "presented his country" with an extraordinary and immense production, entitled *Washington, a National Epic.*

The opening is simple. Washington is taking tea with his wife. The hero cries out,

> "For me as from this chair I rise
> So surely will I undertake this night
> To raise the people."

His wife begs him to take a cup of tea before raising the people, for she was

> "There by the glistening board, ready to pour
> Forth the refreshment of her Chinese cups."

> "Oh my dear wife," says Washington, "my time is not my own
> And I am come, etc., etc."

The world has seen many preposterous epics, but none quite equal to this one.

What shall we say of the great men with whom Mr. Griswold has peopled the American Parnassus, Trumbull, Alsop, Clason, Robert Payne, Charles Sprague, Cranche, Legget, Pike, Hopkinson and some fifty others. One of them, Robert

Payne, represents Washington standing up and with a drawn sword in his hand, repelling with his breast the thunderbolts, "like an electric conductor, directing the lightning towards the ocean where it is to be extinguished." This heroic lightning rod is the *chef-d'œuvre* of machine poetry. Some others, Percival has been still more successful in piling up words without ideas.

Mr. Charles Sprague, cashier of the Globe Bank in Massachusetts, and who leads a very retired life, fabricates laboriously, after the manner of Pope, didactic verses, agreeable enough—he is a republican, American, banking Pope.

Mr. Dana, author of the *Buccaneer*, and Mr. Drake who wrote the *Culprit Fay*, are of a higher order. Mr. John Pierrepont, a lawyer and author of "*Airs of Palestine*," is very moral, monotonous, and unpoetic. Several ladies, Mrs. Osgood, Mrs. Sigourney, Mrs. Brooks under the title of Maria del Occidente, have published poems. Those of the first-named lady are pretensiously puerile, the second is only distinguished by wordy facility, and Mrs. Brooks, author of Zophiel, has a talent which is so fatiguing by its heaps of color, of sound, and of images, the complication of the rhythm, and the fantastic subject, that both mind and ear cry out, hold! The only names which we can single out from this forest of versifiers are Street, Halleck, Bryant, Longfellow, and Emerson.

Street is a descriptive poet, agreeable but diffuse, Halleck, superintendent of the rich Mr. Astor, is the author of *Marco Bozzaris* and of *Red Jacket*, pure and agreeable poems. William Cullen Bryant is far superior.

SECTION II.

BRYANT—EMERSON—LONGFELLOW.

Bryant has created nothing great; his voice is feeble, melodious, somewhat vague; but pure, solemn, and not imitative.

More philosophic than picturesque, the expression of melancholy sensations, born of forest and lake, finds a sweet echo in his verse. The sublime is not his territory; his peculiar charm is a chaste and pensive sadness, which associates itself with natural objects and the beings of the creation; he loves them, and the modest piety mingled with this affection, breathes a pathetic grace upon his verse. Christian and English poet, the gentle solemnity of his poetry emanates from his religious conviction. If he set his foot in the forest, he sees God there.

"Come when the rains
Have glazed the snow, and clothed the trees with ice;
While the slant sun of February pours
Into the bowers a flood of light. Approach
The incrusted surface shall upbear thy steps,
And the broad arching portals of the grove
Welcome thy entering. Look! the massy trunk
Are cased in the pure crystal; each light spray,
Nodding and tinkling in the breath of heaven,
Is studded with its trembling water-drops,
That stream with rainbow radiance as they move.
But round the parent stem the long low boughs
Bend, in a glittering ring, and arbors hide
The glassy floor. Oh! you might deem the spot
The spacious cavern of some virgin mine,
Deep in the womb of earth—where the gems grow,

And diamonds put forth radiant rods and bud
With amethyst and topaz—and the place
Lit up, most royally, with the pure beam
That dwells in them. Or haply the vast hall
Of fairy palace, that outlasts the night,
And fades not in the glory of the sun;—
Where crystal columns send forth slender shafts
And crossing arches; and fantastic aisles
Wind from the sight in brightness, and are lost
Among the crowded pillars."

Sometimes the souvenir of the Indian, destroyed by civilization, gives a more vivid interest to his poems. We can cite, as *chefs d'œuvre* of pathos, "The Indian Girl's Lament," "An Indian at the Burial Place of his Fathers." "The Disinterred Warrior," and "Monument Mountain."

THE DISINTERRED WARRIOR.

Gather him to his grave again,
  And solemnly and softly lay,
Beneath the verdure of the plain,
  The warrior's scattered bones away.
Pay the deep reverence taught of old,
  The homage of man's heart to death;
Nor dare to trifle with the mould
  Once hallowed by the Almighty's breath.

The soul hath quickened every part—
  That remnant of a martial brow,
Those ribs that held the mighty heart,
  That strong arm—strong no longer now.
Spare them, each mouldering relic spare,
  Of God's own image; let them rest,
Till not a trace shall speak of where
  The awful likeness was impressed,

For he was fresher from the hand
That formed of earth the human face,
And to the elements did stand
In nearer kindred than our race.
In many a flood to madness tossed,
In many a storm has been his path;
He hid him not from heat or frost,
But met them, and defied their wrath.

Then they were kind—the forests here,
Rivers, and stiller waters, paid
A tribute to the net and spear
Of the red ruler of the shade.
Fruits on the woodland branches lay,
Roots in the shaded soil below,
The stars looked forth to teach his way,
The still earth warned him of the foe.

A noble race! but they are gone,
With their old forests wide and deep,
And we have built our homes upon
Fields where their generations sleep.
Their fountains slake our thirst at noon,
Upon their fields our harvests wave,
Our lovers woo beneath their moon—
Then let us spare, at least their grave.

The Ages, a poem in the style of Childe Harold, contains a still more remarkable fragment.

Late, from this western shore, that morning chased
The deep and ancient night, that threw its shroud
O'er the green land of groves, the beautiful waste,
Nurse of full streams, and lifter-up of proud
Sky mingling mountains that o'erlook the cloud.
Erewhile, where yon gay spires their brightness rear,
Trees waved, and the brown hunter's shouts were loud

Amid the forest; and the bounding deer
Fled at the glancing plume, and the gaunt wolf yelled near.

And where his willing waves yon bright blue bay
Sends up, to kiss his decorated brim,
And cradles, in his soft embrace, the gay
Young group of grassy islands born of him,
And crowding nigh, or in the distance dim,
Lifts the white throng of sails, that bear or bring
The commerce of the world,—with tawny limb,
And belt and beads in sunlight glistoning,
The savage urged his skiff like wild bird on the wing.

Then all this youthful paradise around,
And all the broad and boundless mainland, lay
Cooled by the interminable wood, that frowned
O'er mount and vale, where never summer ray
Glanced, till the strong tornado broke his way
Through the gray giants of the sylvan wild;
Yet many a sheltered glade, with blossoms gay,
Beneath the showery sky and sunshine mild,
Within the shaggy arms of that dark forest smiled.

There stood the Indian hamlet, there the lake
Spread its blue sheet that flashed with many an oar,
Where the brown otter plunged him from the brake,
And the deer drank: as the light gale flew o'er,
The twinkling maize-field rustled on the shore,
And while that spot, so wild, and lone, and fair,
A look of glad and guiltless beauty wore,
And peace was on the earth and in the air,
The warrior lit the pile, and bound his captive there:

Not unavenged—the foeman, from the wood,
Beheld the deed, and when the midnight shade
Was stillest, gorged his battle-axe with blood;
All died—the wailing babe—the shrieking maid—
And in the flood of fire that scathed the glade,
The roofs went down; but deep the silence grew,

When on the dewy woods the day-beam played;
No more the cabin smokes rose wreathed and blue,
And ever by their lake, lay moored the light canoe.

Look now abroad—another race has filled
These populous borders—wide the wood recedes,
And towns shoot up, and fertile realms are tilled:
The land is full of harvests and green meads;
Streams numberless that many a fountain feeds.
Shine, disembowered, and give to sun and breeze
Their virgin waters; the full region leads
New colonies forth, that toward the western seas
Spread, like a rapid flame among the autumnal trees.

Here the free spirit of mankind, at length,
Throws its last fetters off; and who shall place
A limit to the giant's unchained strength,
Or curb his swiftness in the forward race!
Far, like the comet's way, through infinite space,
Stretches the long untravelled path of light,
Into the depths of ages: we may trace,
Distant, the brightening glory of its flight,
Till the receding rays are lost to human sight.

Europe is given a prey to sterner fates,
And writhes in shackles; strong the arms that chain
To earth her struggling multitude of states;
She too is strong, and might not chafe in vain
Against them, but might cast to earth the train
That trample her, and break their iron net.
Yes, she shall look on brighter days and gain
The meed of worthier deeds; the moment set
To rescue and raise up, draws near—but is not yet.

But thou, my country, thou shalt never fall,
Save with thy children—thy maternal care,
Thy lavish love, thy blessings showered on all—
These are thy fetters—seas and stormy air
Are the wide barrier of thy borders, where,

Among thy gallant sons that guard thee well,
Thou laugh'st at enemies: who shall then declare
The date of thy deep-founded strength, or tell
How happy, in thy lap, the sons of men shall dwell?

Bryant by his contemplative gentleness and gravity reminds one of Klopstock; fantasy and free caprice are found in neither. You wander with them through arcades of verdure which shadow slow and quiet waters; a few waters only gleam in the rare sunlight. In the poems of Bryant, reprinted in London, 1840, 1842, the sermonizing tone predominates.

The summer day is closed—the sun is set:
Well they have done their office, those bright hours,
The latest of whose train goes softly out
In the red West. The green blade of the ground
Has risen, and herds have cropped it: the young twig
Has spread its plaited tissues to the sun;
Flowers of the garden and the waste have blown
And withered; seeds have fallen upon the soil,
From bursting cells, and in their graves await
Their resurrection.

* * * * * * * *

In bright alcoves,
In woodland cottages with barky walls,
In noisome cells of the tumultuous town,
Mothers have clasped with joy the new-born babe.
Graves by the lonely forest, by the shore
Of rivers and of ocean, by the ways
Of the thronged city, have been hollowed out
And filled, and closed. This day hath parted friends
That ne'er before were parted; it hath knit
New friendships; it hath seen the maiden plight
Her faith, and trust her peace to him who long
Had wooed: and it hath heard, from lips which late
Were eloquent of love, the first harsh word,
That told the wedded one her peace was flown.

Farewell to the sweet sunshine! One glad day
Is added now to Childhood's merry days,
And one calm day to those of quiet Age.
Still the fleet hours run on; and as I lean,
Amid the thickening darkness, lamps are lit,
By those who watch the dead, and those who twine
Flowers for the bride. The mother from the eyes
Of her sick infant shades the painful light,
And sadly listens to his quick-drawn breath.

Oh thou great Movement of the Universe,
Or Change, or Flight of Time—for ye are one!
That bearest, silently, this visible scene
Into night's shadow and the streaming rays
Of starlight, whither art thou bearing me?
I feel the mighty current sweep me on,
Yet know not whither. Man foretells afar
The courses of the stars; the very hour
He knows when they shall darken or grow bright:
Yet doth the eclipse of Sorrow and of Death
Come unforewarned.

Ralph Waldo Emerson, a Unitarian minister not now exercising his profession, merits a more particular mention, though he has published but two small volumes of verse and prose. He is the most original man produced by the United States up to this day.

He is not like Channing, nor Prescott, nor Irving. Dr. Channing, known by a remarkable essay upon Milton and Napoleon, wants clearness and measure in his thought, and sacrifices to sonorous pomposity, those serious advantages of prose, solidity and concentration. The charming style of Washington Irving has both monotony and mannerism. Prescott, author of a good History of Isabella the Catholic, procured in Spain original and authentic documents from which he has made a wise and complete composition, not overdrawn, and powerful; one is interested additionally in a work, dictated by a blind father to his daughter who has arranged the materials under the paternal direction. Irving is of the school of Addison, Channing imitates Burke, Prescott is modeled upon Robertson, Emerson resembles Carlyle without copying him; his ideas are analagous though often more hazardous;—the reconciliation of the reforming and conservative minds, morality carried into industry, human dignity restored to the blind masses, and the hideous sentiment of envy driven back to its lurking place. Emerson has published in prose, only a little volume called "Essays"—which, when they fell into the hands of Carlyle so struck him by the analogy of their thought with his own, that he published the little volume in London, where it met with considerable success.

Some of Emerson's poems are charming. A little piece "To the Bee," delicious in its way, is almost worthy of Milton. Through wood and valley goes the bee, happy, active, disdaining whatsoever is malevolent and ugly, seeking the sunlight, the odorous solitudes, the hidden perfumes, the murmur of running brooks, humming through sheen and fragrance. Nothing is more vivid than this picture, a mystic sense and a concealed view of philosophy wind through the luxurious gracefulness of the images. The very rhythm and melody reproduce the golden flight of the bee through the rich foliage.

Thou in sunny solitudes,
Rover of the underwoods,
The green silence dost displace
With thy mellow, breezy bass.

Nor will we destroy by a translation so delicate a combination of music, form, color and philosophy.

More varied than Bryant and Emerson, Henry Wadsworth Longfellow, now professor of Modern Literature at Harvard University, was brought up in Europe and has travelled in Sweden and Denmark. The modern Scandinavian genius seems to have exercised great influence over his thought. Severe intellectual beauty, a peculiar sweetness of expression and rhythm distinguishes his verse, especially the "Voices of the Night."

He is a "moonlight" poet, say the Americans, and attracts the soul by his sad, sweet grandeur. The effect of his verse is often strange, and the colors are so transparent that sentimental romance would willingly claim the merit of them.

No one among the Anglo-Americans has soared higher into the middle air of Poesy than Longfellow, whose most touching poem we will shortly analyze.

Little passion, and great calm, approaching to majesty; a sensibility stirred in its very deeps are exhibited in moderated vibration and rhythm; only the Swedish poems of Tegner can give an idea of the gentle melody and thoughtful emotion. Longfellow appears to us to occupy the first rank among the poets of his country; a distinct savor characterizes him; as you read him you seem to feel the permanent mournfulness of the mighty sounds and shadows of the endless prairie and the woods which have no history.

CHAPTER VI.

EVANGELINE: AN ACADIAN HISTORY.

SECTION I.

HISTORY OF THE ACADIAN COLONY.

"This is the forest primeval. The murmuring pines and the hemlocks,
Bearded with moss, and in garments green, indistinct in the twilight,
Stand like Druids of eld, with voices sad and prophetic,
Stand like harpers hoar, with beards that rest on their bosoms
Loud from its rocky caverns, the deep-voiced neighboring ocean
Speaks, and in accents disconsolate answers the wail of the forest."

Thus does Evangeline, that singular poem by Longfellow, commence. The scene and the actors belong, as the début shows, to the primeval solitudes of the New World. Evangeline is a romance, written in hexameter verse and in English upon a subject historical and French, and adorned with romantic and metaphysical colors by an American of the United States.

It is the end and the beginning of two literatures; the cradle and decline of two poetries; a faint new dawn above an ancient ruin. So go human things, by destruction and resurrection, by complication, alliance, and affinity.

Desirous of renewing its intellectual patrimony, without repudiating the wreck of its antique heritage, the Anglo-

American race attempts since 1846 to create for itself a personal literature and poetry. Irregularity, affectation, want of simplicity as to the means, effect sought for but missed; these are faults to be expected and pardoned. Longfellow's work as incomplete in its order as the chivalric romances of the middle ages, with their irregular and monotonous rhyme, and their defective proportions, which take from their value, is not the less worthy of serious and attentive examination. There we find that worship of native land, that impassioned love for the heaven and earth of America, that moral energy and that spirit of indomitable enterprise which characterize the republican of the States. The sentiment of morality, of purity, love of duty, sanctity of the affections and of home, profoundly imprinted on this poem, form its deep soul and its secret inspiration. All the landscapes are exact; not only is phantasy wanting, but the sentiment born of them is distinct, powerful, full of freshness, of novelty, of life; only the poet has drawn them gentle and elegant; there is no energy.

Generally speaking, what may be criticised in Longfellow comes from the old world. The tokens of vitality and force belong to the new. He gives us too many druids, muses, and bacchantes; the looseness of old Europe, and the mythologic dress float clumsily about the fresh beauties of the child of the forest. There is also too much solemnity and majestic melancholy. A more rustic, more impassioned tone would have suited better for the simple manners of those Normans transplanted to the Atlantic shore, whose memories the poet wished to recal. Evangeline, the name of a young French girl, the heroine, is a first fault; I will wager that the name of the Norman acadienne was Jeannette or Marianne; daughter of a brave, joyous farmer of the colony; she thought little of moonlight, and yet loved her betrothed none the less. The true secret of the artist would have been to find the greatness of passion in the naïve delicacies of a young and rustic soul, and to make them accord with the greatness of Nature: Mr. Longfellow has not gone so far. The Norman and Catholic peasant disappears in the puritan, romantic being of his creation. Thanks to this transformation, borrowed from modern second-rate poets—a defect which is seen throughout the whole work—the old crucifix and the old portmanteau become *household gods!* Here, as in many other quarters, simplicity had been supreme art.

But it is time to speak of the heroine, since there is a heroine. As to the subject, it is charming and far preferable to that of the *Louise* of Voss, or the Hermann and Dorothea of Göthe.

At the end of the world, near Saint-Pierre-de-Miquelon, between latitudes 43 and 54, longitudes 63 and 68, there still exists a small French colony, or rather, the last fragment of a Franco-Norman colony of the seventeenth century. Here, as in Upper Canada, not only do the manners and language belong to the epoch of Louis XIV., but they speak the language of Olivier Basselin, and those huge *cauchois* caps, those reversed boats, with floating sails, appear in their primitive glory. The original type of the race is there intact. "The women are tall and handsome," says the sagacious observer, Judge Haliburton; "the Norman profile still exists in all its hereditary vigor and delicacy; the men are gay, active, vigorous, ingenious, and brave. They cannot read; and they are always suing each other, not by avidity, but to keep their activity in exercise, the mixed Scandinavian and Norman character with its energetic elasticity re-appears in them. They go joyously to sea, and are indefatigable and adroit cod-fishers" Marc Lescarlot, Diéreville, and De Chevrier, have celebrated, in bad verse, the patriarchal manners and the antique virtues of the farmers, fishermen, and shepherds, of whom there remain only about 10,000 in New Scotland—a people ignorant of the lights and sciences of civilization, possessing little capital, and yet happy in their simple houses. Even yet, this little handful holds out against the English pression and the diverse population which has invaded their country. Often chased away by the English troops, they have constantly returned to their fisheries at the earliest opportunity.

The English, wishing to *unfrenchify* them, gave the name of the Mediocre Queen Anne to the Norman town of Port-Royal, but in vain—Annapolis exists only on the maps.

You can easily imagine that our Norman fishermen, being good Catholics, had but little love for the English; and that their Puritan neighbors of Massachusetts and Pennsylvania, looked with cold eyes upon these French Papists. Therefore when, about the beginning of the 18th century, Acadia or New Scotland was ceded to the English, these latter found much difficulty in subduing the Normans given to them by the treaty of Utrecht.

The fact of the cession of Acadia, apparently so insignificant in our annals, is important in the history of the world. It signalizes the first movement of our monarchical and European decay, and of the superiority taken by Britannic society, representing northern force and northern Protestantism. In 1713, after the imprudent wars of Louis XIV., the treaty of Utrecht commenced the decline of our power. In the south, we lost Pignerol and the passage of the Alps; in the north, the Keys of the Low Countries, and the line of fortresses erected by Vauban remained ours. Throughout the 18th century we struggled against decay. In 1735, Lorraine and Bar were reunited to France; in 1739 we had military occupation of Corsica; Minorca was retaken in 1745, and in 1748 we reconquered a little influence in Italy, but these were but partial endeavors, efforts to keep hold of vanishing power. In 1713 we ceded to England, Newfoundland and that little, fertile Acadia of which we are now speaking; it is true that we still kept nearly all the Antilles, Canada, Louisiana, that is, much of North America from the mouth of the Saint Lawrence to the Gulf of Mexico. England in 1740 owned but a thin line of coast from Frederickston to Florida, about the twentieth part of our Canadian possessions. The coasts of Hindostan were yet ours; the rajahs were our vassals, and England had in India, but two unimportant establishments. Madagascar, Gorea, Senegal, Isle of France, Isle of Bourbon and St. Mary's still belonged to us.

Such was the power of France in the world about the middle of the 18th century.

One hundred years flow by, and all is ruined. Our institutions change; the phenomenal rule of Napoleon succeeds to the extraordinary drama of the Revolution. Look at the map of the world in 1830: all our possessions have disappeared: North America, from the Esquimaux to Newfoundland, and Hindostan, except a few square leagues. We have lost in Europe the line of fortresses which protected us on the north, and the important Minorca in the south; we have gained two cities, Mulhouse and Avignon, and a corner of Africa, Algeria. All our strength has been needed for our intestine struggles, our forensic combats, our ministerial changes, our attempts at social regeneration. During this time, England has maintained, with vigilant care, the internal peace of her territory; she has thrown out afar the threads of her power, as the spider throws out and fixes the threads of his web: she has worked incessantly at this tissue so colossal, at this measureless increase. It is very sad for a Frenchman to examine these two lines of conduct, so full of fearful lessons:—here the sovereign power of law and discipline ;—there the numberless faults which have effectuated our decay ; and the greatest of which is our stupid subservience to rhetoricians ; the second, our incapacity to submit to discipline, creator of great nations ; and the last our want of power to love the law, which is the active symbol of the Divine justice and order in the affairs of this world. Love of law and tradition is preserved in England, thanks to which the Anglo-Saxon race has overspread the world. To-day they have a girdle round the earth, commencing at Bank's Peninsula, passing Australia, Hindostan, Cape of Good Hope, St. Helena, Sierra Leone, and Gibraltar; then crossing the Atlantic by Trinity, Jamaica, the Bermudas, it reaches North America, and touches the Pole at Melville's Island—this is the result of the interior peace, and of the gigantic external labor of the Anglo-Saxon.

The Acadian Normans, who were not far seeing, nor great politicians, were yet very good Frenchmen ; and resisted England vigorously.

Never would they march with the Protestant armies, nor fight against their Canadian brethren ; it was simply sublime ; our history does not speak of it. At first there came a great number of English colonists, who settled in 1749 at Chibouctou, which they changed into Halifax. Then by prizes and grants of land, they attracted all the adventurers whom they could seduce, in hopes to destroy or break the spirit of this obstinate race. It had too cruel enemies in the Puritans of Boston, and, at their head, the philanthropist, Benjamin Franklin, who wrote to a correspondent at London, "*We shall never prosper until we are disembarrassed of our French neighbors.*" Chatham, then minister, a man of ambitious and violent genius, knew that he would be popular in London if he would smite the French Catholics, and he yielded to the desires of Franklin. He issued the most abominable order of which political history makes mention.

On the 5th of September, 1655, the bell convoked all the inhabitants of the *commune* into the church of Port-Royal, which was soon filled with unarmed men. The women waited outside in the cemetery. An English regiment, with fixed bayonets, preceded by their drums, entered the sacred place. After the roll had been beaten, Governor Lawrence mounted the steps of the altar, and read the royal commission, countersigned by Chatham.

"You are convoked," said he, in English, to the Acadians, "by the order of Her Majesty. Her clemency towards you has been great; you know how you have replied to it. The task which I have to accomplish is painful and repugnant to me; but it is urgent and inevitable; I must fulfil the will of Her Majesty. All your goods, domains, flocks, lands, fisheries, pasturages, houses, and cattle, are, and remain confiscated to the profit of the crown. You are condemned to transportation in the other provinces, according to the good will of the monarch. You are prisoners."

The Acadians were unarmed and defenceless. Could they have foreseen so barbarous and unheard-of a proceeding, they would have called to their aid eight Indian tribes, who were devoted to them, and who would have aided them with arms, or to find an asylum in the great forest. Five days only were given to them. The soldiers commissioned to guard them set fire to their houses, barns, and the church; they barely left some clothing and a little furniture to this agricultural and fishing people. As they found in all the houses signs of idolatry, that is, the cross of the Saviour, and an image of St. Mary the Virgin, Anglican fanaticism urged on by the neighboring Puritans, pushed barbarity to atrocity. Children were separated from their mothers, husbands from their wives.

The despair of the aged, the resistance of the men, the cries and tears of the women were powerless. "It was," says Mr. Haliburton, "a spectacle more horrible than the sack of Parga, an act, the memory of which is profoundly kept in this part of America, and which not a little contributed to excite republican hatred against the partizans of British royalty."

Yet the movers of this execrable persecution were the patriots, Chatham and Franklin; the instruments of this vengeance upon the Catholics were Presbyterian and Anglican soldiers. Prejudice does not reason.

The condemned departed. Their fair orchards, their French habitations, their enclosures of Norman apple-trees, their rich pastures, the dikes which they had raised to protect their lands from inundation, were abandoned. As the frigates which carried these 15,000 poor Frenchmen away, set sail for Frederickstown, the light of their burning homes was reflected upon their persons, and reddened the waters of the sea. The last touch was given to this barbarism by setting them ashore, here and there upon the beach, like impure beasts who ought to be lost, the father far from the son, the mother from her child. They found each other again as best they could; none but themselves cared for that; anything was good enough for Frenchmen and Catholics. The amiable Franklin did not raise his voice; the philanthropy of the Quakers was not indignant; Voltaire did not disquiet himself; Boston Puritans, and gentlemen of Versailles had something else to attend to.

These poor heroic Normans, protected by their courage, formed here and there, little groups which prospered, thanks to God! Moral energy and religious perseverance are powerful aids. You can still see the wreck of an Acadian Colony at Saint Domingo, in French Guyana and in Louisiana where their colonies were very flourishing. Even at Port-Royal some few obstinately returned, established themselves despite the English, and regained their ancient farms. About twenty embarked for France, and cleared those grey and roseate heaths which hide a fertile soil not far from Châtellerault. In 1820, five chiefs of these Norman-Acadian families, claimed and received from the Chamber of Deputies, a small pension, promised by the National Assembly, and which had ceased to be paid; such good patriots are we, so grateful for grand deeds, since talkers govern us, philanthropists enrich us, and advocates reconstitute us every ten years.

You are perhaps astonished that Chatham should have ordered this infamous affair, and that the worthy Franklin should have approved of it. Many incredulous people must resign themselves to historic proofs which are irrefragable; to what end would be the art of writing and thinking if justice were not rendered now and then. Mr. Macaulay, proves in his recent history of England, that the philanthropic William was deep in the corruptions and intrigues of the venal court of Charles II. Penn excused himself doubtless on the ground of good intentions; such is the human race. The Abbé Raynal who looked upon Penn as a god, would have thought Mr. Macaulay very hardy, for disturbing his admiration.

Events which leave such burning traces in the life of nations, are soon transformed into legends. The Acadians have a very touching legend of their exile, probably true at bottom, as all legends are; it has been treated with talent by Longfellow, who has rather over ornamented this rustic and ingenuous story. The misfortune of Madame Cottin may some day overtake him. She covered with agreeable and tasteful ornaments an interesting Russian tradition: M. Xavier de Maistre destroyed the ornaments, took up the subject afresh, and told the simple history of the Exiles of Siberia; told it so well and so simply, that his narration, a *chef-d'œuvre* of our language, has caused the book of Madame Cottin to be forgotten.

SECTION II.

MR. LONGFELLOW'S POEM.

The Acadians relate, that a young girl of Port-Royal, affianced the night before the order of Chatham arrived, and sent on board another frigate than that which carried her betrothed and her family, was set ashore upon the coasts of Pennsylvania, far from her kindred and friends; an old Catholic priest disembarked with her, and aided her by his councils and cares. They crossed together Delaware, Massachusetts, Maine, in hopes of finding the father and the betrothed—they were now and then helped by some good Catholic souls, and at last, at the mouth of the Wabash, discovered a fragment of their old colony.

Going on board the boat which carried the wrecks of their people, they descended the great Mississippi. It was the month of May. The boat, rowed by Acadian oarsmen, followed the yellow current, and bore the troop of exiles, poor beings who had lost their country, their kin, their fair prairies of Opelousas, and their beloved homes. They were seeking their dispersed families, and for many days, floating down those dangerous waters, they travelled through the solitudes of the profound forest. At night they kindled a fire and encamped upon the shore. Sometimes they encountered a rapid, and their bark shot on like an arrow; sometimes they glided into a lagoon, amid green isles covered with cotton, and the white pelican stalked beside them.

Soon a vast horizon was discovered, the landscape grew flat; they saw the white houses of the planters, the huts of the negroes and the dove-cotes. The majestic river curved towards the Orient, and the boat entered the *bayou* of Plaquemine. There all changes; the wandering waters spread above the clay soil like a vast coat of mail—the cypresses along the bank droop in mournful arches above them; their gloomy boughs covered with eternal moss the black banners and draperies of nature's cathedral. No sound, save where from time to time is heard the measured plash of the heron's foot, or the cry of the screech owl. The cedar and the cypress colonnades are blanched by the irregular gleam of the moonlight upon the waters; all is vague, strange, pleasant as a dream.

Evangeline is sad, says the poet, with

"———Strange forebodings of ill, unseen and that cannot be compassed.
As at the tramp of a horse's hoof on the turf of the prairies
Far in advance are closed the leaves of the shrinking mimosa,
So at the hoof beats of fate, with sad forebodings of evil
Shrinks and closes the heart, ere the stroke of doom has attained it."

The voyage of the young girl to Louisiana is told with a really admirable truth and sentiment of nature. Yet it is spoiled by many affectations and the faded tints of which we have already spoken. A more consummate artist would have avoided big words, and touches of trivial melancholy, *thorns of existence*, *desert of life*, and particularly the moonlight reveries. Still the sentiment, the invention, the movement are true, powerful, and new. What a delicious picture is that of the young girl asleep with her head upon the knee of the old priest, while the rowers sing an old French chant, and strike in cadence the waters of the Mississippi. "Alas, father," says Evangeline, "my love is lost;" and the old priest said:

"Talk not of wasted affection, affection never was wasted;
If it enrich not the heart of another, its waters returning
Back to their springs like the rain, shall fill them full of refreshment,
That which the fountain sends forth, returns again to the fountain."

This is doubtless very refined for an old Norman priest, but the thought is beautiful and the expression just.

The poor child, escorted by her guide, looks everywhere for some trace of her family and her betrothed. She visits the fertile bayous of New Orleans, the green shores of the Delaware, the sterile and stormy plains that lie at the foot of the Ozarks; from time to time, some gleams of hope appear; she learns that Gabriel has become a trapper. She knows even that he has passed her in a boat, one autumn night; but days, months and years pass away. In the search youth has faded, Evangeline grows older, becomes a Sister of Mercy, and gives up her life to the sick. At last, one day, she finds her lover stretched upon a hospital bed and dying; he opens his eyes, sees her, and dies consoled: she soon follows him.

"Still stands the forest primeval; but far away from its shadow,
Side by side, in their nameless graves, the lovers are sleeping,
Under the humble walls of the little Catholic church-yard,
In the heart of the city, they lie, unknown and unnoticed.
Daily the tides of life go ebbing and flowing beside them,
Thousands of throbbing hearts, where theirs are at rest and forever,
Thousands of aching brains, where theirs no longer are busy,
Thousands of toiling hands, where theirs have ceased from their labors,
Thousands of weary feet, where theirs have completed their journey!

Still stands the forest primeval; but under the shade of its branches
Dwells another race, with other customs and language.
Only along the shore of the mournful and misty Atlantic
Linger a few Acadian peasants, whose fathers from exile
Wandered back to their native land to die in its bosom.
In the fisherman's cot the wheel and the loom are still busy

Maidens still wear their Norman caps and their kirtles of homespun,
And by the evening fire repeat Evangeline's story.
While from its rocky caverns the deep-voiced, neighboring ocean
Speaks, and in accents disconsolate answers the wail of the forest."

There is, in this poem, a singular mingling of the factitious and the natural—two contrasting elements, the real and the permitted, one moving the heart by its truth, the other wounding the mind by affectation. All the American portion merits praise. We are carried down the vast Mississippi to the music of mocking birds. The new, magnificent world is not merely described and analyzed, but the poet reproduces it, and communicates to the reader its peculiarity, its vivifying sap, its inner emotion. We have the "red ears of corn, which, signifying lovers, make the girls blush during harvest." We have the Mission vespers, sung in the midst of the wilderness; the Crucifix hangs upon an old oak, only dweller in that solitude; all heads are bared, and the Christ regards them with a look of divine pity, while the sound of the even song mingles with the rustling of the boughs, and the vine clusters droop downward on the forehead of the crucified Saviour. We have the hunter's camp, in the same prairies, amid seas of verdure, and profound bays of vegetation, which mingled with the wild rose and the purple amorphia, float like waves in the light and shade. There go headlong bands of buffaloes, wolves, wild deer, and armies of riderless steeds. There, near the rivers, under clusters of holm, a smoke announced a robber camp, who stain with blood the solitudes of God, and circling above their heads, the vulture expects his prey. Then you have the Acadian farmer, a king, like the good Evander: then when the twilight comes, and the labor hours are over, and stars appear in heaven, you see the flocks and herds, with nostrils open, breathing the freshness of the night, their heads upon each other's necks: patient and self-important, after them comes the dog, marching right and left in his instinctive pride, proud of governing all these, happy to be their protector at night, when the wolves howl and the lambs tremble. Then the moon rises, and the wagons laden with fodder come home. The horses, their manes wet with the dews, neigh joyously, and shake with their robust shoulders the red fringed harness. The patient cows are milked: the laugh of the farmer's men is heard, and the singing of young girls, and the long lowings of the kine. Then silence, and the doors are barred.

As an American idyll this poem is admirable. All that it lacks is passion. The love of the betrothed, its birth and progress, are not indicated. It appears that all the ardor of the poet's inspiration can direct itself only to the country itself, towards the sublime and virgin nature which surrounds it.

In this Anglo-American poet two tendencies are visible; the one, religious, towards the Catholic creed, towards vaster and more liberal Christian ideas: the second, literary, towards the Scandinavian Teutonism. His hexameter verse, which flows with sad solemnity, is filled with numerous, irregular alliterations.

The first effect of this upon an ear accustomed to the rapid English iambics is unpleasant, but one gets used to it. And then one endures the echo of the same consonant at the beginning and in the middle of words, strange as it is to the poetic habits of the South; you find examples in the old Latin and Greek poets, but it is generally avoided by the English.

We in France have never been able to adopt this rhythm, although the ridiculous Guilliaume Cretin tried to naturalize it, and which comes from the German *Meistersänger* of the fifteenth century; a curious fact, to be found in no history of literature. Mr. Longfellow knows Icelandic and Danish and has passed some time on the Scandinavian Peninsula; and, without thinking, he has habituated himself to alliteration, an involuntary form with him, voluntary with the old Scalds, and still preserving a popular influence in the North. The Danish poet, Oehlenschlager has written part of his poem on the gods of the North in alliterative verse.

> *T*i*l*giv *t*vu*n*gne
> *T*rae*l* af E*l*skov
> *At* han dig *at*ter
> *Ast*aeld findet, etc.

So Longfellow,

> *F*uller of *fr*agrance *th*an *th*ey
> And as heavy with sha*d*ows and night-*d*ews,
> *H*ung the *h*eart of the *m*aiden,
> The cal*m* and *m*agical *m*oonlight
> See*m*ed to inundate her soul.

What is strange is that Mr. Longfellow, in writing, never noticed these multiplied alliterations which flow spontaneously from his pen and fill the poem. This involuntary return of English poetry towards its primitive source in the Scandinavian caves is too curious a fact to be passed over in silence.

Thus then, while old Europe regenerates herself as she can, young and less troubled nations are endeavoring art and poetry. Evangeline is not a *chef-d'œuvre*, but its beauties have the gift of life, future life in them. Here are the elements which prevent the death of society and of literature, the most correct notions of justice and morality, the most ardent and thoughtful love of native land.

CHAPTER VII.

OF CERTAIN AMERICAN NOVELISTS AND TRAVELLERS.

SECTION I.

COMIC ROMANCE—TOM STAPLETON—PUFFER HOPKINS—REPLY TO CHARLES DICKENS.

It is amazing how many frivolous or ironical books have issued from the American presses since 1830. The races inheriting from old civilization, seeing before them an unknown world of industry and politics to conquer and to organise, find themselves face to face with ridiculous contrasts, and are naturally given to irony. Roman Gaul commenced thus.

This irony in the United States is still very rude; it will become refined, but at present it is singularly bitter and coarse. Readers upon this side of the Atlantic can only feel disgust for the odious scenes written by two satiric painters of manners, Messrs. Moore and Matthews, authors of *Tom Stapleton* and *Puffer Hopkins*. I read eagerly these sketches of American life by Americans. The impression is a mournful one; it is not popular, but low and aristocratic in the worst sense of that word; faded and corrupted vices, without grace or taste; a coward life which pursues titles, envies fortune, rushes upon success. These manners are destitute of purity, passion, simplicity, elegance or greatness—'tis the lowest shopkeeper of Whitehall, transported into gilded drawing-rooms, and clumsily borrowing the upper vices without forgetting or losing the baser. It is no longer Washington; it has not become Horace Walpole. I cannot express, the disdain and grief produced by these crazy and brutal manners, which belong by their impurity to the scandalous boudoirs of the old world, and smell of the bar-room while claiming to be aristocratic.

Must we look here for the true description of American society. Dickens, Marryatt, Mrs. Trollope, Miss Martineau, being English, should inspire us with little confidence, yet are they much more favorable to America than Messrs. Moore and Matthews, whose *highly popular* novels, published in a sheet called the "Brother Jonathan," with horrible wood-cuts, give for twelve and a half cents the value of three octavo volumes, of three hundred pages each. It is the *ne plus ultra* of cheap printing. Let us add that it is impossible to see anything uglier than these cheap impressions; but the form is worthy of the matter. There was an idea in *Puffer Hopkins*, the man of puff, sailing, with full sheet, the seas of democracy in the bark of charlatanism and fraud, but the grossness of the scenes make the book hideous. Lighter and more frivilous, *Tom Stapleton* accumulates orgies, fights, scenes of drunkenness, broken chairs, and falls upon staircases, mixed with the blackguard scenes and philosophic liberties of *Compere* Matthieu. The author desired to paint the deeds of the amiable good-for-naughts of New York: nobody would like to trust himself alone with those fellows. The club plays a principal part in the drama; Tom is the friend and secret protector of a heroine worthy of himself. When they are not drunk, they fight; when not fighting, they are drunk. All finishes by the hero's profitable marriage, a marriage full of dollars, accepted enthusiastically by a girl won by strength of wrist. A savage society appears in its nakedness. from time to time, through the brutality which composes the main tissue of this work. We regret to see a brave people, one half of whom burn or hang Abolitionists and then blame them, adopting as a favorite book, a work wherein such words are placed in the mouth of the hero.

"Honesty! the word is ridiculous, and means nothing. Each of us does with as little as possible. *Honesty is unnatural.* There is but one law which governs the universe, attraction; it rules even in inanimate things. In the animate creation it is called acquisition, or "theft." The sun would attract all the planets, if he were able. A single man would, if possible, absorb the enjoyment of all his fellow creatures, and would devour them all. There is but one good rule, *Every man for himself, and God for us all!*"

Here is a frank, open, honest, candid, clearly enunciated philosophy. I have always shuddered, less with terror than anger, at hearing in a drama, set by Meyerbeer, that cruel refrain, *Every man for himself, and God for us all!* The Nemeses of savage life rose up before me, dictating those words to that frightful choir, and invoking the destruction of all human ties. The American Author explains this ferocious cry. It is the law of force. Life becomes an universal pillage; the best prey for the strongest, the second best for the trickster. Oh ye hyena-philosophers! born to minister to Heliogabalus or to Genghis-Khan!

If this insurrection against probity, imagination, poetry, and philosophy should become universal, humanity would have but one object, to live, and to fight for a living, *fruges consumere nati*; all would then be in harmony.

On the contrary, as Emerson says, a crusade is wanted against the ME, the egotism, the avidity, the robber-brutality of the day, in favor of intelligence and self-devotion. The devise of this league shall be, *God for each, and each for all!* the device of a great race; the theme which civilizes—the rest should go and rot in the sewers of the last Roman empire. The passage which we quoted above shows that this holy alliance against egotism and its interests would not be amiss; and France, instead of entering upon the way of fatal sensuality, should march at the head of this crusade.

The American authors of light works, people who are not worth Franklin for goodness, nor Irving for amenity, nor Cooper for force and precision, never miss, no matter how vulgar they may be, to take to themselves the title of esquire. This little chivalric distinction ornaments the title pages of novels full of inexpressible triviality; and this ardent taste for noble titles is found among the most fervent adorers of the populace. With his aristocratic leanings the Yankee is susceptible as a provincial; he takes fire the instant that a stranger suggests an imperfection in America. You could make a library of the printed replies to Dickens' Notes. Few of these works have as much wit as wrath. The most remarkable is called "*Change for American Notes, by an American Lady.*" But we are afraid that the lady's change is scarcely current money. Bitter, without originality, she twists all that she knows of the vices and follies of England, and she knows very little. "The men," she says, "are coarse, the women ill-dressed, the houses all alike, and the eternal brick produces ennui."

Indeed, we fear that the lady has not given Mr. Dickens *full "change."*

Nothing is so trivial as remarks upon the impoliteness of custom-house officers, on the multitudes of unfortunates who overrun the streets of London, "which" says she, "is a collection of hamlets, not a city!" Such documents give us but poor instruction as to the course of events, the tendency of minds, the reality of facts, and the lot in store for England. The American lady sees only the surface; the future hid beneath the present, escapes her. Laing, Chambers, Porter, and especially the prophetic Carlyle, tell us much more than the lady's "Change for American Notes."

SECTION II.

JOURNALS AND VOYAGES—WORKMEN POETS—ARCHÆOLOGISTS.

We must look at the republican journals, as well as at the New York novels, to get some light upon the obscure Present, the singular To-come. Therein are certain instructions as to the condition of the Union. In the north the affluence of Irish is enormous, they usurp the territory and create an Irish America. In the south the "negro makes his master tremble."

This double condition of affairs, often produces sanguinary collisions, and the Constitution will get along with them as it can. Already the first cut has been made upon the liberty of the Press and the liberty of the subject, as well as on the laws of probity. Read the Constitution. You will find it humane, just, philanthropic, worthy of Franklin and Washington. It consecrates the rights of the subject and insures his life, it decrees his liberty and that of the press; and now see how this Constitution operates. The public papers are full of documents. The *Clinton Gazette* (May, 1843) tells us that "on Friday evening, May 22d, the crowd assembled to decide the fate of James—accused of having excited the blacks to insurrection. Some voted for whipping, others for hanging. The hanging party had an immense majority. The death of James was voted by the mass of the people. After the unequivocal expression of this sentiment, James was carried to a mulberry tree and hanged upon a branch. We" adds the editor, "entirely approve this measure: the people acted as was fitting." It was about the sixteenth time in six months that the people had so acted.

So much for personal security. As for the liberty of the Press, it is abolished in some places; the crowd is the master; and one dares not print what the master dislikes. A New York journal printed an anti-slavery discourse by Channing; the journal was sold in Charleston; and at once the planters of South Carolina commenced a process against its vender, who was obliged to give a thousand dollars bail. The bookseller had just received a bale of Dickens' Notes, which book does not spare the planters: alarmed, he hastens to insert the following notice in the city papers: "Dickens' book will be submitted to a committee of intelligent members of the South Carolina Association. If they approve of it, I will sell it, if not, I will not." Now is not this committee an embodied "censure of the Press." Not only do these facts exist, but they erect themselves into principles and constitute a theory.

I prefer American voyages to most of the other books coming from that country, excepting, of course, Emerson, Longfellow, Prescott, Irving, etc. The North American is a traveller, but you must learn to understand him. If he travel in Europe, prejudice, national pride, rancor blind or envenom him; he sees badly; judges unjustly and makes mistakes. In the New World he preserves his simplicity, amid the glories of Nature, he reproduces with a truth often piquant and even eloquent, his emotions and impressions.

Stevens' "*Incidents of Travel in Yucatan*," Silliman's "*Gallop among American Scenery*," merit to be distinguished. Silliman's little volume is indeed a gallop: in that society which moves so rapidly, the best books, the most agreeable styles are those which go headlong, careless of philosophy as of fine language. There is, in Silliman's Sketches, a magnificent picture of Niagara in winter; an immense palace of ice suspended and sparkling, a giant motion arrested in the air by magic force, compose one of the most extraordinary spectacles possible. The touch of the American author is easy, rapid and bold; a little incorrect, but warm, and therefore better.

The manners of Yucatan, the strange habits of that lost country, where Indian customs mingle with feudal souvenirs and Spanish traditions, are detailed very truthfully by Mr. Stevens. It is probably the book which contains the greatest amount of instruction on the interesting race of the Maceguas, indigenous in that part of America.

The style of this work is not remarkable for compression energy, or concentration; they have a certain valuable, free touch; and European travellers, so often full of mannerism; valuing themselves upon vastly superior knowledge, have rarely the ingenuous vivacity which forms the charm of Audubon, Silliman, and Stevens.

We come now to a piquant American curiosity. The Lowell (Massachusetts) factories employ only women, and the price of labor is sufficiently high to enable them, after the task is done, to retire to their chambers, read, write, or issue into open air, armed with a green parasol, and promenade with all the airs of a duchess, to the intense amazement of English travellers.

The explanation is simple. Working America needs her

arms, until her day of physical labor shall have passed; it is physical labor which repays her, her intellectual toil is merely factitious. It is true, she possesses colleges and universities which strongly resemble the paste-board decorations which Prince Potemkin showed to his empress. We will give one example: An American collection, with some pretensions to erudition, makes the plural of *dives* not *divites*, but *divēses*, "the *diveses* of our land."

Why should Miss Martineau be astonished that the demoiselles of Lowell take certain airs? They are princesses; their blason is that of their country, a steamboat and a spinning-jenny. This congregation of Massachusetts spinsters had, naturally enough, the idea of forming themselves into an academy, and of presenting to the world specimens of their talents as story-tellers, romancers, poets. In fact, they are women of leisure, these workwomen who realize two or three hundred dollars a-year, wear gold watches, hang a dozen silk dresses in their wardrobes, and can very well spare some moments for gentle melancholy, reverie, and poesy. These *beguinnes* of American industry united to write a sort of *Musen-almanach*, under the title of the *Lowell Offering*.

There you will find all the ideas that can present themselves to idle girls; prose, verse, odes, sonnets, love, caprice, caves, spectres, clouds, and turrets; a singular mixture of blue-stockingism and modern romance.

Anna, Tabitha, Oriana, Lucinda, Gregoria, Alleghania, Atala, Gismunda, Tancreda, Velleda, (where will the pretty names of Arthenice's *cabinet bleu* find rest?) sign mediocre fragments, the best of which would hardly gain admission into the humblest European journal, but which taken together are remarkable.

We have seen in Europe the poetry of working-men,

which, between ourselves, has not half the value of good bread and good boots. The Americans exhibit the poems of working-women, all of which I would unhesitatingly give for a pair of well-darned stockings, or a nicely-hemmed handkerchief. What is the use of it? Success to working-men poets, if they make verse at the command of God, and preserve bright in their hearts the sacred fire of morality, the love of nature and of honesty, virile energy, and the power of devotion!

Only one Lowell specimen deserves to be cited. The idea is largely extravagant, the style elevated and wild, and if the phantasy had fallen into the soul of Jean Paul, instead of into that of a factory girl, the German Mystic would have given it an immense value. But such as they are, these fancies of a brain of eighteen years, of a girl living at the other end of the world, are very singular. The piece is called NO NIGHT, and offers a counterpart to Byron's fearful *Darkness*. In the work of the American girl, the sun never sets, the world is fatigued with splendour, and asks of God repose, obscurity, and silence.

Local archæology has produced somewhat in America. No fraction of the United States so small as not to have an historian; no city so small as not to become visible in octavo or quarto, with engravings. The *chef-d'œuvre* of this particle-literature is a *History of Beverley*, a little town of New England, with engravings, plans, charts, and biographies. One would hardly have imagined that this honest, little city possessed two hundred and three great unknown men. The United States, which have no feudal souvenirs, and therefore no history, whose heroic age was only yesterday, interests itself in minutia, which have not even the doubtful importance of antiquity, nor the melancholy charm attached to the ruins of the Past.

Farther off than Beverly, Halifax, the capital of New Scotland, a city completely stranger to literature, has become piqued. *Sam Slick*, the clock-maker, has constituted himself the Addison of this obscure and distant portion of the British Dominions. British America begins to have some pretensions. Three volumes called "*Colonial Literature*," by G. E. Young, (Halifax,) bears witness to these desires. Mr. Young repeats what Blair, La Harpe, and Batteux have told us too often. Old societies are fertile in philosophy and criticism: one would say that these books which come from afar, were thought, written and printed in some provincial town of England or France. There are some curious facts in William Oliver's "Eight Months in Illinois," an unambitious work from the pen of a workingman in Roxburgshire, printed in Illinois. An emigrant himself, the author gives counsel to those who are to follow him. You see a society just germinating, a country barely inhabited, great inundated prairies, painful cultivation of unploughed soil, and the efforts of a distant colonization, with curious and novel details which interest you vividly.

America republishes for twelve and a half cents the guinea romances of England: the Pictorial Times furnishes engravings, which are used in the sheets which go to the West to sooth the literary appetite of the settlers and the Chippeways. Every State of the Union will soon have its history in ten volumes: Washington's letters, very wise but very insignificant, fill six: Franklin has furnished ten: Jefferson and John Quincy Adams will do likewise.

There is then no want of volumes. The globe is covered with them. Soon the forests will be gone, and they will raise pyramids of books which they do not know what to do with. A quaint and clever man, the *Philosophe Inconnu*, Saint Martin, asks how one shall get rid of all those books which repeat the same idea with a shadow of difference in manner, two thousand years hence. And he proposes in one of his strangest and least known works, the following burlesque and facetious plan. To reduce all existing books to a *pap*, and with this encyclopedic mixture to nourish childhood and youth ; clever men and sages are to be the nurses, and are to receive as reward a grand spoon, according to the grade which each shall attain in this new University—silver spoon, gilt spoon, gold spoon—the highest title to be that of *Grand Spoon !*

The intellectual and typographical state of the world gives some sense to this bit of facetiousness. The literary pap seems to be hardening in advance. All the world seems to write with the same ink, and in some three hundred years, God knows how glad people will be to gather the few books which have an especial character, and which seem born of a human brain, and not of a material mechanism. Ah, what a dearth there is of originality, humor, poesy !

The present superior men of France, America and England who pretend to great honors, seem afraid to show themselves humorists. Only two or three bold ones dare dream, meditate, not dogmatize eternally, but give themselves up to caprice, wander through the flowers of thought and enjoy liberty. All America has not one humorist. England has only Carlyle. Yet, really serious men, men of powerful thought never refuse themselves the indulgence of caprice, as strong natures risk a too long, too rapid ride beneath the noonday sun, so feared by the sickly and the little.

I have very little faith in excessive gravity and moderation of temperament. I do not trust those ladies so virtuous, always so stiff, who dread a crease in their dresses, and fear to read Moliére at the age of forty.

CHAPTER VIII.

SAMUEL SLICK, THE CLOCKMAKER.

PRIVATE MANNERS OF NORTH AMERICA.

It is a piquant curiosity, a book and an excellent book, composed, printed, and published in one of the most unknown cities of the world, between Cape Breton and the Appalachian mountains, on the shores of the Atlantic, in the lap of a slumbering civilization, discouraged, strangled, deadened by the neighborhood of the United States. Who knows of the existence of a capital composed of five or six large white houses and two or three hundred small red ones, in the fortieth degree of north latitude, all ruled by the English viceroy Sir George Campbell, governor of New Scotland.

This capital is called Halifax, and the governor has nothing to do. Happy sovereign. Under his windows, an abandoned cemetery extends its vast silence, and the new writer pretends that it is the best possible symbol of the governor's administration.

In the midst of the ennui which must exist in a society without life, future, industry, wealth, emulation, by the sound of the murmuring sea, in a climate now vigorous, now burning, lives, not as you might fancy, a lyric poet, a romantic fairy-tale writer, nor yet an epic poet sublime as the ocean, but, what is more rare, a great observer, an original philosopher. If one were to tell me that a work possessing a grain, a single grain, a poor and miserable scruple of originality, had appeared in Java or Madagascar, I think I would have the courage to learn the language of those countries. Here the trouble was less, the harvest more abundant. To enjoy a new pleasure it was only necessary to accustom myself to the Yankee dialect, a sort of patois composed of subtractions and multiplications of syllables, of consonants doubled and vowels elided, and not presenting any formidable difficulties. The Scottish patois, turned by Burns and Ramsey into a poetical language, is an hundred times more difficult.

It was therefore a cheaply purchased vivid enjoyment. I studied Mr. Haliburton's work diligently. In less than a week, I understood all the points of the Yankee dialect; and my labor was amusing and useful even in the philologic point of view.

The philologists who cultivate with exemplary patience, and with an assiduity, rather meritorious than profitable, the garden of Greek, Hebrew, and Persian roots, should occupy themselves with the actual changes taking place in modern tongues. They would discover some of those most interesting facts possible in the science which they cultivate. In lieu of operating upon etymologic corpses, they could exercise themselves upon a living subject. It is a pleasure to note, as they rise, the variations introduced into language by different people, whether these be in the idiom or the pronunciation. We are not uttering hypotheses but realities, not piled up theoretic conjectures, but incontestable facts.

This is the true object of veritable philology. Few think so. They edit Celtic dictionaries, but cannot stoop to pick up the words formed or deformed every day under their eyes. No Englishman, whom I know of, dreams of collecting in a dictionary all the dialects of his language, which are now *patois*, or *brogues*, and cannot claim the title of separate tongues —the dialects of Cumberland, Lancashire, Sommersetshire, the Scottish, Irish, Yankee, and even the strange jargon of the Hindoostanee half-breeds. Mr. Haliburton's book, "The Clockmaker," gives at a glance all the American elegancies. I have said, it is a remarkably good book.

It is not a romance, history, drama, philosophic treatise, voyage, story, or declamation ; this patois-book, written by a colonist of Halifax, full of adages à la Sancho Panza, and of stories worthy of Bonaventure Desperiers, is simply an admirable book. The author explains the sketchy, existing civilization of the United States ; the ricketty, unhealthy civilization of Canada, and the profound torpor of the neighboring British provinces. He enters into the secret details of private life, and exhibits all which English travellers have left in shadow. Nearly all travels in the United States are unsatisfactory. An English tory, accustomed to be surrounded by veneration and respect ; a fashionable actress, living on the lucrative enthusiasm of the republicans ; a romantic female economist, who regrets that she does not find in America, the reality of her illusions, these are guides little worthy of esteem or trust ; their observation is but skin-deep : they give us but sterile epigrams and frivolous satire, instead of any insight into a civilization unexampled in history, into a society, scarcely formed, yet of incontestable greatness.

It cannot be too often repeated to Europe and her preoccupied statesmen, that there are two nations and two territories meriting the closest attention ; they are mistresses of unknown power ; the future is theirs ; the nations are young, the countries poorly peopled, but they have much to do, and they grow rapidly: I speak of America and of Russia.

Both grow too rapidly to understand the secret of their increase: both are too simple to be believed, when they speak of themselves.

The painters, orators, sculptors, poets and historians of the United States, keeping their eyes fixed upon Europe, and oppressed by her mass of glorious memories, lose the courage necessary to draw from a living source personal ideas and fresh sentiment. The engraver's art is cold; the painter's disposition methodical; the preacher's eloquence recalls the amplifications of college; the parliamentary debates offer an indefinite succession of pompously vulgar harangues. Common-place, that fearful disease of subservient intellect, spreads itself like a grey cloud over a literature yet vague, pale, diffuse, decrepit, even in its cradle. The muse repeats with flat sweetness, Cowper's mournfulness, Wordsworth's morality. The local patriotism of each province, condemns the historian to a minute and slow exactitude, which forbids him to write annals, but allows inventories, and devotes six volumes to the genealogy of Pittsburgh or Nashville, and six others to explanatory documents. When, lately, the Quarterly Review, in its sympathy for Brother Jonathan, attempted to laud the talent of American Orators, the editor produced a pleasant contradiction; the lie was constantly given to his predetermined eulogy, by the fragments which he was compelled to cite. There were oceans of words rolling over deserts of ideas; metaphors rained in torrents, melodramatically thunderous expressions sounded in the solitude and mist; nothing was new, nor simple, nor energetic, nor delicate, hardly an idea of measure and of numbers. Absence of taste would not be astonishing in a nation just trying its wings; but one is surprised to miss hardihood, spontaneous effort, and grandeur of style or of ideas.

Yet its founders were energetic. Between Florida and Maine, the Atlantic and the Rocky Mountains, live the republicans, the sons of Washington, the grandsons of the indomitable Puritans, the great-grandsons of the Saxon and the Teuton. The energetic activity which for years has precipitated the movement of these athletæ, has not yet lost its first impulse. Everywhere they build bridges, raise cities, dig canals, the steam engine flies, popular assemblies are formed, new districts are won from savage life, the wilderness yields, the prairies are cultivated, the forests cleared, ports open, manufactures spring up from the earth, and the triumph of Saxon civilization goes on. Clearly the heroes of this triumph have no lack of genius, but they do not write it; they use it. Now they are in the mêlée of industry, in the heat of the battle, and so will they be for some time to come. Thinking, is for the idle man. These people have no time. Their literature is factitious and not their own; they have no national leisure, that essential basis for a national literature. They do not yet get the impression of that grand Nature which surrounds them, or if they do it, it has no force: nothing concentrates it in that ardent and silent furnace which by a grand alchemy, transforming sensation and thought, gives birth to Art, Poetry, Eloquence, and, diadem of an achieved society, crowns a ripened people.

They then are not to be consulted, for they do not yet understand themselves. Nor is it their aristocratic enemies who love to deny the power of the democrats once their colonists.

In the work under consideration, Mr. Haliburton supposes an Englishman travelling in British America, to meet a clockmaker, Sam Slick of Slicksville in Connecticut; and they journey together. Sometimes in a light wagon, sometimes on horseback, Slick and his new friend visit New Scotland, Acadia, Maine, and all that portion of North America disputed for by Great Britain and the States. They knock at the door of the cabin, visit the farm, halt at the taverns; lose no occasion of involuntarily judging men, themselves unobserved. None of the originalities or singularities of this new society escape Slick. He trades with everybody, and, thanks to his ready speech, he sells an enormous quantity of wooden clocks; above all he boasts of knowing human nature. And how he judges men and things!

Since the personages of Sir Walter Scott, nothing has been better done than this character of Sam Slick. This Connecticut Clock Pedlar, is an excellent and clever creature; without cleverness in *our* way, that old cleverness turned rather rancid and stale, withered by its transformations, its passage through college, Rome, Greece, Egypt and some thirty ages of affiliation; but a naïve, native cleverness, which comes from experience, as the spark comes, gleaming, from the flint, vivid, short, penetrating, not troubling itself about words; a republican Parnurge.

This man travels through the States, leaving on the road, for ready money, his wooden clocks. His nose is pointed, his forehead high, its form erect and well-formed, his embrowned face smiles through its freckles, his eye gleams with penetration and with vanity. He unites the qualities of the merchant, the traveller, the diplomatist, the courtier, and the savage. Member of a society which admits no masters, yet possesses nothing but masters, he flatters everybody, sure of deceiving them. Active, industrious, vigorous and inflexible in mind and body, he yields to no one, has need of no one. In a commercial country, which exists and grows only by a continued effort of agriculture, industry and trade, he knows that it is to everybody's interest to respect the law; therefore he has all the honesty of the merchant, the regularity of the banker, and the exactitude of the clerk. He never cheats his customers; he *takes them* in. His pleasure is to make use of his penetration to induce them to dupe themselves; he has marvelous traps for the cupidity of others; he is ravished when a customer, trying to dupe him, cheats himself. He excels, in lending a charm to the speculation of his fellow-citizens, in exciting their desire, irritating their ardor, to hide the book for a moment, then to let it reappear, and to entice them by a prey of which they soon become the prey. He does not *catch* any one; he is not so foolish. He plays the simple, an excellent role in life, yet manages to make the others catch themselves. Were he less boastful and less patriotic you might take him for a Norman; less crafty and litigious for a Gascon. But such as he is, he is delicious.

Sam Slick has not married: it is, he says, too hazardous a market, he only speculates where he is sure. The graces of the fair sex move him, and he yields to their seductions but moderately, master of his passions and his tastes, and enjoying life, American fashion, without risking his capital. This portion of practical and experimental good sense is sharpened in him by the habit of trade: he loves his horse without feebleness; courts the beauties on the road without endangering his heart; likes his grog or his mint-julep, but never gets drunk. He is a sage. One regrets that he is tricky. But what will you have? 'Tis commerce. Would you compare him with Sancho, he is less ingenuous and farther advanced; a Sancho who may not have a Don Quixotte. No deceptive imagination, no distant illusion can get Sam Slick out of the track of interested observation, calculating flattery, and commercial seduction. It is to him rather an art than a trade, he loves the philosophy of it more even than the profits. He despises men because he deceives them so often, which uplifts him in his own eyes.

He spreads his nets like a hunter or a politician, preferring success to profit. When the fish is taken, the angling finished, and the money in his pocket, he laughs less from avarice than self-love, and then he examines piece by piece, with charmed eye, that thousand-wheeled clock, that soul whereof the mainspring is self. His analysis is worth more than those of Dugald Stewart or Emanuel Kant. He sincerely loves his country, of which the institutions, in perfecting the fine faculties of which we speak, has made of this Clockmaker a national personage, a symbol, a resumption, a type. But his patriotism does not blind him. Ultra-American, vehement friend of the federal republic, despising other nations, certain of a superiority which place the United States immeasurably above Europe, his eyes are nevertheless open to the abuses, faults, dangers, and miseries of his country. He reasons about them as about everything else, pertinently, coldly, without twist or rhetoric, going to the bottom of the matter, taking facts for facts and phrases for phrases. When he is not trading he relates, smokes, gets on his hobby, and piques himself on his clever acts, and laughs at his dupes as he touches his faithful horse with the spur, and endoctrinates the Englishman in his theories, memories, loves, hopes, the condition of the country, the Americans, Canadians, New Brunswickers, and *Blue Noses*, as he calls the people of New Scotland, a little known province to which by the way Haliburton belongs.

Our Briton and Sam Slick follow the shores of the Atlantic, and having run through New Scotland, enter Maine. On the road, every individual whom they meet, all the anecdotes which the scenes recall to the Clockmaker, all the memories with which his experience is armed serve to explain the moral position of the British colonies, and the republican states, their past, their present, and their progress. He never bothers himself with theory but sticks to facts after the manner of Franklin, the Socrates of his country. Here you find twenty personages better than Cooper's, borrowed not from the exceptional life of the wilderness, but from the real society which agglomerates and progresses in the scarce-built villages, the scattered farms : those actors who hold no long discourses on politics, religion, commerce, or agriculture represent exactly the march of interest, and the development of mind.

Like Sam, they talk Yankee, a patois of calculation, prudence, interest, commercial speculation, trickiness which flutters midway between cheating and probity. As you study it, you see how the passions of men enter into the dictionary of the people, and by what imperceptible process idioms change shapes as they are found in new manners. The Clockmaker never answers a question by an assertion positive enough to compromise or bind him. Take this sketch.

"A man entered the room, carrying a small bundle in his hand, tied up in a dirty silk pocket-handkerchief. He was dressed in an old suit of rusty black, much the worse for wear. His face bore the marks of intemperance, and he appeared much fatigued with his journey, which he had performed alone and on foot.

* * * * * * *

"Then, taking a survey of the Clockmaker and myself, observed to Mr. Slick that he thought he had seen him before.

"Well, it's not onlikely ;—where ?

"Ah, that's the question, sir ; I cannot exactly say where.

"Nor I neither

"Which way may you be travellin? Down East I expect.

"Which way are you from then? Some where down South.

"The traveller again applied himself to brandy and water.

"Ahem! then you are from Lunenburg?

"Well, I won't say I warn't at Lunenburg.

"Ahem! pretty place that Lunenberg; but they speak Dutch. D—n the Dutch; I hate Dutch; there's no language like English.

"Then I suppose you are going to Halifax?

"Well, I won't say I won't go to Halifax afore I return, neither.

"A nice town that Halifax—good fish-market there; but they are not like the English fish a'ter all. Halibut is a poor substitute for the good old English turbot. Where did you say you were from, sir?

"I don't gist altogether mind that I said I was from any place in partikilar, but from down South last.

"Ahem! your health, sir; perhaps you are like myself, sir, a stranger, and have no home; and, after all, there is no home like England. Pray, what part of England are you from?

"I estimate I'm not from England at all.

"I'm sorry for you, then; but where the devil are you from?

"In a general way folks say I'm from the States.

"Knock them down then, d—m them. If any man was to insult me by calling me a Yankee, I'd kick him; but the Yankees have no seat of honor to kick. If I hadn't been thinkin' more of my brandy and water than your answers, I might have known you were a Yankee by your miserable evasions. They never give a straight answer—there's nothing straight about them, but their long backs,—and he was asleep in his chair, overcome by the united effects of the heat, the brandy and fatigue."

Does one speak of the United States, of the Republic, of Webster, Clay, Jefferson, John Adams, Bunker-Hill, or the heroes of the Revolution, this dialect, which is always bargain-making with the thought, this response which *juggles* half their signification, keeping always for itself a concealed passage, by which it may wriggle out of its obvious meaning, this dialect gives place to positive assertion; to the most comical mixture of shop talk and college emphasis. "Calculate your best," says Sam, "it is sartain sure that we are letter 'A,' No. 1, among the nations; first column, without tare, deduction, subtraction, or damage. I speculate that them who don't agree to that, can't do a sum in simple addition, and don't know the first rules of cipherin'. It is clear that we have the most splendid location between the poles; it's ginerally acknowledged. The greatest man livin' is General Jackson; he goes ahead of Napoleon Bonaparte by a long chalk. I don't mention Van Buren, Webster, Amos Kendal, and a whole raft of statesmen, who are up to every thing. England can lick the world, and we can lick England." This last sentence is the well-beloved of Sam Slick, and finishes all his harangues.

"The folks of Halifax," says Sam, "take it all out in talking—they talk of steamboats, whalers, and rail-roads—but they all end where they begin—in talk. I don't think I'd be out in my latitude, if I was to say they beat the women kind at that. One fellow says, I talk of going to England—another says, I talk of going to the country—while a third says, I talk of going to sleep. If we happen to speak of such things, we say, 'I'm right off down East; or I'm away off South,' and away we go jist like a streak of lightning

"When we want folks to talk, we pay 'em for it, such as our ministers, lawyers, and members of Congress; but then we expect the use of their tongues, and not their hands; and when we pay folks to work, we expect the use of their hands, and not their tongues. I guess work don't come kind o' natural to the people of this province, no more than it does to a full bred horse. I expect they think they have a little *too much blood* in 'em for work, for they are near about as proud as they are lazy.

"Now the bees know how to sarve out such chaps, for they have their drones too. Well, they reckon its no fun, a making honey all summer for these idle critters to eat all winter—so they give 'em Lynch Law. They have a regular built mob of citizens, and string up the drones like the Vixburg gamblers. Their maxim is, and not a bad one neither, I guess, 'no work no honey.'"

"*The Blacks and Whites* in the States show their teeth and snarl, they are jist ready to fall to. *The Protestants and Catholics* begin to lay back their ears, and turn tail for kickin. *The Abolitionists and Planters* are at it like two bulls in a pastur. *Mob-Law and Lynch-Law* are working like yeast in a barrel, and frothing at the bunghole. *Nullification and Tariff* are like a charcoal pit, all covered up, but burning inside, and sending out smoke at every crack, enough to stifle a horse. *General Government and State Government* every now and then square off and spar, and the first blow given will bring a genuine set-to. *Surplus Revenue* is another bone of contention; like a shin of beef thrown among a pack of dogs, it will set the whole on 'em by the ears.

"You have heerd tell of cotton rags dipt in tupentine, haven't you, how they produce combustion? Well, I guess we have the elements of spontaneous combustion among us in abundance; when it does break out, if you don't see an eruption of human gore worse than Etna lava, then I'm mistaken. There'll be the very devil to pay, that's a fact. I expect the blacks will butcher the Southern whites, and the Northerners will have to turn out and butcher them again; and all this shoot, hang, cut, stab, and burn business will sweeten our folks' temper, as raw meat does that of a dog—it fairly makes me sick to think on it. The explosion may clear the air again, and all be tranquil once more, but its an even chance if it don't leave us the three steamboat options, to be blown sky high, to be scalded to death, or drowned.'

After this Sam lights his cigar.

"But," says the other speaker, "the testimony of all my friends the travellers is against you."

"'*Your friends!*' said the Clockmaker, with such a tone of ineffable contempt, that I felt a strong inclination to knock him down for his insolence—your friends! Ensigns and leftenants, I guess, from the British marchin regiments in the colonies, that run over five thousand miles of country in five weeks, on leave of absence, and then return, looking as wise as the monkey that had seen the world. When they get back they are so chock full of knowledge of the Yankees, that it runs over of itself, like a hogshead of molasses, rolled about in hot weather—a white froth and scum bubbles out of the bung; wishywashy trash they call tours, sketches, travels, letters, and what not; vapid stuff, jist sweet enough to catch flies, cockroaches, and half-fledged galls. It puts me in mind of my French. I larnt French at night school one winter of our minister Joshua Hopewell (he was the most larned man of the age, for he taught himself een amost every language in Europe;) well, next spring, when I went to Boston I met a Frenchman, and I began to jabber away French to him: 'Polly woes a French shay,' says I. I don't understand Yankee yet, says he. You don't understand! says I, why it's French. I guess you didn't expect to hear such good French, did you, away down east here? but we speak it real well, and its generally allowed we speak English, too, better than the British. 'Oh,' says he, 'you one very droll Yankee, dat very good joke, sare; you talk Indian and call it French.' But, says I, Mister Mountshear, it is French, I vow; real merchantable, without wainy edge or shakes—all clear stuff; it will pass survey in any market—its ready stuck and seasoned. 'Oh, very like,' say he, bowin as polite as a black waiter at New *Orleens*, 'very like, only I never heerd it afore; oh, very good French dat—*clear stuff*, no doubt, but I no understand—its all my fault, I dare say, sare.'"

"The fact is, the American of the United States has funds, quickness and good appearance—quick as a fox, supple as an eel, sharp as a weasel. I oughtn't to say it, but it's known. He eclipses creation; he's worth ready money."

At this last expression Sam is silent, eloquence can go no further, and he delicately changes the subject.

But Sam has reason to be proud. Never has the real situation of the United States, so dangerous, so flourishing, so active, been exhibited so profoundly and simply. And so he treats every topic, "My rules," says the philosophical Clockmaker, "are not numerous, but they're sure, they go right to the point, and that's a fact. *Everything can be ciphered. No man nor woman can resist soft sawder. What is that to me.* With them three rules you can go to the end of the world, and no mistake."

He has not the good nature to profess for political life that admiring esteem which we Frenchmen, new to it, bestow upon it. "When one is used to politics," he says, "one never goes straight; it's impossible. Politics turns and twists us. You can't trust people of that trade. They always walk crooked, like porters with heavy burdens. At last they get bent. The politician who is loyal, honest, sincere even to his friends is a marvel. Did you ever clean your knives with brick-dust? It is a long and bad way; the blade gets bright, but the steel wears out; it's so with politics.'

SECTION II.

HISTORY OF AHAB MELDRUM, THE KORKONITE.

Alabama has plenty of those cities, which spring out of the earth as if by the blow of an enchanter's rod, which have more streets than houses, more houses than inhabitants. There, as in the other States, the worship and clergy are not supported by the State but by individual contributions. If a minister be abandoned by his flock, the church becomes a store-house, the parsonage goes to ruin, and that is the end of the matter. This is called the "Voluntary System," of which Sam Slick has more than one story to tell.

"I recollect when I was up to Alabama, to one of the new cities lately built there, I was awalkin' one mornin' airly out o' town to get a leetle fresh air, for the weather was so plaguy sultry I could hardly breathe a'most, and I seed a most splendid location there near the road; a beautiful white two-story house, with a grand virandah runnin' all round it, painted green, and green vernitians to the winders, and a white palisade fence in front, lined with a row of Lombardy poplars, and two rows of 'em leadin' up to the front door, like two files of sodgers with fixt baganuts; each side of the avenue was a grass plot, and a beautiful image of Adam stood in the centre of one on 'em—and of Eve, with a fig-leaf apron on, in t'other, made of wood by a na*tive* artist, and painted so nateral no soul could tell 'em from stone.

"The avenue was all planked beautiful, and it was lined with flowers in pots and jars, and looked a touch above common, I tell *you*. While I was astoppin to look at it, who should drive by but the milkman with his cart. Says I, stranger, says I, I suppose you don't know who lives here, do you? I guess you are a stranger, said he, ain't you? Well, says I I don't exactly know as I ain't, but who lives here? The Rev. Ahab Meldrum, said he, I reckon. Ahab Meldrum, said I, to myself; I wonder if it can be the Ahab Meldrum I was to school with to Slickville, to minister's, when we was boys. It can't be possible it's him, for he was fitter for a State's prisoner than a State's preacher, by a long chalk. He was a poor stick to make a preacher on, for minister couldn't beat nothin' into him a'most, he was so cussed stupid; but I'll see any how; so I walks right through the gate, and raps away at the door, and a tidy, well-rigged nigger help opens it, and shows me into a'most an elegant farnished room. I was most darnted to sit down on the chairs, they were so splendid, for fear I should spile 'em. There was mirrors and varses, and lamps, and picturs, and crinkum crankums, and notions of all sorts and sizes in it. It looked like a bazar a'most, it was filled with such an everlastin' sight of curiosities.

"The room was considerable dark too, for the blinds was shot, and I was skear'd to move for fear o' doin' mischief. Presently in comes Ahab slowly sailin' in, like a boat droppin' down stream in a calm, with a pair o' purple slippers on, and a figured silk dressin'-gound, and carrying a'most a beautiful-bound book in his hand. May I presume, says he, to inquire who I have the onexpected pleasure of seeing this mornin'. If you'll gist through open one o' them are shutters, says I, I guess the light will save us the trouble of axin' names. I know who you be by your voice any how, tho' it's considerable softer than it was ten years ago. I'm Sam Slick, says I,—what left o' me at least. Verily, said he, friend Samuel, I'm glad to see you; and how did you leave that excellent man and distinguished scholar, the Rev. Mr. Hopewell, and my good friend your father? Is the old gentleman still alive? if so, he must anow be ripe full of years as he is full of honors. Your mother, I think I heer'd was dead—gathered to her fathers—peace be with her!—she had a good and a kind heart. I loved her as a child; but the Lord taketh whom he loveth. Ahab, says I, I have but a few minutes to stay with you, and if you think to draw the wool over my eyes, it might perhaps take you a longer time than you are thinking on, or than I have to spare;—there are some friends you've forgot to inquire after tho',—there's Polly Bacon and her little boy.

"Spare me, Samuel, spare me, my friend, says he; open not that wound afresh, I beseech thee. Well, says I, none o' your nonsense then; show me into a room where I can spit, and feel to home, and put my feet upon the chairs without adamagin' things, and I'll sit and smoke and chat with you a few minutes; in fact, I don't care if I stop and breakfast with you, for I feel considerable peckish this mornin'. Sam, says he, atakin' hold of my hand, you were always right up and down, and as straight as a shingle in your dealin's. I can trust *you*, I know, but mind—and he put his fingers on his lips—mum is the word;—bye gones are bye gones—you wouldn't blow an old chum among his friends, would you? I scorn a nasty, dirty, mean action, says I, as I do a nigger. Come, foller me, then, says he;—and he led me into a back room, with an oncarpeted painted floor, farnished plain, and some shelves in it, with books and pipes and cigars, pig-tail and what not. Here's liberty-hall, said he ; chew, or smoke, or spit as you please ;—do as you like here ; we'll throw off all resarve now ; but mind that cursed nigger ; he has a foot like a cat, and an ear for every keyhole—don't talk too loud.

"Well, Sam, said he, I'm glad to see you too, my boy ; it put's me in mind of old times. Many's the lark you and I have had together in Slickville, when old Hunks—(it made me start, that he meant Mr. Hopewell, and it made me feel kinder dandry at him, for I wouldn't let any one speak disrespectful of him afore me for nothin', I know,)—when old Hunks thought we was abed. Them was happy days—the days o' light heels and light hearts. I often think on 'em, and think on 'em too with pleasure. Well, Ahab, says I, I don't gist altogether know as I do ; there are some things we might gist as well a'most have left alone, I reckon ; but what's done is done, that's a fact. Ahem ! said he, so loud, I looked round and I seed two niggers bringin' in the breakfast, and a grand one it was—tea and coffee and Indgian corn cakes, and hot bread and cold bread, fish, fowl, and flesh, roasted, boiled, and fried ; presarves, pickles, fruits ; in short, everything a'most you could think on. You needn't wait, said Ahab, to the blacks ; I'll ring for you, when I want you ; we'll help ourselves.

"Well, when I looked round and seed this critter alivin' this way, on the fat o' the land, up to his knees in clover like, it did pose me considerable to know how he worked it so cleverly, for he was thought always, as a boy, to be rather more than half onder-baked, considerable soft-like. So says I, Ahab, says I, I calculate you'r like the cat we used to throw out of minister's garret-winder, when we was aboardin' there to school. How so, Sam ? said he. Why, says I, you always seem to come on your feet some how or other. You have got a plaguy nice thing of it here ; that's a fact, and no mistake (the critter had three thousand dollars a year); how on airth did you manage it? I wish in my heart I had ataken up the trade o' preachin' too; when it does hit it does capitally, that's sartain. Why, says he, if you'll promise not to let on to any one about it, I'll tell you. I'll keep dark about it, you may depend, says I. I'm not a man that can't keep nothin' in my gizzard, but go right off and blart out all I hear. I know a thing worth two o' that, I guess. Well, says he, it's done by a new rule I made in grammar—the feminine gender is more worthy than the neuter, and the neuter more worthy than the masculine; I gist soft sawder the women. It 'taint every man will let you tickle him; and if you do, he'll make faces at you enough to frighten you into fits; but tickle his wife, and it's electrical—he'll laugh like anything. They are the forred wheels, start them, and the hind ones foller of course. Now it's mostly women that tend meetin' here; the men-folks have their politics and trade to talk over, and what not, and ain't time; but the ladies go considerable rigular, and we have to depend on them, the dear critters. I gist lay myself out to get the blind side o' them, and I sugar and gild the pill so as to make it pretty to look at and easy to swaller. Last Lord's day, for instance, I preached on the death of the widder's son. Well, I drew such a pictur of the lone watch at the sick bed, the patience, the kindness, the tenderness of women's hearts, their forgiving disposition —(the Lord forgive me for saying so, tho', for if there is a created critter that never forgives, it's a woman; they seem to forgive a wound on their pride, and it skins over and looks all healed up like, but touch 'em on the sore spot agin, and see how cute their memory is)—their sweet temper, soothers of grief, dispensers of joy, ministrin' angels. I make all the virtues of the feminine gender always—then I wound up with a quotation from Walter Scott. They all like poetry, do the ladies, and Shakspeare, Scott, and Byron are amazin' favorites; they go down much better than them old-fashioned staves o' Watts.

'Oh, woman, in our hour of ease,
Uncertain, coy, and hard to please,
And variable as the shade
By the light quivering aspen made;
When pain and anguish wring the brow,
A ministering angel thou.'

If I didn't touch it off to the nines it's a pity. I never heerd you preach so well, says one, since you was located here. I drew from natur', says I, a squeezin' of her hand. Nor never so touchin', says another. You know my model, says I, lookin' spooney on her. I fairly shed tears, said a third; how often have you drawn them from me! says I. So true, says they, and so natural, and truth and natur' is what we call eloquence. I feel quite proud, says I, and considerable elated, my admired sisters,—for who can judge so well as the ladies of the truth of the description of their own virtues? I must say, I felt somehow kinder inadequate to the task too, I said,—for the depth and strength of beauty of the female heart passes all understandin'.

"When I left 'em I heerd 'em say, ain't he a dear man, a feelin' man, a sweet critter, a'most a splendid preacher; none o' your mere moral lecturers, but a real right down *genuine* gospel preacher. Next day I received to the tune of one hundred dollars in cash, and fifty dollars *pro*duce, presents from one and another. The truth is, if a minister wants to be popular he should remain single, for then the gals all have a chance for him; but the moment he marries he's up a tree, his flint is fixed then; you may depend it's gone goose with them arter that; that's a fact. No, Sam; they are the pillars of the temple, the dear little critters.—And I'll give you a wrinkle for your horn, perhaps you ain't got yet, and it may be some use to you when you go down atradin' with the benighted colonists in the outlandish British provinces. *The road to the head lies through the heart.* Pocket, you mean, instead of head, I guess, said I; and if you don't travel that road full chissel it's a pity.—Well, says I, Ahab, when I go to Slickville I'll gist tell Mr. Hopewell what a most precious superfine, superior darn'd rascal you have turned out; if you ain't No. 1, letter A, I want to know who is, that's all. You do beat all, Sam, said he; it's *the system that's vicious, and not the preacher.* If I didn't give 'em the soft sawder they would neither pay me nor hear me; that's a fact. Are you so soft in the horn now, Sam, as to suppose that the gals would take the trouble to come to hear me tell 'em of their corrupt natur' and fallen condition; and first thank me, and then pay me for it! Very entertainin' that, to tell 'em the worms will fatten on their pretty little rosy cheeks, and that their sweet plump flesh is nothin' but grass, flourishin' to day, and to be cut down withered and rotten to-morrow; ain't it? It ain't in the natur' o' things, if I put them out o' concait o' themselves, I can put them in concait o' me; or that they will come down handsome, and do the thing ginteel, its gist onpossible. It warn't me made the system, but the system made me. *The voluntary don't work well.*

System or no system, said I, Ahab, you are Ahab still, and Ahab you'll be to the eend of the chapter. You may decaive the women by soft sawder, and yourself by talkin' about systems, but you won't walk into me so easy, I know. It ain't pretty at all. Now, said I, Ahab, I told you I wouldn't blow you, nor will I. I will neither speak o' things past nor things present I know you wouldn't, Sam, said he; you were always a good feller. But its on one condition, says I, and that is that you allow Polly Bacon a hundred dollars a-year —she was a good gall and a decent gall when you first know'd her, and she's in great distress now at Slickville, I tell *you.* That's onfair, that's onkind, Sam, said he ; that's not the clean thing ; I can't afford it ; it's a breach o' confidence this, but you got me on the hip, and I can't help myself ; say fifty dollars, and I will. Done, said I, and mind you're up to the notch, for I'm in earnest—there's no mistake. Depend upon me, said he, and, Sam, said he, a shakin' hands along with me at partin',—excuse me, my good feller, but I hope I may never have the pleasure to see your face ag'in. Ditto, says I ; but mind the fifty dollars a-year, or you will see me to a sartinty—good b'ye."

A year after Sam Slick and his companion found themselves entering Thebes, not the Egyptian nor the Grecian city, but a little hamlet formed of five or six wooden houses, to which the inhabitants had given that illustrious name, probably with a view to annoy and bother future geographers. All the doors were shut, not a man was in the streets. In the midst of the general silence, you saw the mason's trowel standing in a heap of mortar, the scaffolding up, the joiner's tools as if just laid aside and everything denoting a sudden cessation of labor. At last they found a tavern open, and in it's only room the tavern-keeper smoking. "I calculate," said Sam, entering, "that you ain't the only inhabitant of this location." "I reckon not," was the reply, "they are all gone to the woods to hear the preacher of the new Korkornites." "I guess," says Sam, "I never heard of them fellers afore. What is a Korkornite?" "They can tell you themselves ; I don't know. All that I know is, that there's a religious bee, which they call a meetin' or a *stir.*"

"All people have their stimulants: the Chinese take opium, the Dutch schiedam, the English gin, the Irish whiskey. Now, we Americans who go ahead, we take 'em all, tobacco, rum, green tea, politics, and religious excitement. Every new sect has its revival. I've got four children; the first is a Hicksite, the second a Universalist, the third a Socialist, the fourth a Shaker, and I reckon that if I should have a fifth he would be a Korkornite."

Curious to see the affair, Sam and his companion follow the directions of the innkeeper. Near a bridge on the not yet cleared property of a settler, and on the edge of a forest, the shadows of whose giant trees fell upon the strange scene, some twenty wigwam-like tents had been erected, and therein were sold liquor, tobacco, and cakes as at a fair. In the centre a sort of barn made of planks served for theatre to the chiefs of this revival: and their shrill, shrieking voices aroused the far echoes of rock, shore, and forest; some hundreds of men seated upon the trunks of felled trees, talked of religion or politics, and drank mint-julep or grog while waiting the return of their wives and daughters, who filled the barn. Slick and the Briton managed to effect an entrance into this, at the moment that a person mounted the table which served for pulpit. He was meagre, pale, attenuated, hollow-eyed, his head was bound in a red handkerchief, which increased his palor, his neck was bare; and his whole mien so mournful and resigned that he looked more like a criminal going to be hanged than a minister of the gospel. It was unpleasant to look at him. All were still. Then he slowly pronounced a few words; then murmured inarticulately, then an axiom or two, raising his voice gradually, and then entering upon his subject, which was a picture of the fearful tortures reserved for the damned. His gestures became animated, his eye kindled, his language grew fierce and vehement, he perspired freely, and at last took off his coat. This done, he recommenced his infernal description, in which the images, borrowed from all that is revolting and hideous in the physical life, inspired so profound a disgust, and were so utterly senseless, that Slick and the Briton left their places and quitted the barn, while frightened women were fainting, howling, and falling hysterically into each other's arms. "I speculate," said Sam," that I have seen that chap somewhere. He calls himself Concord Fisher, but it's a false name, I know." Nor was he wrong.

The next day this terrible preacher came to the tavern, without his red handkerchief. "Samuel," said he, "I recognized you yesterday; and you're just the man I wanted to see. I am Ahab Meldrum. My dear friend, we preach temperance, for nothing else goes down in these parts; but it is easier to preach than to practice. I can't do any more: for heaven's sake give me a glass of brandy.

"That's good, I guess," replied Sam, "you eternal hypocrite. Why the devil can't you drink your brandy like everybody else, like a man, hands up, above board, without cheating or trickery? I don't like all this parade."

Nevertheless Sam gave him some of the comfortable liquor, and when he saw him a little revived, said:

"Well, Ahab, what the deuce are you doing here. The last time I saw you the preachin' trade was good, and you was doin' pretty well with your new rule of grammar that the feminine gender is superior to the masculine. Come, don't cry, Ahab, what's the use of that? Bolt your brandy and tell me all about it.

"Alas," replied Ahab, sobbing, "it didn't end well. The fathers and mothers thought that their girls came too often to submit their consciences to me and to struggle against the evil Spirit. Judge Lynch got under way, and would, I reckon, have hung me up at the door according to your republican ideas of justice, when I got timely notice, and cut my stick. Now I am a Korkornite, and have a magnificent success. But I lead a deuce of a life, and I kill myself with screaming, drinking water, and acting. I reckon I'll become a Socialist. They are not hard, and their rule will suit me; everybody does as he likes. What do you think, Sam? Can one make something out of it? Is it a good thing? Will it last? When I speculate, I like to have all the chances on my side."

"Ahab," said Sam, "you make me tremble. You're a real devil. Turn farmer or merchant, and quit your preachin' trade."

"I," cried the now half-intoxicated Ahab, "I'll never put up with a common trade. Hurrah for Socialism, it's easy, it's free, and it's the fashion." And he fell under the table.

It is by this sort of example that Sam Slick initiates the reader into the popular genius of the nation. He visits the manufactories as a draughtsman, and "takes off the factory girls." Politics, the arts, commerce, are his, personified and living. It is an excellent method—no hypothesis, but all experience.

What is the result of this laborious observation, the most attentive, profound, and naïve, to which the New World has ever been submitted? It does not generalize certain results, and lean upon deductions and conjectures, but penetrates into the secrets of manners, discovers the slightest springs of the on-going elaboration, and weighs with care all the elements which constitute American society. The result is, that nothing is as yet complete in these regions, and the formation now in progress, advancing with a formidable quickness, devouring time and space, yet ever seeing time and space before it, has not yet performed the half of its work.

We southern Europeans, to whom languishing and degenerate Rome bequeathed a language which we afterwards mutilated, institutions which we deformed, and memories which we adored as pedants—we, wear wrinkles in our cradle. The Americans inherit no material civilization. Behind and before them are the forest and the ocean. Therefore their physical activity is unlimited. But they are heirs of so much intellectual civilization, that it crushes them ; and they cannot advance one step upon the way. Directors of industrial civilization, they follow intellectual civilization. You must study this prodigious movement, and this complete nullity in Haliburton's book.

But by what eccentricity, you will say, do you go to the limits of the world, not far from Newfoundland and Labrador, to find a book which is not literary, not written in English, and does not treat of the great interests of humanity ? . The life of Tennesee planters, New Scotland colonists, is of very little importance to us. What new legislation, what ingenious system do you bring us. What new light upon human destiny, is *formulized*, as the modern thinkers say, in this useless work ? Surely none. But we do not stand in need of systems and theories—those baloons floating high and low in our atmosphere for our amusement ought to suffice us. Continue this easy amusement, the last charm of feeble minds, and make plenty of laws ; Europe awaits a great many still. Build with enthusiasm those paper edifices, those sublime card-castles. Leave to other minds *their* pleasure.

Never, until ours, has any epoch been night and day visible and transparent in its most secret motions. Now we can hear the inner mystery of the world, feel its giant pulsations, watch with mournfully ardent interest the palpitations of that central and living point, which is the heart of humanity, and which is called civilization ; observe whether it be displaced, and whither the life goes; in a word, we seize as it flies, and stenograph, that eternally improvising drama called History, which other men will one day try to write. In the olden times, the rarest intelligences could not succeed; men saw but two steps before them. Julius Cæsar knew poorly what was happening in Persia and Armenia; and the internal affairs of India and Samothrace were nearly unknown to sovereign Rome. Now, all the springs that move society do their work before our eyes; the world is of crystal. It is a glorious joy to listen to the deadened and measured sound of those wheels, and to share in those regular transformations, which were once taken for unexpected and mysterious phenomena.

So we may leisurely contemplate that easily explicable miracle, the peopling and fertilizing of North America; its attraction to itself of the life and force of decaying Europe, and its disposition to destroy all foreign possessions in its neighborhood. Vast hive of laborers, storehouse, shop, farm, arsenal, manufactory, workshop, it fancies itself a democracy and is only a fabric. Its leisure hours have not yet arrived; the giant does not yet know his strength. But what keeps off the solution of the problem is, that America extends its limits by the magnetism of example. Texas is hers: the old French of Canada incline to be hers; languishing New Scotland expects a new life, if, in her turn, she become a republic. So the terms of the problem are multiplied. The other side of the seas, all is to come, all is hope, ardor, while on us the Past weighs heavily, and we fret ourselves amid the ashes.

Of the two new and threatening societies now being formed, one under the laws of the Czar, the other under the invocation of Washington, the more interesting, by its energy, traditions, Teutonic descent and free form, is North America.

CHAPTER IX.

THE FUTURE OF NORTH AMERICA AND OF THE UNITED STATES.

SECTION I.

RESUMÉ.

We have exposed without indulgence, it may be with some severity, whatever is incomplete in the civilization of the United States; unsatisfactory or hollow in the arts, sketchy or rude in their social position, factitious or chimerical in their literary pretensions. We have reproduced them as in an inventory without accepting them blindly, without taking the responsibility of their own partial criticism, nor yet the severe appreciation of English travellers, more attentive to the faults or absurdities of their transatlantic brethren than is becoming among relatives. While the English analyzed so passionately, the Americans worked on; and what proves that they were endowed with life is that one by one the spots disappeared, the feebleness vanished and the bitter criticisms of English travellers became less applicable.

What then was the element of strength, which *lived* at the bottom of the American Institution?

A moral and traditional element, which I have exhibited in the first chapter of this work, and of which I have now only to indicate the development.

SECTION II.

THE BEE—FORMATION OF AN AMERICAN VILLAGE.

Towards the borders of Arkansas or Illinois, in the profound and inexplored solitudes at the foot of the Rocky Mountains, you may see on some fine summer day, the arrival of a family whose entire furniture is contained in a wagon drawn by a small horse; sometimes the husband and wife form the association, sometimes one or two children serve to complete the republic. The father chooses the *location.* Here is a river, oaks, and turf; but what next? He has no tools, and to build his log house he needs time, workmen and money. He has no arms but his own and his wife's, maybe those of Jonathan and Samuel, his sons, not yet grown. The old settlers, in the neighboring forest, who have long had their log houses, and who know the country, go to see the strangers, not merely to salute but to aid them. No preparation, no making ready, no tumult, no vain phrases. Time is precious. They say little, but content themselves with the most simple things; they imitate the Bee; they work together for the profit of the new-comers. This real and active fraternity has borne great fruit. The oak falls, is dressed and rolled to its place; the house grows; a roof only is wanted, and fifty ready arms soon construct it. When the harvest comes in, the wheat must be threshed; again the comrades come, and a week's work is done in one day: what would have cost the solitary settler a month's toil is accomplished in the twinkling of an eye. The new settler returns what he has received; and when new ones come they receive the same services. You borrow your neighbor's horse, and he your plough, everybody helps everybody else, and misery reaches no one.

These habitudes constitute the moral life, i. e. the essential and fundamental life of America. They begin, at first, in a community of five or six log houses. The idea of God and of the Bible are present to all these men, Saxon or Scottish, German or Dutch, coarse men if you will, and for the most part Calvinists. Next, they must have a church; and, to build one of logs, a new *Bee* is formed. All the world, Quakers and Armenians, Methodists and Catholics, help. The clumsy wooden pulpit will be occupied by the nomadic preachers who may traverse the desert. It is not only a community, but a communion. The sympathetic law of Christ makes itself understood in that rudely-constructed edifice; meetings become frequent and regular; they pray together. Some souls have scruples; the Calvinistic leven is there, severe and analytic, full of dreamy doubts, nor docile to the yoke of thought. Is it then thus that men should pray to God? The dissidents, however, claim the right to their peculiar dogma, and a second church is built, forming a new community. The Quakers' chapel is burnt, and the Catholics lend them theirs; the Presbyterians do the same for the Anabaptists.

If we search for the true constitutive elements of the *Bee*, which has just built an American village under our eyes, we will find three—the element Christian and Calvinist, adapted to association; full of charity for one's neighbor and of sympathy for his sufferings;—the Germanic element, patient, victorious, laborious, attached to the soil and to tradition;—and the element of enterprise and boldness, younger than the other two of which it is born, and which it fecundates without destroying. Combine these three elements as you will, they will always preserve variety, liberty, and attachment to tradition: leaving to Religion absolute independence; to politics the liberty of federative groups; and in private and public manners, encouraging equality of relations, individual independence and voluntary association. The United States, at present, are but a development of these three principles.

Community is everywhere without injury to liberty. The work of the *bee* recommences in the phases of civil life; they meet to settle the manner of repairing the bridge, placing the ferry-boat, settling the school-fund, laying out the road, clearing the forest. As to the tax, that is soon settled; everybody knows that he needs the bridge and the ferry-boat, and so pays his part. Then new voluntary associations, or rather deliberative meetings to decide upon the position and support of a tribunal. At first all the heads of families take part, then the number of voters becomes too great, and a chamber of representatives is formed to take care of the little interests of the commonwealth. These interests multiply. The trappers steal the horses and cattle, the Indians fire the barns, and a militia is organized. Assurance against fire becomes indispensable. All this is done progressively, with order and by the same process—always the *bee*. There is no government, each being able to govern himself, none desiring the vain and mournful care of governing the others.

So grows an American village. Nothing resembles it in France or in Europe. There, mutual aid is not thought of; all wish to command, and never have they seen "the gathering of the bee." Read the *Polyptique d'Irminion*, naïve picture of the eighth century; there are nothing but graduated slaves, whose misery is soothed by Christianity. It matters little whether the peasants group about the château or the abbey; first the Roman, then the German, then the lawyer or perhaps the abbot, have governed the young village, and aided or impeded its progress; but no service rendered by equal to equal; ever benefit or oppression, gratitude or vengeance. And now that eighteen centuries are gone, look at the moral condition of a French village; the loveliest country in Europe lives in a state of universal hostility. All hatreds ferment with all interests; the schoolmaster hates the curé, who excommunicates the schoolmaster; the miller is jealous of the neighboring manufacturer, and he is full of envy towards the representative, the cultivator, the vigneron. Count the adverse elements, the furious dissonances made to howl and fret together by our civil wars; near the Suzerain, to whom the Restoration has given back his estates, lives the assiduous reader of Voltaire, proprietor of some national property bought during the Revolution; not far from him is the General of the Empire, who elbows the advocate of the overthrown Restoration; finally, some relics of the Revolutionary whirlpool, faithful to their creed of 1793, are neighbors of the young Communist, who hates the unity of Spartan democracy. These layers touch each other repulsively: Society full of hatred! Concert of vengeances.

The French or Italian hamlet cannot govern itself. It has neither the instinct nor the science of autonomy. Nursed in another cradle, formed of other elements, it wears the old stamp of authority, or, if you like, of servitude. Rival and jealous passions ferment there with the memories of ancient wrongs; not that the souls are worse, but that the customs are bad.

Without that moral predisposition which gives the faculty of self-government, republican institutions could not exist two years, even in the United States. It is the Germanic and Christian sentiment of active solidarity, or real community, of fraternity close and a little wild, which sustains and vivifies them! The *Bee*, a voluntary association of individuals and families, marches always on; after establishing the tax, it institutes the sub-treasury, which becomes the local bank, an easy transformation. This bank issues local notes, makes each man's money profitable, and lends to the laborer who wishes to buy a horse or a plough. Everybody being a banker, no one wishes to destroy the state. The water-course near moves the mill whither each brings his corn, or his planks to be sawn: then more mighty mills arise, attracting everybody's capital, the widow's, the orphan's, the journalist's; who dare burn those mills, which belong to all? Capital does not accumulate as in France; the money, which they greatly love, passes through a thousand hands; specie is never idle, a great banker seldom exists. Confidence is the mainspring. Rhode Island, for her 100,000 inhabitants, has 65 banks, of which the capital varies from $100,000 to $2,500,000, the total reaching $50,000,000. And the shares are by statistic report distributed thus:

Women,	shares 2,438
Mechanics,	673
Farmers and Laborers,	1,245
Savings' Banks,	1,013
Teachers,	630
Private Estates,	307
Charitable Institutions,	548
Corporations,	157
Public Officers,	438
Sailors,	434
Merchants,	2,038
Retailers,	191
Lawyers,	977
Doctors,	326
Churchmen,	220
	11,645

Thus everybody owns something; every man who works is a capitalist, buys one share, then a second, and ends by the purchase of a store or a vessel. The bank pays its own expenses, the community profit by the rest.

It is surely convenient for the laboring man to have near him, the shop where money is sold, where farmer and mechanic can be supplied according to their means and credit. The inhabitant of the smallest place need not send his savings to the great city for investment. In almost every town in America, tailors, shoemakers, widows, orphans, making up some hundred and fifty capitalists, are all owners of the local bank which lends at 6 per cent., and pays it back in dividend. The shareholder helps his trade with what he borrows, and augments his capital by the industry which this capital supports. What member of the community so humble, so ignorant as not to be interested in the preservation of a society which is but an aggregation of individual interests.

The log-houses disappear. Cities are seen. The speculator and the capitalist, always eager, turn to their own advantage the situation which they did not create, and which they may injure or destroy, if the essential force of manners do not triumph over all else. You see men who have or who desire money, using this young society as a gaming table. They ruin or enrich themselves: their fortunes crumble or increase like mountains of sand that rise or disappear at the will of the desert-wind: the basis rests immutable. The *Bee* still lives and labors; there still exists the same mainspring of moral and physical energy which borrows and lends with equal facility, the same activity of mutual aid, the same Christian spirit of strife against evil; of brotherhood in that strife, of equality in duties and expenses, of free will in expansion. One expects nothing from the state: what is the state? One does not dream of Utopia; why should one? No one curses a Past which possessed all the seeds of American self-government, that is, the greatness of the United States. He is a true Englishman, that American shipbuilder who agrees with the rail-road proprietors, with the engineer, the mechanic, the settler, without fancying that he needs a government to protect him, and in whose soul is a rooted belief that the best society is that where everybody agrees to command nobody.

Take from America her spirit of Christian brotherhood, of antique Teutonism and of hardy enterprise, or any one of the three, and her prosperity will disappear.

Large and fertile neighboring territories, some nominally republican, others subject to a distant metropolis,—Mexico or Canada,—one with institutions copied from the United States, the other under British dominion, but with French memories: these will arrive at nothing. The Spanish republics vegetate in convulsive torpor. The French Canadian farmer, full of heart, bravery, often of cleverness, sociable, charitable, ingenious, has not been able to create a society nor even to sustain himself. "Nothing," says Lord Durham, "is more striking than the difference of situation, cultivation, and riches, between the two fractions of the same country, inhabited and cultivated by two different races. The Canadian territory towards the great Lakes is perhaps the best in America yet it yields scarcely anything. The vast peninsula in Upper Canada between Lakes Huron and Erie, comprising the most fertile grain-land on the Continent is left to nature. Between Amherstburg and the sea, the selling value of the soil is infinitely greater in the English United States than in old French Canada. The difference in some parts is as 1000 to 100. The acre sold for a dollar in Canada is worth five or six, two steps off in the United States. Opposed to the old French city of Montreal, where all is repose and silence, rises and grows the young Anglo-American city of Buffalo. Buffalo is of yesterday, Montreal dates from the 16th century. Everywhere the same contrast; here, forests cleared, fields cultivated, houses built, farms made the most of by the Anglo-Americans; there, an infructuous solitude, where a few colonists vegetate in poverty, scattered wrecks of old French families, without the spirit of enterprise, without roads or markets, and separate from each other by considerable intervals." It is the same Christian and Teutonic genius of voluntary association, of sympathetic industry which, in Ireland, opposes the riches of the imported Scots to the poverty of the old Irish.

Persuade a Norman, Picard, or Gascon peasant to deposite his weekly gains in a central bank! Tell that vigneron who distrusts the smith, that smith who loves not the doctor, that doctor who detests the curé, to form an association—they will do nothing of the kind. All community of interest is impossible, since each treasures up what he can gain, and is on his guard against his neighbor. Suppose besides that the University man is at war with the Churchman, the tax-gatherer with the instructor, and that the thundering voice of the journals reanimate incessantly these mutual hatreds; beneath the ashes which covers and smothers them; what harmony can come from such an accumulation of antagonisms.

Listen to writers of statistics;—they tell us that in France a population of 35,000,000 produce only 520,000,000 bushels of corn of all sorts in a year; that they raise cattle in greatly inferior disproportion to the number of men; that with the finest ports and the most admirable sail, France is relatively poor. The moral main-spring ruined; the spirit of enterprise wanting, or working wrongly; the tavern taking the place of the church; present enjoyment absorbing the future; the spirit of family attacked; no local nor popular banks; a profound demoralization seizing upon the manufacturing towns;—all this comes not from the Present, but from the Past; and thus the loss of power, which for two centuries has not ceased to impoverish France, is sufficiently explained. What statistics could give a complete list of the capital wasted by our useless and unhappy wars, our false theories, our inactivity, our carelessness. Between 1803 and 1815 our strife with Europe cost 6,000 millions of francs and 1,000,000 men; we paid the allies 1500 other millions, and lost in products destroyed by two invasions as many more. In twelve years 9000 millions of francs. Go back to 1800 or to 1789 you will find a sum almost as great exhausted by the wars of the Revolution, and the destruction of industry. Therefore in spite of the progress of science and of light, the wound is very painful.

"I have often," says the engineer Cordier, "traversed twenty square leagues without finding a canal, a route, a manufactory, or even a domaine. The whole country seemed a desert, or a place of exile abandoned to the unfortunates whose interests and necessities are equally ill-understood, and whose distress increases constantly because of the high price of transport, and the low price of products." "The unfortunate condition of the French working classes," says the British Consul Newman, in his report to the British Commissioner of the poor laws, "has no better proof, than the resolutions recently taken by the manufacturers and the Breton farmers, to employ none who would not leave in their hands a weekly sum for the support of their wives and children. They are generally quick, active people, who make good soldiers, but the moral culture is null; nearly all the small farmers come back from the fair half-drunk, and the week's money is spent by Monday."

"It is known," says another report, "that the abuse of paternal power has enfeebled the population of the department *du Nord*. A father uses his child to gain a few more centimes. He sends him to school but leaves him there only until his feeble arms become of some use to his parents. And this child, worn out before he is grown up, curses, as you can imagine, a father who has shown him no pity."

See then what the most active, ingenious, generous race of Europe has done with the fair land which God gave it. The race is not to be accused, but the Past. The tradition was erroneous.

Despite the ameliorations of the last sixty years in material interests, it is plain that the old Celtic spirit is not yet vanquished, a spirit prompt in war, in art, yet mentally disorderly, incapable of self-government, and kindling the war which labor now wages against capital.

In the United States, contrary traditions have produced contrary effects. On-going in its force, trusting itself, expecting nothing from one's equals, demanding nothing from government, succoring one's neighbor, and being succored by him; these form the secret: these are the English habits, which, under an aristocratic form have made the prosperity of Great Britain and which America now carries out to their fullest extent.

Hence comes universal hope, general industry, ardent desire for the advancement of the race. Born of the Christian and Teutonic elements, these three forces abound in America: Charity, Good Sense, Activity. From the combination of these three forces, not one can be spared without injury to the organic play of such a state as the Union; love, intelligence, power. A proud and sympathetic tradition becomes self-government, resolves itself into the government of province by province, commune by commune, municipality by municipality, of each group by itself, of man by man.

The true device of the United States is not "every man *for* himself," a motto of destruction, but "every man *by* himself and *for* all;" a motto of sympathy and creation. Nothing astonishes and scandalizes, I will not say an American, but a peasant of Norway, Denmark or Scotland, so much as to hear that there is in the old Roman countries a unit Power, which acts for everybody, supports the schools, pays the clergy, builds the bridges, sustains the theatres, sells tobacco and salt, erects hospitals, keeps whole armies of clerks to copy and endorse letters. The Teuton peasant is still more amazed when he learns that if the government were to withdraw its aid, everybody would revolt.

He does not understand our two habitudes;—the rage of wishing to be governed, and that of biting the hand that governs us.

SECTION III.

GROWTH OF THE AMERICAN REPUBLIC—FIRST AND SECOND ERA OF AMERICAN CIVILIZATION IN THE UNITED STATES.

That tradition of liberty in unity, order in independence, has no need of laws to exist in America. The manufacturer is free to employ or dismiss his workmen, the workman to accept or refuse the price; the capitalist to do what he pleases with his money, the farmer and the merchant to capitalize their gains. The State and the law never interfere; moral law, the main-spring, is in the character of the people. There is no forced and theoretic association, but a sympathy of fact and habit, an Anglo-Saxon *clubbing*, perpetual, ineffaceable as their manners, which governs the whole country, and without which self-government would be a chimera: they unite everywhere mutually to aid one another. It is so thoroughly a memory of race, a Germanic tradition, dating from the epoch of the *Rachinbourgs* and of the *Wittenagemot*, that the Irish, so abundant in the States, have difficulty in getting on: their habits of disorder and isolation often compromise the destinies of the Union. Even among the half-savages, who, skin-clad and armed with an axe, go to clear the forest, this creative sentiment exists; they too associate to create, never to destroy. They constantly reproduce the phenomenon of voluntary association, which we find on a larger and more active scale in civilized cities, for instance, the Puritan city, Boston.

In 1844, says Mr. Mackay, the English ship Britannia, carrying despatches, and bound to quit the port on the first of February, was caught in ice seven feet thick at the docks and two feet thick at its extremity seven miles out to sea. The vessels lying in the clear water were loaded from carts driven from the shore. So soon as this blockade became known, a *bee* was gathered as rapidly as if in the woods of Ohio or Tennessee. This opulent and literary city arose to deliver the British mail-boat. The *workies*, commanded by engineers, traced a canal in the ice seven miles long by two hundred feet wide; two furrows, seven inches deep, were drawn by a plough, ice blocks an hundred feet square, were sawn out and pushed toward the sea. This enormous and dangerous operation was performed in two days; but already new ice, two feet thick, had formed. The Bostonians came to see how the Britannia, now armed with an iron cuirass, would overcome this obstacle. She managed to break the ice, and advancing at the rate of seven miles an hour, issued triumphantly from the port, amid the hurrahs of twenty thousand Bostonians. Tents were erected on the shore, the *élite* were there in sleighs. A thick couch of snow covered the ice; the sun rose, and joyous shouts filled the air, as they pushed the boat with long poles, or followed it, in row boats, to the sea. To complete the good work, of which an engraving perpetuates the memory, Great Britain offered an indemnity, but the Bostonians gallantly refused.

It is surely curious, and useful to examine how such manners were formed, what institutions they have produced, how they sustain each other, what vices have been introduced or have resulted from them; what is the actual progress of a society so organized, and towards what future it marches. To find the actual source of these manners, we are to read neither Franklin nor Jefferson, personages of the second epoch of America, but the Narratives of the first Pilgrims, "Extracts of early documents relative to the old Puritans," and the ridiculous or fanatical books of the preachers, from 1630 to 1680, Increase Mather and his friends. The strange story of the Astorian expedition, by Alexander Ross, and the "History of the United States," by Hildreth, will show us in spite of what obstacles the Puritan genius was developed.

Finally, passing by a crowd of English travellers who deal merely in useless satire, or in parody of the institutions and their faults, you should consult the work of Mr. Mackay, "The Western World," where the statistic anatomy of the country, at present, is examined with extreme care, and the work of the American, Mr. Carey, a book wearisome by its doctrinal tone, its apologetic excess, its panegyric, or rather its metaphysical apotheosis of the American Union. These works, which explain the true origin and actual character of this great people, are to be followed by some sixty volumes of contradictory narrative, Mrs. Houston, on the West, Revere and Wilkse on California, Lanman on the Alleghanies, MacLean on the Rocky Mountains. By comparing these works, which differ in tendency, object and details, we can discover the Future of America, and the secret of her elevation, which is not her political institutions, as some imagine, but sympathy, reason, energy; not by blind fury against the Past, but by the development of tradition; not by the abolition of the Christian spirit, but by Christianity, not by laws but by manners; not by theory but by facts, not by revolutions but by evolutions. No American State is revolutionary; all association is *evolutive*. Now all "evolution" is, in itself, organic, all revolution inorganic, one full of life, precedes Life; the other, mortal, gives Death. Revolutions are crises which always kill nations by destroying their principles, evolutions are advancements, which save by developing the germs of a people.

The bee-hive which covers America did not issue suddenly from the earth, nor is it the fruit of metaphysical combinations. The mighty seed was in the colony founded by Sir Walter Raleigh in 1585, and which lasted but a little while, because the Christian element was feeble in it. In 1606 came an hundred English Calvinists. In 1619 the first colonial assembly was convoked, and decided as sovereign upon the colonial interests. The Puritans of 1620 continued the work with more authority and austerity. Minding danger and toils but little, they planted their tents upon a rock bathed by the ocean, surrounded by sterile sands, under a vigorous sky; there, happy in free, mutual labor, they gather their first *Bee*, enact laws, choose magistrates, act by representatives, recognize a nominal king, allow the metropolis to call itself their mistress, and in reality organize a republic They pay their taxes and ask nothing more.

The first epoch of the colony is from 1620 to 1715, a period quite savage. In 1732, the age of Voltaire, there was not one portrait painter in America; not a press until 1640. They were busy in clearing the forests, with difficulty enough; to excite themselves in the combat with Nature, they had chosen the most rebel soil. The first college was founded and endowed with £800, by the minister, John Harvard, in 1639, and is now the most celebrated in the United States.

The first press, in the same locality, Cambridge, printed in 1640 a detestable translation of the Psalms of David. There was not a single Anglo-American city until 1564. In all North America, there were for a long time but two cities, St. Augustine, founded by the Spaniards in Florida, and Santa Fé, which still exists. A century later, the entire population was only 134,600 souls, not to count the Indians who were never numerous, at greatest some 300,000. The title of "New World" was just.

Between 1615 and 1715, the rejected of Europe, the refractory elements, the banished, the discontented, regicides, adventurers, Catholics driven away by Protestants, Protestants by Catholics, some dreamers, many poor folks who knew not what else to do, came to mingle with the Anglo-Saxon Puritans who fled from the religious tyranny and oppressive monopoly of James VI. and his son. The manly and organizing spirit of the Puritans governed all. The colonists formed groups, *lees*. Difficulty was great, poverty extreme; they honored toil, prayer, severity of life and probity.

During this phase, barbarous if you like, but certainly heroic, this people, enterprising, commercial, colonizing, sea-loving as their fathers were, changed neither their spirit nor their race. All commerce is perilous, therefore they have courage; all cultivation is fatiguing, so they have perseverance; all association is annoying, therefore they show devotion. The old Teutonic and Christian spirit grows root and branch, like the oak, which is its emblem. If London and Whitehall regulate the soil and make the laws, Tradition, in despite of those laws, organises a community, not a republic of old

Greek heroes, or Roman patricians, but a Northman's *Commonwealth*, a word which does not indicate riches held in common, but the *weal*, the *well-being* of all. It was already all republican; in the charter-governed provinces which elected their own magistrates and deputies; in the crown provinces which chose their own representatives, and in the provinces held, by royal grant, by individuals who strove in vain to annul or modify the results of election. One mind and one soul vivified these three political establishments. All the colonists wished to govern themselves and they did so.

From 1643, in the days of Louis XIV., the colonies formed a league offensive and defensive; each sent two commissioners to the Congress of the Confederation. In 1676 a thoroughly republican charter, accorded to Rhode Island, finished the work, so much in conformity with the old affinities of the race. The metropolis, obedient to the middle-age corporations, could not destroy the same principle in the colonies, the free spirit of corporation.

Shaftesbury and Locke took part in the political destiny of the colonies. The laws meditated by Locke, dictated by his tolerant and rationally free mind, remained in force until 1842, and the whole republican Constitution of this state, comes from this philosopher, the friend of William of Orange.

I have said that they were poor. The grandfather and father of Franklin took pay in *wampum* for want of specie. The little gold and silver brought by the May-flower had soon found its way back to the metropolis in return for her products. New emigration brought a little more, but money was soon wanting; they were forced to trade with corn, flour, cattle, even with furniture and houses, if they were in debt. A special law ordered the value of objects of trade to be appraised by "three *intelligent* persons," one chosen by the debtor, one by the creditor, the third by the judge. They paid with beaver skins and musket balls, which latter were worth a farthing each, and were current to the amount of a shilling. The Dutch of Manhattan taught the Puritans a more commodious means, the use of the shell-work called *wampum*. Three black grains or six white ones made a penny; these were made into strings worth from threepence to six shillings.

So went on the arduous work of civilization, not by wealth but by resolute labor, by the *bee*, by mutual aid, by individual respect, by the liberty of each province. Every township, centering in itself, free to exist as it could, faithful to its personal customs, was yet obedient to the great Christian laws. There was no unique and absorbing centre; no theoretic pretension, no rhetoricians, no disciplinary unity. The idea of property was everywhere distinct, giving to each family the greatest possible happiness, to each village the greatest possible wealth; to each province the greatest possible influence and commerce. All these groups, balanced by their mutual strength, had a common and general elective motive power; hope, life, activity. Nothing violent, ambitious, chimerical or hazardous; there was only the simple and normal development of the Teutonic genius, of the Christian institutions of the Middle Ages, their essence, their variety, their strength and their freedom.

Not only are the useful and fertilizing elements of this great epoch still found in America, but the fiercer Middle Age elements are neither wanting nor annulled; they form a part integral, of the solid germ from which a new civilization must spring, and possess all the qualities requisite, resistance and endurance.

It is not the absence but the excess of Christian sentiment which has founded America; there it is perpetuated under the form of mitigated fraternity. The Puritan of 1620, a protestant inquisitor, who went to struggle against Nature, only to escape the religious tyranny of Europe, would make us quake to-day, estimable as he was. Armed, in his turn, with fire and sword to smite all heretics, wizards, and witches, this martyr of Catholic or Anglican persecution, became, as soon as he found himself free, a fearful persecutor. The first epoch of American civilization is full of his cruelties. The principal types are the famous Increase Mather, and his son Cotton, two figures colder than Calvin and bloodier than Knox. The first Colonists coarse, violent, fierce and austere, of implacable severity, pushed credulity and fanaticism to the extremity of barbarity. Honest they were, serious, sincere, manly; they could fight against savages, cold, hunger, distress, if need be, against the very Devil; indeed, they had a peculiar taste for a combat with that personage. If they did not discover him on their way, they went in search of him, and frequently gave themselves the pleasure of burning a witch. Yet they did not destroy American Society, they founded it. Fanaticism is the exaggeration of Faith, but not its poison; a formidable astringent, it proves the social vitality of which it is the excess and the abuse.

The old municipal registers of some of the towns in Massachusetts, between 1640 and 1680 have been reprinted. "Jane Edwards is to be imprisoned for having pressed Jonathan Williams' hand.—The little Johnson shall have thirty stripes and be put on bread and water, for sleeping in church.—Mary Merivale shall do public penance, bare-footed, for pronouncing the name of God without respect."—As for witch histories, they abound from the beginning and recall the history of Urbain Grandier and the possessed of Loudon. "Between 1688 and 1692" says a chronicler, "we had in Boston a fearful and singular example of the wiles of the demon. In a respectable family, four young children, the eldest a girl of thirteen, and the youngest a boy of nine, were attacked with demoniacal convulsions, which presented all the symptoms given by the best writers upon the subject. These children complained of being bitten, pinched and tortured by invisible beings; they barked like dogs and *miaouled* like cats. The frightened father hastened to send for Dr. Oaks, a renowned theologian, and a great physician of souls, who declared that the children were possessed. An old Irish woman, a servant in the house, was denounced as a witch by the eldest sister, who had quarrelled with her; the other children confirmed the testimony of their sister. The four ministers of Boston, and the one of Charlestown, met in the house and made long prayers, by which the youngest boy found himself considerably soothed. The others persisted and the Irish woman was imprisoned. Being asked if she was a sorceress, she replied "she flattered herself that she was." As she was very poor and of lowly estate, she fancied that her relations with the demon would procure her some credit. She was hanged.

This occurred during the voyage of Increase Mather to London whither he had gone to ask aid for the colony; he had left behind him a worthy son, Cotton Mather, aged twenty-five, as ardent as his father in pursuit of the demon. He took an active part in the execution of the Irish woman, and then desiring to examine more closely the diabolical operations, he caused the eldest girl to be taken to his house, where he lodged her, watched all her actions, followed all her motions, and wrote a journal about her which still exists, printed, under the title of "Memorable Providences manifested on the subject of possession and sorcery." In a special document, joined to this work, the four ministers attest the truth of all therein contained, and Cotton adds a thundering preface, wherein he does not fail to uplift himself against those

Sadducees who will not believe in the Devil, and are consequently *Atheists.* The book was reprinted in London, with a preface by the worthy Baxter.

For fifty years, an epidemic of demoniac possessions vexed Massachusetts. Four years after the young girl, retired into private life, had ceased to be the object of popular curiosity; the whole village of Salem was possessed. Curious scenes took place in the church. Rival women arose and accused each other of sorcery in the temple itself. Many innocents perished, and the affair was only put a stop to by tortures.

At the moment that these fierce ideas began to be softened, when the Christianity of these men, quitting this exalted fanaticism, became a more humane and prudent, even a finessing charity, in 1715, Franklin was nine years old Activity was preserved, energy had not disappeared, the religious spirit existed in men's hearts, as powerful, and less sharp. Franklin and Washington, apostles of toleration, gentleness, and pacific activity, began to rise and grow in the midst of this reactionary movement, submitted to a new impulse. Franklin represents the second epoch which now expires, and which was signalized by the American independence.

SECTION IV.

THIRD ERA OF NORTH AMERICA—VESTIGES OF PURITAN FANATICISM—MORMONS AND MILLERITES—CATHOLICS IN THE VALLEY OF THE MISSISSIPPI.

A third era is commencing. Now that colonization, finished on the Atlantic sea-board, goes on triumphantly in the Valley of the Mississippi, and from the great northern lakes to Sierra Nevada, the new reaction manifests itself: it is an impulse towards enterprise, war, conquest. The old faith, in its rigor, has left few traces: activity has become extraordinarily energetic: charity and concord have transformed themselves, little by little, into patriotism. the love of glory and of war break forth strongly. Still the Past lives in the Present, and the old Puritan germ is not dead. Nine tenths of the citizens of the United States are still Protestants: the Northern States preserve some Puritan sap; those of the South lean towards tolerance, towards Presbyterianism or towards Catholicism, of which the activity concentrates itself in the fertile Valley of the Mississippi. All the North, especially where the Mathers lived, dislikes the pacific element of this modified protestantism which is so general in southern and western cities, which is protected and favored by men of instruction, the capitalists, the whigs, or, as they may be called, the moderates or conservateurs. The new element of warlike enterprise, peculiar to democrats, to country-folk, to workmen, to the active, vehement mass, always eager to change the Present, mingles easily and well with the old Puritan element. Hence, that strange enterprise of the Mormons, who are trying to reconstitute, in the Rocky Mountains, the Biblical, patriarchal unity of power; and hence the sect of Millerites, Millenium people, who in their turn took refuge in the White Mountains.

The Millerite and Mormon follies are marks of the alliance of the popular genius, with the old Puritan leaven.

The Prophet Miller announced the end of the world for October 23, 1844; but as the event did not correspond with the prediction, he put it off until October 23, 1847. The popular masses of the North were shaken, and the fanatic movement extended as far as Philadelphia. Farmers neglected their labor, and public officers were appointed to rescue their harvests. In signing their receipts, they would say, "I trust that this is the last time." Concord, a little village of New Hampshire, was entirely drawn into the movement. Between Plymouth and Boston several proprietors sold their estates, and gave the money for the construction of a tabernacle wherein were to be gathered all the faithful, clad in white for their ascension. The Bostonians made a good affair of it. In many shop-windows you read, "White robes of every texture, size, and shape, for the ascension on the 23d." Some Methodist preachers and some journals encouraged this strange hallucination. Some New Yorkers passed the nights of the 23d and 24th awaiting the trumpet of the angel. A young girl, having received from her betrothed a precious necklace, desired to consecrate it to preparations for this ascension. Accordingly, she took it to a jeweller, to whom she revealed her motive. "Why," said he, "here are some silver spoons which I am now engraving for your minister; so that you see he does not believe in his own predictions."

In the most public part of Boston they built a huge shantee, capable of holding two or three thousand persons. The edifice was about to fall, and the magistrates interfered and required them to build it more strongly. The crazy troup, passed the night in it in prayer, robed in white, and singing,

> I'm all in white; my soul is clear,
> I'm going up; nought keeps me here

The flower-decked room was lighted by seven-branched candlesticks, and hung with Hebrew texts. The night passed, the morning came, nobody "went up," and the society became bankrupt. The hall became a theatre, and Mr. Lyell was amused to hear there, Hecate singing in the play of Macbeth,

"Hark, I'm called! My little spirit, see,
Sits in a foggy cloud and stays for me."

Charlatanism, speculation, hyprocrisy mingle in these customs, and make out of them what they can. A preacher establishes himself in a village, kindles the minds, inflames the hearts, and makes the credulous contribute. Rigor is pure mockery in many pretended fanatics. " Madam, " said an innkeeper, gravely, to Mrs. Houston, "this is a religious house; prayers take place regularly, but if you do not wish to assist at them, we will shut our eyes to it."

Variety, liberty, tradition reign then in America in the religious sphere, as well as in the political. The free division of the Protestant sects, themselves sub-divided into constantly sub-dividing sects perfectly realizes the prediction of Bossuet. The Methodists count 1,200,000 communicants and 7,009 ministers; the Baptists a few less; the Presbyterians 350,000 members and 3,000 ministers; Congregationalists 200,000 members and 1,800 ministers; Evangelical Lutherans, mostly Germans, 145,000 communicants and 7,500 ministers; the Episcopalians 86,000 communicants and 13,000 ministers; the Universalists 60,000 communicants and 700 ministers. The Presbyterians, conservators of the severe tradition, despite their numerical inferiority, are the richest and most influential; the Baptists and Methodists are distinguished by an ardent zeal often excessive.

The Catholic movement in this country merits attention. Repulsed at first by the general sentiment of the English Protestant Colonists, the Catholic emigrants who gave to their settlement Maryland, the name of Queen Mary Tudor, and to their capital that of Lord Baltimore, were on the defensive for a century; nevertheless the very principle of Protestantism and Germanic independence protected them in their isolation. Now they count nine hundred priests and 1,750,000 laymen. Not only do they nearly equal in numbers the most flourishing Protestant sect, but in the large cities they have powerful congregations; considerable rural districts are entirely Catholic, and the valley of the Mississippi, with its rapidly doubling population cannot help being theirs. Already are the Sisters of Charity at work in the wilderness; nineteen twentieths of the valley are sown with chapels; the cross hangs from the branches of the old trees, the mass is celebrated by the Missionaries amid those antique shades. At St. Louis and at New Orleans the best schools are Catholic; and nothing is so visible as the perfect capability of conciliation of Catholic dogma with that personal independence and social energy which the regions of Southern Europe have so irreparably, wrongly refused to favor.

A witness of this usurpation of its dominion, the old Puritan spirit awakes in *revivals*, which are religious fevers common among the Baptists, and excited by Nomadic preachers. Amid tears, sobs and convulsions four or five hundred men are plunged into the waters of regeneration. Debauchées, prodigals, adulterers, seat themselves before the people upon the "anxious seat," and confess their crimes. This fury of moral regeneration seizes sometimes upon whole provinces. Sometimes calmer parties take part against the instigators of these revivals, and cite them before the Courts of justice as "troubling the peace," or as "slanderers," if some rather vivid personality may have been uttered. "I saw one," says a traveller, "whom a band of musicians were playing out of town with the Rogue's March. A fight ensued, and when the parties came into Court and the Judge enquired why the accused had not quitted the place without noise, he replied,

"'I have my idea; the devil has his.'

"'But you break the peace.'

"'Nehemiah refused to yield to the enemies of the Lord.'

"'But,' said the judge, 'you should have followed the example of St. Paul, who had himself let out of a window in a basket. It is a more peaceful and modern precedent.'

"The laugh that ensued gave the victory to the magistrate."

One sees that such manners do not result from political mechanism.

Beneath universal suffrage and the appearance of a democracy, tradition exists. The old sap circulates in the veins of that society composed of millions of Anglo-Saxons worthy of their fathers, and who, hammer and axe in hand, continue their work and clear up an immense field for their future;—their instruments are moral and value far more than iron or steel.

SECTION V.

THE POLITICAL SYSTEM BORN OF TRADITION AND CUSTOM—FEDERATIVE HARMONY—DANGERS—WHIGS AND DEMOCRATS—FEDERALS AND ANTI-FEDERALS.

It is a profound error to regard the American institutions as new, simple, or reducible to an abstract type. It is precisely the contrary. Diversity, inseparable from liberty, is their proper characteristic. They are old as the Europe of Charlemagne, varied as humanity, practical as Reality.

The Mississippi Catholics and the Mormon Protestants, the Texan so vividly and wrathfully painted by Jonathan Sharp; the Blue Nose of Maine, the butt of Sam Slick, the

Alabamian, whose bony energy frightened Mr. Mackay, and forty other varieties of the American species crowded in that continent, having not only diverse manners and customs, but ever-conflicting interests, need a legislation and a political formula of a complexity equal to their varieties. It is not by an ingenious labor, by a judicious arrangement of the political wheels that so many cogs play within one another, that so many little spheres describe their respective elipses without striking and breaking one another. Admit that all men are equal, and the war of interests becomes naturally legitimate, society would be but one carnage, if the customs of which we have spoken, if the traditions of the Protestant hive and its laborious bees did not prevent the universal destruction, inevitable result of the strife of so many opposing interests. Now thirty-one States move freely, each in its sphere, all enclosed by the common sphere, and if there be shocks and unfortunate gratings, still the development of the national prosperity goes on.

How has this difficult end been attained? Is it by the *a priori* system, the metaphysical unity, the philosophical method? Have they divided the States by Domesday Book? or made partial or general revolutions? or broken violently the old feudal system?

The Americans have effaced the word "King," and that is all. The electoral system is the same; the States are governed by their ancient laws. They have not passed a garden-roller after the various characters and customs. They have developed not strangled.

As the corporations of the Middle Ages were governed by their own laws, which their neighbors had no power to change, so each State has its own constitution, suitable not only to the needs of the day, but elastic enough for future acquisition. There are then thirty-one local politics, thirty-one executives, legislatures, judiciary powers. All this goes on, not without collision, but without effort. The Americans have not fancied that they could violate the Teutonic and Christian traditions of their Anglo-Saxon race, nor separate the idea of liberty from the idea of variety. They have not made their institutions as philosophical dreamers. But bringing to the task the experience of the colonist and the practical simplicity of the peasant, they have continued that which succeeded so well with their fathers; what was worth nothing to them they rejected.

They were advised to constitute a deliberative chamber, on the old Roman model, a unitary, and therefore, despotic way: two chambers they did create, both emanating from universal suffrage, the one representing the principle of federal union, the other consecrated more particularly to local interests. Each of these branches of legislative power respects the other, without checking it; each has its proper limits, its determinate circumscription; out of these limits, neither can act. They had not the strange idea of concentrating power in an assembly, that most tyrannic of tyrants. Should either house surpass its powers, the Supreme Court breaks the decree or the law so made. This duality of the American chambers has been the great safe-guard of the country in all the dangers which it has run; has prevented them from blundering legislation, that is from shaming the sacred character of the law, by violence or passion. What is remarkable is, that in destroying the title of King, and the duration of hereditary power, they have compensated for the relative feebleness of his position by the real power given to the President. His veto, that right of annulling against which such an outcry was raised at the commencement of the French Revolution, can repulse any sort of bill from both houses, unless two-thirds shall take part against the President —a thing almost impossible.

Thus the executive power is joined to the legislative; the Americans not having to dispose of the stable elements of the British Constitutional Monarchy, have replaced the want of antiquity by energy of action. Hardly a session passes without the use of his right by the President, yet no one is astonished: the Americans play fair: habituated by race to the political dice, they are amazed neither at gaining nor losing, provided one plays openly and loyally.

The Lower House is directly elected; the Upper is chosen at second hand. The House of Representatives is renewed every two years, and now consists of about 230 members; every ten years, after the census, this representation is enlarged. The senators are chosen by the State Legislature, each of which sends two, precisely as in 1642, when the Provincial league was formed under the monarchy. It is easy to understand this political mechanism, rooted in the Past, and corresponding to the varieties of race, ideas, and customs which distinguished the first colonies. The Lower House represents the nation and the individuals who comprise it; the Upper House, the individual States.

Is the American Government then not one of abstract forms, but a living reality? No: it is the legitimate and inevitable development of the Past; favorable to variety, liberty, and human expansion; nor less favorable to the spirit of family, to Christian cohesion and brotherhood. Just as families assemble in isolated groups to form their *bees* in the frontier districts; as the subdivided sects and fractions of sects rally under one common banner, so do these two elements of dispersion and concentration, originating in German, Christian tradition, constitute the political mechanism of the United States, and preserve the energetic vitality of the Union. Every member of the community supports his distinct opinions and interests, manufacturers, planters, Northern men, Southern men, abolitionists, workmen, farmers, capitalists; each opposes his neighbor, and brings to the strife a crazy verbal zeal, little terrible in reality. Every township, every district, county, state, forms a sphere isolated and concentric, all united in the great sphere of the Union. In every one of these circles, they quarrel, but with little peril. There are few inflammatory discourses or tumultuous assemblies, even on election days; they vote in small groups, and in one day all is accomplished. In Vermont, where the principle of dispersion is pushed to the extreme, and where each township used to be represented, it so happened that in one township there were found but three electors—father, son, and servant, "who," says Mr. Mackay, "mutually elected each other; the father to represent the interests of property, the son the rights of the future, and the domestic the rights of labor."

Thus political life is not an universal fever, and does not act by furious fits. Occupying little time and little space, it does not prevent the farmer from cultivating his lands, nor the woodcutter from using his axe; a man is a member of the community precisely as he is father, son, or husband, without ceasing his ordinary occupations to be so. A thousand personal and local considerations; a thousand peculiar interests arm one man against the tariff, another for it; one for slavery, another for the agricultural interest-question, sub-divided and localized *usque ad infinitum*, these interest only fractions of the community. A man is a politician in his district, who is never in his county, and who will never see Washington; and, finally, the moment that the central legislature takes up an agitating question, the movement ceases in the provinces, and no matter how violently the blood may boil at the heart, the pulsations growing feeble as they reach the extremities lose all power to disturb the regular and normal life.

Such is the federative harmony of this grand whole which you would strive in vain to bring to imperial or monarchical unity. Having as political elements only family groups scattered over an immense continent, the Americans proceed by the powerful self-concentration of each group, a system which the Union has well substituted for a centralization which would destroy it. I imagine a purely central movement in a society of so many million souls habituated to variety of active and free personal exercise of their will, would open a gulf that would swallow up all.

Social life, monarchical or republican, is only a varied harmony which concentrates on a certain number of points, its normal and regular forces, and balances them by one another.

Excessive dispersion or excessive concentration would destroy the social body. Some Americans fear one of these, others are alarmed for the other. Hence their great fundamental division into whig and democrat. The democrats, (which word is not to be taken in its European sense), oppose all centralization; go for dispersion; want the annexation of other countries, Canada, Mexico; and will never rest until all North America be one great hive, with its separate cells.

"Instead of calling themselves democrats," says Channing, "a word which has no meaning in modern language, they should be named *disseminators*." They preach the division of the Union into small groups, into concentric spheres, which shall effectually absorb all the surrounding force to give it sail again energetically. They represent mobility, activity, change; they willingly oppose capital and its holders, especially manufacturing capital. Men of action, they further war, and are not particular about ideal or theoretic equity. Once in motion, they cannot be arrested even by a certain amount of injustice. It is they who show least courtesy to foreign nations," and I think," says Mackay, "that they would not hesitate to violate the constitution." This party is the symbol of extreme will and of ardent life. The invasions of Texas and Mexico, political crimes, were earnestly and unanimously supported by this party.

What makes its strength, is the Puritan element, which in many circumstances it possesses, and that need of popular aggrandisement, of warlike conquest, and of hardy passion which characterises the *third* epoch of America, and which is now. To consolidate the Central Government, and to oppose dispersion, is *Whig* politics. Such are nearly all moneyed men, manufacturers, capitalists, large proprietors; it is they who instinctively supported the National Bank, attacked by President Jackson; it is they who fight for the interests of capital in opposition to those of labor, especially of agricultural labor. Twenty other questions—slavery, manufactures, railroads, come into these opposed politics. In subsidiary questions, democrats and whigs mingle or become individually independent. Some Pennsylvania democrats join the whigs in the commercial question, while some of the Western whigs lean to the opinion of their adversaries on that topic.

At the extremity of the whig party are found those who defend capital at all hazards, the gentlemen; at the extremity of the democratic party, the nullifiers, who wish to give to each State the power of nullifying an act of Congress; there are also *separatists* who hold to a right to quit the Union when they please. These last tend toward the total destruction of the Union. The whigs call their adversaries *loco-foco*, from an accident which happened in one of their meetings;

in revenge, the democrats call them federalists, an injurious title, which they refuse to accept.

What proves the complexity of American institutions and the play of parties is, that the nullifiers and *separatists* are checked not by any political force, but by interest. They are not sentimental or theoretic democrats, but cotton planters impoverished, or menaced by the protection of Northern manufactures. South Carolina, centre of this party, which was lately headed by Mr. Calhoun, an Irishman by race, of extraordinary energy and will and great mental power, has given great trouble to the rest; the Charleston militia were ready to resist Congress, musket in hand, when the affair was settled by General Jackson. Then a few words pronounced in the House of Representatives made the Union tremble. An orator, after long inflammatory debates, spoke of dissolving the Union, a measure of which a vague presentiment may have been felt, but the actual presence of which struck the Assembly with a solemn terror. Pale, with lips trembling and crisped at his own words, stood the orator. All were still. Perhaps the divorce of loving and impassioned hearts was about to be pronounced—the suicide of America!

The Americans know well that the element of variety and liberty will never grow feeble among them: but, above all they cherish the element of association; what indeed would become of that great body without it? without that element of true Christian fraternity?

SECTION VI.

MECHANISM AND STRATEGICS OF PARTIES.

You see how delicate and of necessity how fragile is this federative mechanism, where the two elements of variety and unity keep each other constantly in check.

You must maintain in these thirty-one groups, so distinct and often divided by interest, the purely moral power of cohesion; arms will be useless. Some years ago the Legislature of Pennsylvania was assailed by a troop of rioters who put the members to flight, not without danger to life; a part of the population of Philadelphia were in accord with them, and the Harrisburg militia half in their interests. Until now the national sentiment favored and cherished by Congress has prevailed; the lower house represents the Union, the Senators the individual States, while equally acting in their collective capacity. Thus a basis of fundamental unity reunites all diversities, and will continue so to do until interests too violently hostile, definitively breaking the chain, shall establish separate republics—a thing not impossible at some distant date.

We have shown to what past origin this wise and complex equilibrium belongs. The same strategics long ago used by the Mother Country are still employed by the Americans; if a question interest the entire country each party struggles to get first possession of it. The democrats are generally the more active: in getting the question of Oregon and Texas they surpassed their enemies. The old corruptions of English politics have not been blown away by these federal republican institutions. In 1840, General Harrison was made President by rather unorthodox means. What they called the "Log Cabin Agitation" consisted of excellent dinners and breakfasts, cider, beer and ham, seasoned with political songs and served in log-cabins. The electoral corps in the country, is somewhat more independent, but at the same time more credulous. The Irish, who crowd from Belfast and Tipperary, to become American citizens, being very abundant in market, cost but little. Votes are often bought, and there are slang terms appropriated to this political jockeyism—*pipe-laying*, for example. The elector and the corrupter sit down together in a tavern, the former smoking a *pipe*. The other offers for it six, ten, twenty dollars. As long as it rests between the voter's lips, he is virtuous; when he *lays it down*, he is sold.

These singular habits, inevitable corruptions, abuses, vices, caprices, wills isolated, ever wakeful, ever ready to resist the yoke, give much trouble to the heads of parties; some fraction constantly strives to detach itself, some member of the army tries to go alone. They submit only at the last extremity and on the most vital questions. Then all these boiling waves enter one bed, and roll onward with irresistible force. Wo to him who would stem it. Independence ceases, discipline begins, and with it, tyranny. In all subsidiary questions be free, do as you please, lampoon your chief, attack the President, no one will hinder you: but once that the party is in full march, fall into your rank, sustain the standard, and fight. Even then, you may be somewhat undisciplined and eccentric, but you must not desert.

The Teutonic nations understand thoroughly well this mixture of liberty and discipline—old parliamentary tactics of Great Britain it is—a singular combination of dispersion and cohesion utterly incomprehensible by the Roman people.

The chief of a party does not lead, but is led ; they push him, and he is forced to march. The least sign of want of loyalty brands him ineffaceably, and a thousand indignant plumes and furious voices awake against him. His political life is destroyed. If, on the other hand, he be faithful to his party, so will the party be to him. "May he be hanged who would not stay by his President," said a fierce democrat to a recent traveller.

" But you make your President greater than Louis XIV."

" Well, the President is ourselves."

" Then you have all his faults, eh ? Even the Mexican war ?"

" Why, we demanded the Mexican war ; it is glory and power."

" Nevertheless it was an arbitrary and reprehensible thing."

" What of that ; no party voice dared speak against a measure which pleased the people and soothed its love of aggrandisement. If any one had spoken against it, he would soon have felt the popular choler."

" What did Webster and Calhoun think of it ?"

" They took very good care not to tell their thoughts. They are surrounded by rivals ready to seize upon their lightest words and to destroy their influence by making them unpopular."

This is the bad side of these English traditions. Each State exercises so much influence upon its citizens, that in a country of unlimited liberty originality is difficult. One or two rebel spirits like Fennimore Cooper have tried to differ in opinion from the mass, but they were put under the ban.

Hence the subjugated individualities are intellectually effaced, an anti-literary position, detestable for the arts and the exercise of thought, but excellent for the great combat with nature: hence, too, the difficulty found by superior minds in attaining the highest position. The crowd of little minds, and of envious people, often agrees to elect mediocre people, and from this come *presidents by compromise.* Among these are mentioned the democratic Mr. Polk, and the whig, General Harrison. There are other motives for nominating the insignificant. Many a man while remaining faithful in important matters to his party, gives it in lesser points which interest perhaps his own State or province. He wounds not his party, but some section or fragment of it. He displeases so and so, and if he have much talent or activity he displeases everybody. Thus each party seems to prefer a candidate for the presidency, not the most clever man, but him who possesses most negative qualities. These are disagreeable to no one, abolitionist, slaveholder, nullifier, federalist; but remain offenceless and uncommitted amid the jarring opinions of East, West, North, and South.

In a continent where free variety is so powerful, a Capital, in the European sense of the word, is as impossible as a king, The political metropolis, Washington, a desert half the year, has no importance as a city. New York, Philadelphia, Baltimore, Charleston, Cincinnati and St. Louis, are strangely placed near the borders of their respective states, and the legislature meets in none of them. Of all the large cities of America Boston is the only one which is a political centre. The very character and tradition of each city has been preserved intact: the quiet gravity, modest dress, and moderate gayety of the Philadelphians, a certain degree of calm elegance, which sometimes approaches artificial simplicity, recall Franklin and his friends, and contrast with the headlong turbulence, out door life, balls, amusements, constant reunions, and the dress often exaggerated of New York. "Who is that personage with the yellow waistcoat, and the unequalled frill?" asked a lady traveller. "It is a Connecticut farmer." "What! from *the land of steady habits?*" "Yes, but he has been in New York."

The physiognomy of Boston is no less singular—it is not astonishing that this city should play a part almost as aristocratic in the commercial life of the country. It is more English than London. To believe a Bostonian, you would suppose that English was spoken only in that city. There are still maintained customs old before the revolution; they chant the nasal hymns of Cromwell's Puritans and sit at table long after dinner. "I have seen in the streets of Boston," says a recent traveller, "the true Covenanting Calvinist and the English gentleman of Addison or Steele. Do not allow yourself to make a remark unfavorable to the country. John Bull become American is more sensitive than ever.

The Bostonian has reason to be proud of his city. Culture of the intellect, severity of manners, probity and economy are honored there, and few cities of the Union possess so many distinguished men.

It is to the puritan city that the honor belongs of having introduced into the manufacturing life, a regularity of custom and the purity of family manners; of having conciliated the most active industry with respect for liberty and the rights of humanity, in a word of having moralized capital. It is not by theory but by practice that the Bostonians have arrived here, following the path of Christian tradition. They have not ceased to honor capital profoundly; but they have offered a perspective and recompense to the laborer whom they employ, the rights of property and the culture of lands purchased by his economies. Land is so plenty in the United

States that it is no very difficult thing. The field is moral: capital is less so. The field is religious, it attaches one to the soil, and elevates man. The trickeries of which one complains in America come from free capital, from the bold speculator; but as the moral base of the cultivated field is gigantic, it balances or rather bears down the frauds and adventurousness of capital, which at least, it moralizes.

SECTION VII

THE LOWELL FACTORY GIRLS — BOSTON—THE BLACKS— PRIDE OF RACE.

One knows what manufacturing life is in France, and how the females so engaged exist, how many victims are thrown to prostitution, and what strange and abominable trades are invented by the crowding of men in the great cities. One knows what manner of education the children of the people receive in the streets and places, and how a young girl's intellect is developed in the same sphere. Laws, governments, ministers, administrators whom they are incessantly accusing can do nothing against the easy seduction, the vile reading, the misery which presses, the example which corrupts, the indifference which vitiates, the jealousy which gnaws, the desired enjoyments and the iniquity that aggravates the evil.

To cure these wounds there is nothing but the Christian principle which Calvinism has pushed to severity and which consecrates the labor of all, by basing it upon man's feebleness and his natural imperfection. This is not the moral basis which French chivalry has left to the workman and woman of France. The Child of the people, quick generous, clever and easily amused, of whom so mournfully gay a portrait has been sketched by Mr. Robert Guyard, is neither less industrious, nor less endowed that her American sister at Lowell; but she is otherwise placed. "She never drops the needle until three o'clock on Sunday; mass or other religious office do not exist for her: she prepares her little dinner and thinks of the ball as the negro forgets his *cous cousou* for the dance; finally she is happy, she goes to the ball, which is no great crime. A storm arises, the fair white frock is ruined, the week's labor is ruined. So she says, "one is forever buying yet never has anything." But on Monday next, the white frock is refreshed, and brilliant and ready for the dance." To this poor girl, when Catholicism does not guide her inexperienced youth, who has no asylum in the convent, for whom old family feeling has no protection, whose sanctuary is the ballroom, let us oppose the Lowell factory-girl, daughter of some farmer or workman, and employed by Bostonian capital Employing her strength and capacity, the manufacturer moralizes and enriches her, a great phenomenon worth some study.

The first curious fact is that a population of 30,000 now replace that of 200 which Lowell possessed in 1820. This creation of yesterday situated at the junction of the Merrimack and Concord rivers, is the second city in Massachusetts and perhaps the twelfth in importance of the Union. In 1816 there were but a few cabins. Now the spinsters of Lowell turn some two hundred thousand spindles; nearly all the important mills belong to corporations, eleven in number a little time ago. The principal one, called the Merrimack Company, owns the great canal which conducts the water power to the mills. Not only does it own the canal and the mills but all the land below the falls. Queen of the industry there, this company is the mistress or lessor of all the others. In 1844 these companies made 100,000,000 yards of printed cotton, dyed 15,000,000 yards of the same stuff, and used an eighth part of the cotton produced in America.

As you approach Lowell, you find neither smoke nor putrid exhalations. nor crooked streets: no insalubrity: a pure nature furnishes a healthy atmosphere, plenty of water, and the anthracite coal which is used there, does not produce such masses of black vapor as hang over Manchester and Sheffield. All is tranquil or even gay. The freshness of the faces, the smiles of the women, the regular animation of the town and the extreme cleanliness of the streets seduce you. If you enter the establishments you find contentment upon all faces. Schools are numerous: the poorest can send their children to the primary schools, of which there are thirty; while eight upper seminaries furnish the more wealthy with a more complete education. The workmen who love knowledge have founded what they call a "laboring man's hall," where they are taught reading, writing, and modern languages. A population of 30,000 send to school 6000 children.

The life of the Lowell women is still more remarkable. As an American never employs infant labor, the factory girl is not taken until she is fifteen years old. She gains nearly $2 a week or more and her board. She is paid monthly. As she has little to pay for lodging or dress, she puts her savings into the bank, lets it grow to a thousand dollars or so, marries some one going westward, helps her husband to conduct some new prairie-farm and dies at an advanced age, after bringing up ten or eleven children. There is nothing like the European chance-life; the sentiment of religion and of family is preserved. There is some little pedantry joined to all this, as in Geneva and Glasgow. These moral factory girls are wrong in becoming *blues.* Mrs. Trolloppe calls them the "*Precieuses ridicules* of Industry."

The Bostonians are proud of Lowell, founded as it was by

their capital, and which agrees well with their Puritanism and grave regularity. As basis of the prosperity of the model manufactories, we find the great matter of which we have already spoken, the respective liberty and mutual dependence of the States. Lowell grew by the suffering of South Carolina. The enormous and almost prohibitory tariff of 1828 assuring to capital placed in a certain way, much greater profits than to any other investment, produced the grand institutions which we have just described; manufacturing population sprang from the soil and the manufacturing capitalist soon grew rich: the corporations of Lowell increased rapidly: gigantic fortunes were made; among others, that of Mr. Appleton, a person much esteemed in that country, some noise was made about it yet it was productive of glory and benefit to America. The slave states reproached the north with using the high tariff for their own profits at the expense of the consumers; and were in turn accused of maintaining slavery, of breaking the first laws of humanity, and of compromising in the eyes of the world, the federal integrity, the moral unity and the honor of the land.

And here presents itself the problem of slavery. Legally the question is small. The constitution has recognised the right of self-government in each State, makes the question of slavery a question of local administration, and Congress has no power to issue a decree of emancipation. To this the abolitionists reply that Washington is situated in a slave State; that the rules of Congress permit and enjoin it to determine upon measures essential to its repose and dignity, and that in maintaining slavery it destroys equilibrium and wounds justice. In this thorny and narrow enclosure rest, without power to get out, parliamentary discussion and trickery; outside of the circle, you find the true causes of the difficulty.

They, like all that belongs to the United States, are rooted in tradition, respect for State rights and above all in the spirit of race.

Not only do the blacks serve as instruments necessary to the grand conquests of the Americans, but in certain localities it would be difficult or impossible to replace them: the pride of blood pushed to the extreme in the South, prevents their being considered as brethren, almost as men. The negro is not of the race, not the fellow, not like the son of Japhet, and nothing can elevate him to such rank. To conciliate this anomaly with their principles, the Puritans of the North claim the right of separating themselves from the blacks, as the Mormons separate from the Anabaptists or the Catholics. Therefore the Africans are left in possession of their own churches, taverns, waggons, and balls. Once emparked, the blacks remain so; and even when the traces of blood become faint, the white man will not yet acknowledge the equality of the mulatto or the quadroon. There is no example of marriage between a white and a creole; their union is illegal in the slave States. But if one do form such a marriage, he is not considered sufficiently punished by the public contempt, but is deprived of his rights as citizen. Before the marriage can be concluded he must swear that he has negro blood in his veins, that is that he has no civil rights. Mrs. Houston cites the example of a young man, "who injected some negro blood in to his arm, in order to swear, and so obtain the hand of a wealthy quadroon."

The trace of African blood, the sign and color of the nails never disappear. The Emperor of Hayti would not be received in a tenth-rate hotel in the States. So the black prince, Boyer, found it through the United States even at the Astor House; nor was either box or parterre of the theatre open to him.

The more one goes southward, the more this Teutonic leaven, this pride of white blood, which the northern Puritans have somewhat softened, is visible. The immense estates, the aristocratic life, the elegant tastes of Maryland, Virginia, Georgia, Florida, the habit of having slaves, who spare the master all personal exertion, the fear of seeing all wealth and power concentrated in the north, of which the superiority is already threatening; the unruled proceedings and fervor of the abolitionists, the impossibility of giving to the planters an equivalent for their slaves, the insalubrity of certain provinces for the white man, all concur to maintain slavery in the United States. Even in the north, vivid scruples, and a profound repulsion, prevent the adoption of any decided measures in favor of Emancipation.

They fear to dissolve the Union, to irritate the south, and to detach it forever. They do not wish to check that progress which has not yet made the tenth part of its advance, and for which the African lends his arms and his blood. Democrats and Whigs agree to push on Agriculture, supplant their English cousins in all markets, and conquer natural obstacles by enormous works, that sometimes render a State bankrupt: they agree to *tap* the West, by canals, which pierce the Continent, unite the Alleghanies to the Atlantic, and level the high lands that separated them ; to continue the already numerous lines of railroad, and to precipitate the movement of material civilization. What odds, then, whether there be slaves or not.

SECTION VIII.

ACTIVITY OF THE COUNTRY—CONQUEST OE SOIL—RAPIDITY OF COMMUNICATION.

You know that the device of the Americans is, *Go ahead;* Moral justice does not always arrest them; impossibility does not frighten them; "*let us try*," they say. They do try, and once in twenty times, they succeed. As soon as the object is recognized as important, the American goes at it with a surprising vigor and zeal. They are talking, now, of a railroad from the great Lakes to the Pacific, a gigantic and yet practicable scheme, which would make of America the great high road between Europe and Asia, and would turn to profit thousands of now barren leagues. That is enough to command the serious attention of American legislators, and the project will probably be carried out.

In such a country the electric telegraph is of course popular; according to an almanac for 1848, there were, in 1847, 2311 miles of electric wire in use, 2586 in construction, 3815 projected; in all, 8712. Now, a station at Cape Ann communicates European news to Washington before the vessel has reached Boston. A pulsation of five hundred miles of wire, tells the Congressman what is going on in Paris or London. "Being one day at Washington," says a traveller, "I went idly into an office of the Telegraph, and asked about the weather at Boston, 500 miles distant; in three minutes I learned that the weather was fine, but the heat great, and that a storm was gathering in the north-west." The opposition of newspapers gives much employment to the electric telegraph. An editor places two boys, one on foot, the other on horseback, on the bank, to be approached by a news-bringing boat. A third agent on board, encloses the written news in a bit of hollow wood, flings it to the foot boy, who picks it up and hands it to the cavalier, and he, in turn, departs full gallop for the telegraph office. But a competitor ties his message to an arrow which is shot further, picked up quicker and gains the race. To watch this space-devouring eagerness which possesses the Americans, one can foresee the day when European news will pass, in the twinkling of an eye, from New York to San Francisco, and those of Asia be sent back. The extremities of the world will touch, and Rome will converse with Benares across the United States. Hence the immense number of American advertisements. The London Times seldom has more than eight hundred; you find twelve, fourteen hundred, in an American paper. They wish to push conquest in every direction, to experiment, to try every chance. At the age of fifteen, the man learns that he is to be the architect of his own fortune. The ties of family are so elastic, and virility begins so early, that it is a hard matter to tell where youth ends or minority ceases. They talk politics while still in long clothes; the lisping infant speculates. Vague dreams of ambition float through the mind; they are fascinated by the name of Gerard who began without a cent and ended with millions. The babes are politicians or intriguing factionaries. Each hopes to get rich, to make one leap from deepest poverty to largest opulence. The national morality suffers from this; activity and energy are developed at the expense of the calmer virtues. The soil is cleared, the forests fall, the climate changes, ports are dug, progress is accomplished, but all this does not make amiable men. Impatience to acquire, and love of lucre, prevent the culture of art, and that happy disposition which is content to give and receive enjoyment. Nothing but money and the enterprize which wins it are respected. Often the father is considered by the son merely as a once useful object, to be put into a corner like a bit of old furniture. By this destruction of domestic sympathies, the race is spread in every direction, digging canals, raising dikes, draining marshes, making new families, who will be scattered in their turn. The American loves to go as far away as possible; sometimes neglecting fertile lands, because too near his birth place.

This *go-aheadism* is indispensable where everything is done against nature. But one out of three thousand parts of the territory is cultivated and an original voyager has given an idea of the proportion by saying that the cultivated parts are to the uncultivated, as the seams are to the stuff of a coat. Such a situation requires all the force of youth; and this youthfulness of American character exhibits itself in a thousand different ways. In extreme vivacity, in a susceptibility often exaggerated, a thirst for new sensations, and sometimes a light and frivolous humor.

Therefore America abounds in adventurers from every country, among whom the quaintest go the South, the boldest to the North.

SECTION IX.

SCENES OF VIOLENCE AND MURDER—AUNT BECK AND HER SONS—THE ASTORIAN COLONY—THE YANKEES.

The most unheard of things take place in the forests of the Rocky Mountains and the uncivilized world of Texas, Oregon, and California. A new impetuous life goes on by the gigantic streams, the immense spaces of the West. The more one advances towards the Pacific, the more one encounters the phenomena, the efforts, the painful prodigies of a colossal birth. There is something frightful in the reign of brute force in the midst of that fresh nature. The grotesque too mingles with it, and the frightful is often grotesque.

"There is a very gay-looking woman," said a traveller to a Mormon, pointing out the mistress of an inn near Mobile.

"Yes," replied he, "she is one of our saints and sanctity always produces gaiety. She has not been one of us long. She came from afar, and when she goes out I will tell you the story of this she Macbeth. If you like horrors, the story of Aunt Beck will satisfy you." And when the woman had left the room the Mormon began his story.

"You can only find such people here. She is of Irish and of Scottish extraction, with the sublety of the former and the obstinate violence of the latter. She came here with her husband, one of our first colonists, and with six sons, five of whom were strapping fellows of six feet, and the other a blond-haired boy like a woman.

"The strength of the five was a glory to the father; they formed for him an army of brigands who spread terror through the country, and all went well until the preference of the mother for her last and delicate child gave offence to the father, who merely despised the graceful boy. Then followed the jealousy of the five. As he grew up, he rendered this hatred more fierce by refusing to accompany them on their excursions and by openly exhibiting his dislike to their manner of life. At sixteen he had never yet joined them and the mother began to find it difficult to protect him. One day the father handed him a gun and ordered him to attend him with his brothers; and on his firm refusal flew into a violent rage.

"'Won't you," he cried, "then I will tie you to that post and flog you till you yield.'

"'Do so,' said the boy.

"The father then sprang upon him and with one blow upon the temple laid him dead at his feet. Then the mother changed to a tigress. With a bowie knife in her hand she flew at her husband and stabbed him repeatedly; then at her sons, two of whom fell while the other three fled to the woods and became more savage than ever. In a few months there were none left living but the mother, who has become a convert to Mormonism, and as you see is predestined to sanctity."

All those inexplored forests, and those wild rocks have witnessed analogous scenes—and so the progress goes on, mingled with crimes stained with human blood.

Washington Irving has disguised with idyllic colors, the terrible and devouring march of colonization in those savage spots where the civilizing bee is not yet known. But to know well the unequal combat of man with these vast forests, these mighty waters and with primitive human ferocity, the work of

M. Alexander Ross should be read, "Adventures of the first settlers on the shores of the Columbia river."

Thirty years ago a German, named Astor, gave part of his vast fortune to the foundation of a colony, whose history has been written by Irving. Though then the effort was unsuccessful, nature now begins to yield to the force of mutual labor.

The Astorian expedition sailed in a vessel called the Tonkin, commanded by a person of extreme violence, severity, and cruelty—on board were European sailors, some Indians, some German shopkeepers and some New York tradesmen. Among them was Mr. Ross. The captain's cruelty revolted every body. He threw one sailor overboard in a passion, and putting eight others into a small boat, compelled them to cross the bar of the river, where all perished; finally some of his partners and some passengers having displeased him, he set them ashore on a desert island and sailed on. Then he put the rest of his passengers upon the Oregon shore and coasted along to the northward, there to meet an horrible death. They bought furs from the Indians, paying them with cutlery and glass beads. One of the savages having slighty injured a grating with his knife and fled, the captain ordered his chiefs to give him up, but they only smiled They were then imprisoned and refused either to eat or drink. In the morning the culprit was caught, the chiefs set free and presents offered to them but disdainfully refused. The next day not an Indian appeared, but the day afterwards came an invitation to Messrs. Ross and Mackay to visit them. These persons consented, and were asked if the captain were still angry. They were told "no," and that they could come on board freely. Accordingly they came the next day in considerable numbers.

The captain received them kindly, but was told by Mr.

Mackay that he ought to take some precautions. He however said, "I have given them one lesson, and they dare not move." Meantime the trading went on, the Indians throwing their purchases into their canoes. By and bye the women went over the side, and pushed off their canoes, as the men raised the long war-whoop and attacked the defenceless crew. Mr. Mackay had armed himself with pistols and now shot two of the savages, but was soon dispatched and thrown overboard. Mr. Ross leaped into the sea and was picked up by the women. In five minutes all was finished: not a single white remained on board but the armorer Stephen Weeks, who had defended himself with an axe and then taken refuge in the magazine, where he set fire to the powder, and blew himself, the ship, and 175 savages into eternity. Mr. Ross was set on shore and made his way through the woods to the mouth of the Columbia river.

Here new disasters met him; the Astorian expedition had not measured its strength. Everything in this world is an art. To plant, or to cut down a tree, to build a house, or a hut, to sow, to reap, each of these have cost mankind centuries of education, for humanity becomes great only by progress, accumulation and skilful employment of knowledge. The axe knew not where to smite in these tangled wildernesses, and there was not one woodman among them, so that their apprenticeship was a hard one. It cost them a month to clear an acre, and "in that time," says Mr. Ross, "my black hair had become grey, I had grown old in the strife." These hardy and imprudent pioneers disappeared in a few months; all were dead except Ross who lived to recount their sufferings and to destroy Mr. Irving's charming eclogue.

It is only after such disasters that the *bee* is formed, the first adventurers being sacrificed to prepare the way for it.

Burning forests, massacres, bear and wolf-fights, quarrels with other adventurers fill the volumes of Lanman and Reve, as well as the curious work entitled "Jonathan Sharp, or the adventures of a Kentuckian." If we are to believe him, the Texan bandits have no equals in the world. The northern Yankee, complete type of the ancient colonist, speculative, quiet, cautiously curious, full of cold bravery and great sagacity, is of higher grade, yet is far from the refinements of civilization. It is easy to understand that the propriety and politeness of advanced society find little favor with such people. Pretension must meet pretension, blow be rendered for blow, invasion for invasion, impertinence for impertinence. This greatly annoys the English, who cannot be made to understand the difference between Grosvenor Place and the Alleganies. The Americans understand it. They do not expect a trapper to resemble a Cardinal at the Vatican, nor the speculator, dining in the three or four hundred taverns between Texas and Toronto, to resemble the gentleman or the dandy. It is among the politicians, the diplomatists, the men of letters, at Boston or Philadelphia, that you are to seek the gentler and polished forms of North-American civilization. In the Southern States you find the opulent and animated life of the English country gentleman: Gothic towers, ornaments of the *renaissance*, green lawn and feudal terrace greet the traveller, who admires in these republican families the varied knowledge, the literary taste and the refined elegance of Europe.

SECTION X.

THE QUESTIONER—SCENE IN A STAGE-COACH—THE ENGLISHMAN.

In taverns and hotels, in the midst of the active movement of industry, on the high ways and railroads you find symptoms of an infant civilization, which, however, are neither rude nor coarse. The working and trading classes often exhibit an ingeniously impertinent inquisitiveness, and travellers often complain of it. " Sir," said a Vermonter to his neighbor in a stage coach, "are you a bachelor?" "No." "Are you married?" "No." Then you are a widower?" "No."—Here ensued a pause broken angrily by the questioner. "If you are neither bachelor, married, nor widower, what the devil are you?" "Divorced; and now let me alone!" The questioner then turned to a person with a wooden leg and said, "I would like very much to know how you lost that leg?" "Well, I will tell you if you will promise to ask no more questions.'" "Well, I promise." "I'll tell you then; it was bitten off."—"Oh," muttered the Vermonter, "how I would like to know *what* bit it off."

Travellers' books are full of such scenes. The Scotch Dr.. Mackay, getting into a coach, was followed by a little man in brass-buttoned blue coat, bristly grey hair, and most inquisitive little eyes. He chewed tobacco and spat much, to the great disgust of the Doctor—and at last—" Good morning, stranger," said he—" Good morning!" replied the doctor, glancing at him and astonished to see him looking intently out of the opposite window. "How are you?" said the American, with a furtive glance immediately withdrawn. "As well as one can be in such warm weather." "Do you chew?" "No." "Snuff?" "No." "Smoke?" "Sometimes." "It is a dirty habit," said the other, squirting out a jet of tobacco juice, some of which fell on his trowsers, and was wiped off with his sleeve. "All use of tobacco is uncleanly," said the doctor, looking at the sleeve. "You are not a Scotchman are you?" "You might be mistaken?" "It is because you have a plaid." "Yes that looks Scottish." "I was right then?" "I did not say you were wrong." "When I make a mistake, stranger, I'll give you leave to tell me."

This polite conversation was interrupted by the Doctor making some notes. But the little man slapping him on the shoulder said, "I like the Scotch." "Ah!" "I'm Scotch myself." "Indeed!" "Yes; that is, I was born here; so was my father and grandfather, but my great-grandfather came from Scotland." "I see that you have ancestors?" "Oh, that don't count here—we go for what's above ground, not under it: how long have you been in the country?" "Some months." "How long are you going to stay?" "That depends." "On what does it depend?" I would not have time to tell you." "But we can travel on together," "No." "Are you on governmental business?" "Who knows!" "I don't think you are a merchant, and you don't seem to be travelling for pleasure; it is singular." "Yes, it is singular." "Very singular; will you leave the country soon?" "When I have seen enough of it." Fortunately the city of Augusta came in sight. "Ah," cried the doctor, "is that Augusta?"

"Well, I guess," replied the other, "that it may be somewhere near the location which they call Augusta."

In the midst of a civilization so active and varied, here so moral and simple, there so rude and violent, woman represents elegance and grace; she represents too the progress of population, element of future force. Travellers are astonished to see the people so often accused of rudeness of manners and of coarseness, exhibit a chivalric love for their women. In the States, the women, though in fact neglected, enjoy as we have said a singular consideration; young girls demand this, the women receive it. Where there is no gallantry and the manners are in general pure, the domination of the boudoir is without danger.

In 1847, a stout, robust, self-important English traveller, secured the first place in a coach, and established himself in it to read the paper.

"Sir," said the proprietor opening the door, "here are some ladies, will you be good enough to take the other side." The Englishman looked stupified, while the other continued, "Very sorry, sir, but the best place is always for the ladies." Then spake John Bull.

"Sir, I took my place at Cumberland and paid for it. It is mine, and all America shall not take it from me." Then with a volley of d——ns, he fell back in his place.

"As you please, sir," said the proprietor, "you may keep it if you like to all eternity," and he closed the door. In about ten minutes John Bull opened it and looked out. They had quietly harnessed the horses to another coach, and it was now quarter of a mile ahead.

SECTION XI.

WOMEN—EDUCATION OF CHILDREN—LITERARY PROGRESS.

A delicate and quickly fading beauty, early marriage and absolute independence, the exaggeration of German and English tradition, and the deference always accorded to the activity of youth, explains the excessive influence of young girls in American society. Mothers are put upon the shelf. Hence comes the frivolity found in society, submitted to by the gravest men and complained of by Miss Martineau and Mrs. Trollope. "I have seen old politicians," said a traveller, "talking ribbons and dancing for half an hour, not by gallantry but for politics' sake."

This petticoat government makes very undisciplined children, who will not always obey even the doctor's orders, "and many children," says Mr. Lyell, "are lost in consequence." The perpetual revolt and tumult of a nursery is abominable. Yet this indulgence has a good reason. They begin life so early, that it is almost only in infancy that the parents can show them any tenderness. This indulgence to children and respect for women, comes from the sentiment of love of race and compensates for the faults we have mentioned.

Literature, as we have said, is little favored by such a movement. The only wonder is that it has produced so many men illustrious in the various departments of literature, Bryant, Longfellow, Prescott, Cooper, Halleck, and Stevens, a man little known in France yet meriting to be so by the brilliancy of his coloring and his liveliness. Instead of requiring the man of letters to become a politician; instead of despising him for resting in his natural place, the Americans esteem those who are writers. Paulding was made a minister, Bancroft, Everett, and Irving, ambassadors, and honored their mission precisely because they had not begged for it. Instead of cheapening their scientific remunerations, the Americans exaggerate them, and their national pride understands that intellectual power should be sheltered from dependence upon the democracy. An aged member of the *Institut*, receiving 1200 fcs. a year; masters in science paid with $1000, as in France would seem to them absurd. The celebrities of the country are invited to the Lowell Institute to give twenty lessons for $2,000, or $100 an hour. Nevertheless popular instruction goes on—countless journals cover the country, which adopts the discoveries, lights, even the frivolities of the Old World.

The European literature is curiously treated in the United States. "In the scarcely cleared regions of the West, traversed by the railroad, children haunt the stations, shrieking out, "'New Novel by Paul de Kock, Sir?'" or some other such matter.

SECTION XII.

RESUMPTION—ACTUAL TENDENCY OF THE STATES—FUTURE OF THE ANGLO-AMERICAN REPUBLICS.

Through the phases of public or private life which we have noticed, education, politics, enterprise, position of woman, religion, passions, debates, we have always found the three elements of the past,—Teutonic, Puritan, Anglo-Saxon, Christian—variety, liberty, tradition, labor, energy, charity. These virtues, make the force and power of present America, which lives and grows by them, not by her political institutions. The object of these institutions is to protect, but not to interfere with the development of these living forces; if there be little government, there are characteristics, and it is where characteristics are wanting, that a government is needed.

The Irish with their love of disorder, the French with their administrative habits, and the Germans with their antique respect for hierarchy, are all being absorbed—the northern people more easily than the southern—in the general stream of antique Anglo-Saxon liberty. What is called "the American Revolution," "War of American Independence," are words, phrases useful to orators. The Anglo-Saxon colonies, independent from the beginning, attended a favorable moment to declare themselves free; grown strong, they refused to pay taxes to those who did them no good; they were right. Since 1715, they were more than ready for a republic; the reality existed before the appearance; the name came after the thing. But they did not lay down their arms; it is now half a century, that, aided by the Germanic and Christian sentiments, with English respect for law, they produce cotton, tobacco, Indian corn, railroads and dollars. Faithful to Teutonism and Christianity, faithful to their language, in which the word *people* has no such sense as is given to it by Roman nations, but means, *fellows*, *folk*, **volk**, a term which embraces rich and poor alike, the most powerful and the feeblest member of the community; a race of brothers, knowing that there is no real association without sympathy, they, like their fathers, practise those words of A. Kempis, "You must suffer much annoyance and trouble, to live peacefully together."

In Switzerland, Norway, Denmark and Iceland, as in America, the Christian German idea has produced association. Herds and flocks are in common, the gain of cheese and milk is shared; and this community comes not from law, but from custom. The Americans think, like their Calvinist forefathers, that man is feeble, has need of help and charity, and should assist and labor with his fellow. With such dispositions, the form of government is unimportant; they possess already what is indispensable—religious love for humanity, unconquerable antiquity and respect for law. Without these moral elements of a social organic body, the Mexican and Peruvian Spaniards, who tread on gold and silver, more tolerant, civilized, sociable and amiable than the Mathers and Smiths, have fallen into degradation and decay. The present political mechanism of the States of the South, to speak properly, does not exist; that of the Anglo-French possessions is languishing, contradictory and incomplete; that of the United States vigorous, complex and effective.

I have shown in all the chapters of this book what America will become; a mightier Europe!

The space between the Alleghanies and the Rocky Mountains is six-fold greater than all France. Add to this the three hundred and ninety leagues of the old States, and the new Western territories recently acquired, and even the imagination is surprised. It is the tenth part of the globe. Thus no American sees his country in his village church, but in the race and society to which he belongs. The New Yorker goes to New Orleans, the Louisianian to Kentucky Leave him only the laws and customs which allow a free development of the American form, and he is at home. Laws, soil, land, customs, memories, desires, institutions, pride, passions, qualities, all agree. The partial democracies which compose the union are as solid and stable as the best organized States: their roots are in the soul, their sap in the customs. Yesterday obscure, walking with bold step in the unknown, America cares little for the Present; the Future is hers. A fact governs her life; it is Expansion, activity, energy, tendency to variety, *go aheadism*. Her moral vigor, identical in its causes and essence with Rome's inner force under the Scipios, or that of France under Louis XIV., or of Spain under Isabella, or of England under the Georges, moves in a vaster sphere. The American soul, profoundly identified with the institutions of the country, desires only what can result from them and from national customs. Everywhere one works, lives at the hotel, marries young, loves adventure, fears bankruptcy but little, but fears less danger or death; and land is never wanting to the courageous American.

To this vast social experiment now being made in the States, you must add the eternal physical effort of Nature. Rivers change their beds, Niagara rolls back, the forests fall, the prairies burn, the temperature becomes milder and more temperate, the miasma loses its fatal force, the means of subsistence increase, the population doubles in twenty years, and yet all this is but a preparatory work. The heroic age, the war age is at hand; this mighty race has yet much to do.

The tendencies of North America, are, on one hand towards conquest, on the other, towards the expansion of the federative groups, and by no means towards the formation of monarchies.

The States may break up into two or three different federations, when the individual States become too numerous.

Already the inhabitants of the valley of the Mississippi have a desire to separate. Texas, California, and Oregon, now wild and unpeopled, will one day form another sphere.

It is possible that Cuba, Florida, and all the Slave States will form one group; Canada and the old Northern States another, and the third will be in the far West.

Before 1845, the advance of civilization had not passed a line which, drawn from the head of the Gulf of Mexico to Lake Superior, angled off to the mouth of the St. Lawrence and comprised a third of North America. Now the possession of California is one of the most important facts of our day, not only because of the precious metals, so abundant there, but because of the solidarity which it confers upon the various portions of the New World.

While America thus goes on, what of our Europe? What future is reserved for that old country which Franklin called the "good Grandmama"?

Are the decrepit children of our worn-out world wise in attempting, despite their Past, to imitate the American self-government? Will they succeed?

We doubt it.

Already the south of Europe has recognized its incapacity to receive the burden of half-democratic, half-oligarchic institutions, which have raised Great Britain so high.

As for the Anglo-American institution, a bold development of the same kind, it demands more moral vigor and energetic action. Do we possess these indispensable elements in France ?

The Future will tell.

FINIS.

INDEX.

www.ingramcontent.com/pod-product-compliance
Lightning Source LLC
LaVergne TN
LVHW020220110826
845151LV00003B/773

* 9 7 8 1 4 2 5 5 3 1 9 7 3 *